D1627635

GOOD HOUSEKEEPING
# MICROWAVE
## ENCYCLOPEDIA

# GOOD HOUSEKEEPING
# MICROWAVE ENCYCLOPEDIA

S U S A N N A   T E E

EBURY PRESS · LONDON

At the time of going to press, it has been strongly recommended
by the Ministry of Agriculture, Fisheries and Food
that cling film should not be used in microwave cooking.
When a recipe requires you to use cling film, you should cover
either with a lid or a plate, leaving a gap to let steam escape.

Published by Ebury Press
Division of The National Magazine Company Ltd
Colquhoun House
27-37 Broadwick Street
London W1V 1FR

First impression 1986
Second impression 1986
Third impression 1987
Fourth impression 1988

ISBN 0 85223 512 7

Text copyright © 1986 by The National Magazine Company Limited
Illustrations copyright © 1986 by The National Magazine Company Limited

All rights reserved. No part of this publication may be reproduced,
stored in a retrieval system, or transmitted in any form or by any
means, electronic, mechanical, photocopying, recording, or otherwise,
without the prior permission of the copyright owner.

The expression GOOD HOUSEKEEPING  as used in the title of this book is
the trade mark of The National Magazine Company Limited and The Hearst
Corporation, registered in the United Kingdom and the USA, and other
principal countries in the world, and is the absolute property of The
National Magazine Company Limited and The Hearst Corporation. The use of this
trade mark other than with the express permission of The National Magazine
Company Limited or The Hearst Corporation is strictly prohibited.

Editors: Fiona MacIntyre and Miren Lopategui
Design: Peter Bridgewater Associates
Illustrations: Robert Schone
Photography: Martin Brigdale, Melvin Grey, Paul Kemp and Charlie Stebbings
Phototypeset by MS Filmsetting Limited, Frome, Somerset
Printed and bound in Italy by New Interlitho, S.p.A., Milan

# CONTENTS

# INTRODUCTION

The main advantage of basic microwave cooking is, of course, speed: it takes only a quarter to one-fifth of conventional cooking times – a jacket potato, for example, will be cooked in just 4-5 minutes. However, with this cooking method, unlike conventional cooking, the larger the amount of food you're cooking, the longer it takes, so there may in fact be little time-saving if you are cooking for large numbers. When cooking for one or two, on the other hand, the time-saving is enormous.

Many foods are not only cooked more quickly in a microwave but are also cooked more healthily than in conventional cooking. Fish and vegetables, for example, retain their shape, texture and flavour far more when cooked in the microwave, and also retain more valuable nutrients that are so often lost through conventional cooking methods such as boiling.

Microwave cookers are highly energy-saving. The cooking times are so short that there are enormous savings in fuel. Most cookers run off a 13 amp socket outlet and cost only a few pence per hour to run on full power.

In addition, microwaving is a very clean form of cooking. As the walls of the cooking cavity never get very hot, the food won't burn on to them as in a conventional oven. This makes cleaning very easy (see p. 9). A particular advantage in kitchens where there is little ventilation is that you don't get the condensation problems you would when using a conventional hob.

Microwave cookers are very compact. Even the largest model will sit comfortably on a work surface and the very small models are still large enough to cook food in reasonable quantities while occupying very little space. They can also be used hand-in-hand with the freezer to thaw and heat ready-prepared dishes, with no loss of flavour, texture or quality.

There are, however, limitations to microwave cooking, too. The method of cooking, with its lack of direct heat, means that foods won't become brown or crisp. For this reason, some forms of baking could be considered unsuccessful – a loaf baked in the microwave, for example, will not have the crisp crust it acquires in a conventional oven. There is also a limit to the amount of food you can put in a microwave at any one time.

## HOW A MICROWAVE WORKS

A microwave cooker is basically a metal-lined box which, when plugged in, converts the electric current into microwaves using a device called a magnetron. Microwaves are high frequency, short-length, electro-magnetic waves, similar to TV radio waves.

## UNDERSTANDING POWER OUTPUT AND OVEN SETTINGS

Unlike conventional ovens, the power output and heat controls on various microwave cookers do not follow a standard formula. When manufacturers refer to a 700-watt cooker they are referring to the oven's POWER OUTPUT; its INPUT, which is indicated on the back of the oven, is usually about double that figure. The higher the wattage of a cooker, the faster the rate of cooking, thus food cooked at 700 watts on full power cooks in half the time of food cooked at 350 watts. That said, the actual cooking performance of one 700-watt oven may vary slightly from another with the same wattage because factors such as cooker cavity size affect cooking performance. The vast majority of microwave cookers sold today are either 600, 650 or 700 watt ovens, but there are many ovens still in use which may be 400 or 500 watts.

In this book HIGH refers to 100% full power output of 600-700 watts;
MEDIUM refers to 60% of full power;
LOW is 35% of full power.

Whatever the wattage of your cooker, the HIGH/FULL setting will always be 100% of the cooker's output. Thus your highest setting will correspond to HIGH.

However, the Medium and Low settings used in this book may not be equivalent to the Medium and Low settings marked on your cooker. As these settings vary according to power input we have included the following calculation so you can estimate the correct setting for your oven. This simple calculation should be done before you use the recipes for the first time, to ensure successful results.

Multiply the percentage power required by the total number of settings on your cooker and divide by 100. To work out what setting MEDIUM and LOW correspond to on your cooker.

*Medium* (60%) = % Power required
$\times$ Total number of cooker settings $\div$ 100
= Correct setting, i.e.
$= \dfrac{60 \times 9}{100} = 5$

*Low* (35%) = % Power required
$\times$ Total number of cooker settings $\div$ 100
= Correct setting, i.e.
$= \dfrac{35 \times 9}{100} = 3$

If your cooker power output is lower than 600 watts, then you must allow a longer cooking and thawing time for all recipes in this book.

Add approximately 10-15 seconds per minute for a 600 watt oven, and 15-20 seconds per minute for a 500 watt oven.

No matter what the wattage of your cooker is, you should always check food before the end of cooking time, to ensure that it does not get overcooked. Don't forget to allow for standing time.

Microwaves have three important characteristics: 1) they are reflected by metal, 2) they are able to pass through most other materials, and 3) they are attracted to moisture. These three characteristics form the basis of how the cookers work.

As soon as the cooker is switched on, microwaves are generated and enter the cooking cavity where they are reflected off the metal walls. As they bounce off the walls, they pass through the food containers and into the food itself. Here, they cause the water molecules in the food to vibrate millions of times per second, thus producing a great amount of heat. It is this heat which cooks the food. (*Note:* the magnetron only generates microwaves when the oven door is closed and the correct controls have been operated – and then only for the duration of the pre-selected time, so that as soon as the timer switches off or the cooker door is opened, microwaves cease to be generated. The food, however, will continue to cook, not by the action of microwaves but by the conduction of heat within the food. This is why many microwaved dishes require a certain amount of standing time after being removed from the oven.)

## TYPES OF MICROWAVE

A wide range of microwave cookers is available, from small models with two or three power settings, to large, more sophisticated versions with a number of different settings.

All, however, fall into three main categories: countertop microwaves; double oven microwave cookers and combination ovens. Your choice will obviously depend on the price you are prepared to pay, the requirements you have, and the size of your kitchen.

The most popular are the countertop models. The advantage of these is, of course, that they take up little space. Some countertop microwaves have a rack or shelf incorporated inside, thus offering two cooking positions. These, however, are more complicated to use than those without. Usually the food on the shelf gets more of the microwave energy than that on the base so you have to select foods which will cook together satisfactorily. Remember, timings will be different if cooking more than one item at a time.

Double oven microwave cookers are available as either free-standing cookers with hob, or as a double oven unit, housing a separate microwave and conventional oven, but no hob. Both offer the advantage of complementary cooking in one unit. (You can, for example, start cooking a joint of meat in the microwave and then brown it in a conventional oven.)

Combination ovens are appliances offering both microwave and conventional cooking facilities in the same oven.

## STANDARD FEATURES

All standard microwave cookers have an on/off control or button which switches on the power and, in most basic cookers, also activates the interior light and cooling fans. They also have a 'Cook' or 'Start' button which switches on the microwave energy for cooking, heating and thawing food. This will only work when the cooker door is completely closed. (When the door is opened, the microwave energy is automatically switched off. To continue cooking, the door must be closed and this control switched on again.)

The length of cooking is controlled by a timer which may either be mechanical or digital. When the pre-set time is reached, a buzzer or bell sounds and the cooker will switch off automatically. Again, the cooker will not work until a cooking time is selected and the appropriate control is switched on.

Door design varies from manufacturer to manufacturer – most have side-opening doors, although drop-down and slide-up varieties are available. There is usually a transparent mesh panel in the door that enables you to watch the food as it cooks. The cooker cavity – or the actual cooking space in the cooker – is a smooth, metal-lined box which may have a plastic or paint coating. Some models have removable glass floors or shelves and many have removable turntables; these models are the easiest to clean.

Finally, all cookers have some sort of a vent to allow a proportion of moisture to escape from the oven during cooking. Some models also have air filters through which cooling air for the components will pass into the oven space and cool the inner components of the oven. It does not affect the food. These filters are removable and should be checked and cleaned periodically according to the manufacturer's instructions to see that they are kept free from grease and dust.

## SPECIAL FEATURES

In addition to the standard fittings, some microwaves have more sophisticated features which, though they will affect the price, may nevertheless be worth considering.

### AUTOMATIC PROGRAMMING
A feature which allows more than one power setting to be programmed at once, so that a number of cooking sequences can be carried out on the one setting. The cooker can be programmed to, say, start off cooking the food at a HIGH setting, then to complete the cooking on a LOW setting; to come on at a set time and cook the food so that it is ready when you come home; or thaw food and then automatically switch to a setting for cooking.

### BROWNING ELEMENT OR INTEGRAL GRILL
This provides a convenient way of giving microwaved food a traditional brown appearance, either before or after cooking. It is usually situated at the top of the cooker and works in the same way as a conventional grill. It is only useful for those for whom the microwave is their main cooking appliance.

### DEFROST CONTROL
An automatic defrosting control which provides even thawing of frozen foods. When used in conjunction with the timer, the microwave energy in the cooker is automatically cycled on and off to allow rest periods in between short bursts of microwave energy. These short, gentle bursts ensure the thawing is carried out at an even rate which ensures that the food thaws without cooking. (In ovens without this defrost control, this will have to be done by hand.)

### TEMPERATURE PROBE
An instrument which allows the cooking to be determined by the internal temperature of the food being cooked rather than by time. One end of the probe is inserted into the thickest part of the food and the other end is plugged into a special socket in the cooker cavity. The desired degree of cooking (temperature) is then selected. When the internal temperature of the food reaches the required point, the microwave energy is automatically switched off or reduced to a lower setting. The temperature probe is particularly useful for large, dense foods such as joints of meat and whole poultry.

### STIRRERS
Stirrer blades, paddles or fans are built into the roof of most microwave cookers and help to distribute the microwaves around the oven cavity; some ovens have a rotating antennae.

### TURNTABLE
The turntable is a rotating platform which automatically moves the food around the cooking cavity and can contribute to more even cooking. (It will, however, still be necessary to reposition some food by hand – see Cooking Techniques, p. 10.)

### VARIABLE POWER
This allows greater flexibility by enabling the cooking speed to be varied, in much the same way as changing temperature in a conventional oven, thus allowing much greater flexibility. Settings vary according to the microwave model, and are described in a number of different ways such as HIGH, MEDIUM, LOW, graduated numbers or terms such as Roast, Bake, Simmer, Defrost, Reheat.

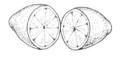

## SAFETY

In the past, many people have been worried about the safety of microwave cookers. These fears, however, are completely ill-founded. Microwave cookers are completely safe. In the first place, the microwaves themselves are non-ionising (ie they do not build up in the body in the way that ionising X-rays and gamma rays do. They therefore do not damage food chemically or build up in the cooker. In addition, microwave cookers have several built-in safety measures. The microwaves themselves will not be produced unless the door is completely closed. The doors are fitted with special locks, seals and safety cut-out switches that automatically switch the power off as soon as the door is opened a fraction and the lock also prevents the cooker from functioning if the door seal is broken for any reason. In addition, the cookers are effectively sealed against leakage of microwaves, as they are built to very precise specifications.

When buying a microwave, however, it is sensible to look for one which has been approved by a technical approval board.

Never tamper with any of the controls or try to repair them if they cease to work properly; call in a qualified microwave service engineer. Some people feel happier if their microwave cookers are checked over professionally once a year.

## COOKER MAINTENANCE

As a precautionary measure, keep a glass or cup of water in the oven when it is not being used for cooking just in case the oven is accidentally switched on. (If the cavity is empty when the oven is switched on the component parts may be damaged.)

Metal must never be allowed to come into contact with the inside of the microwave cooker. This means that you must not use metal containers for cooking food (unless specifically allowed by a manufacturer); nor should you wrap or cover food completely with foil. If you need to shield food to prevent overcooking, use very small parts of foil over the thinnest parts of the food, and use it with the dull side outermost. Make sure the foil is smooth and does not touch the sides of the microwave as it will damage the cooker. If foil is used incorrectly, it will cause sparks which will damage the cooker.

Whichever type of cooker you opt for, it is important that any vents are kept uncovered. If they are at the top of the oven, for example, the oven must not be sited under a cupboard or shelf; if the vent is at the back, then the oven must not be placed against a wall.

Note: some cardiac pacemakers may be affected by microwave energy, though this applies mainly to the earlier types of pacemaker which are no longer supplied. Nevertheless, before buying a microwave oven, check with your doctor.

## CLEANING

When cleaning the cooker it should be disconnected from the electricity supply. The outside of a microwave cooker will not need much cleaning – just a wipe with a damp cloth or according to the manufacturer's instructions. (Outside vents should also be wiped over occasionally to remove condensation but be careful not to splash water over them.)

The inside of the cooker will need more attention. Even though the walls of the oven never get that hot, so that any food that spatters will not burn as in a conventional oven (unless they have conventional heating elements), nevertheless, the oven will still have to be cleaned every time it is used, since any food left on the oven walls may affect microwaving. This, however, is much easier than cleaning a conventional oven – just wipe with a damp cloth, being sure to pay particular attention to the door seal so that it is clean at all times. If the oven walls become heavily soiled, do not use abrasive cleaners or knives on them as these will damage the surfaces. Just place a cup or bowl with a little lemon juice in it in the oven and heat to boiling point. The steam that is produced should soften any stubborn particles.

Removable turntables and shelves should be washed in a bowl of warm, soapy water and wiped dry before being replaced in the cooker.

If the cooker has a browning element or if the model combines microwave with convection cooking, more vigorous cleaning may be required but only use the special cleaners recommended by the manufacturers.

## CONTAINERS

An ever-increasing variety of cookware specially designed for the microwave is now on the market. Some containers, such as those made of soft plastics, paper, pressed polystyrene or bags such as boil-in-the-bags, roasting bags and cling film, are disposable; still more are designed for permanent use and are made of glass, earthenware or hard plastics. Many of these can be used in conventional ovens or placed in the freezer as well as in microwave cookers.

You will also find that many of the bowls and dishes you normally use in the kitchen are perfectly suitable for microwave cooking. In order to be used in a microwave cooker, the container must be made of a material which allows the microwaves to pass through it to the food, absorbing little or no microwave energy itself, it must be resistant to the heat of the food placed inside or on it, and it should be the right size and shape.

To test that containers are suitable for use in a microwave oven, place the dish in the microwave together with a cup of water. Heat for 1½-2 minutes. If the water is hot and the dish cool it can be used in the cooker; if the reverse is true, the dish should not be used. When testing plastic containers, only allow 10-15 seconds, just in case they start to melt.

### SHAPE

Food cooks more evenly in rounded dishes, as these allow even penetration by the microwaves. Round dishes are a better choice than square, oval or rectangular ones in general, but if you have to use a container with corners, avoid one with square corners, as microwaves will cluster in these and result in uneven cooking.

Ring moulds, as long as they aren't made of metal, are ideal for heating or cooking foods which cannot be stirred, to equalise the temperature during their time in the microwave oven. They are especially good for cakes and desserts because they allow microwaves to penetrate the food from the centre as well as the sides, top and bottom. If you don't have a ring mould, you can always improvise the shape by placing a glass tumbler in the centre of a round dish.

Straight-sided containers are preferable to those with sloping or curved sides as they will cook foods more evenly; large, shallow dishes will cook food more quickly than deep narrow ones as the food can be spread out, giving maximum exposure to microwaves.

### SIZE

Size of container is also important. You must use larger containers for microwave cooking than you would for conventional cooking, and you should never fill any dish more than two-thirds full. This allows for liquids which may boil up during cooking and provides ample space for stirring mixtures which need it. Dishes used for light cakes and puddings should not be more than half-filled, otherwise the mixture may spill over the edges.

## COMPOSITION

**China and pottery** Glazed china plates, cups, saucers, bowls and mugs can be used in the microwave. However, you should avoid using china that has a metallic decoration such as gold or gold leaf as arcing could occur. Fine bone china should only be used for reheating foods for short periods as it could crack with excessive heat. Unglazed pottery and earthenware are porous and can be used, but as they slow down the cooking of food they are best avoided.

**Glass** Ovenproof glass and glass ceramic dishes are the most commonly used microwave containers. Clear glass dishes are especially useful if you are unused to a microwave oven because you can actually see the food as it cooks. Ovenproof glass measuring jugs are also very useful, as they can be used for measuring and mixing as well as for cooking. Ordinary glasses and glass dishes are only suitable for heating foods for a short time as they could crack from the heat of the food. Do not use cut glass or leaded glass in the microwave.

**Metal** Metal or foil containers should NEVER be used in a microwave cooker unless specifically allowed by the cooker manufacturer. This is because metal reflects microwaves and the microwaves would therefore never be able to pass through to the food. Metal (and containers decorated with gold or silver) could also cause arcing.

**Paper** Paper cups and cartons, and plain white plates and napkins can all be used in the microwave for short cooking times, although longer cooking may cause them to burn. Coloured plates and napkins should be avoided as the colour in the dye may run on to the food. Greaseproof paper and absorbent kitchen paper can be used as coverings for fatty foods to prevent them spattering, or they can be placed underneath breads and pastries when they are reheated to prevent them from becoming soggy. When using waxed and plastic-coated cups, always follow the manufacturer's recommendations, as some may melt if used in the oven.

**Plastics** Boilable, rigid plastic containers that are dish-washerproof are normally suitable for microwave cooking, though preferably only for shorter cooking times. It's not always easy to tell exactly what sort of plastic the container is made of; in such cases, use the container test on p. 9 to make sure the container is suitable for microwave use.

Cream cartons, yogurt pots and ordinary plastic bags will melt in a microwave, but plastic freezer bags and freezer containers can be used for short periods of thawing or reheating if a slit is put in the top of the bag before heating. Specially designed boiling bags, roasting bags and cling film can all be used, but they must be pricked to allow steam to escape and prevent the build-up of pressure which may cause the bag to burst.

**Wood and wicker** These may be used for short-term heating, but will dry out and crack if exposed to microwaves for a long time. Wooden bowls or spoons used in the microwave should be rubbed occasionally with vegetable oil to keep them in good condition.

# SPECIAL MICROWAVE ACCESSORIES

## BROWNING DISHES

These are used to sear and brown foods whose short microwave cooking times mean that they cannot brown properly. They are ideal for foods which are normally grilled or fried such as steak, chops, beefburgers, sausages and chicken portions. Browning dishes look like ordinary ceramic or ovenproof glass but have a tin oxide coating on the base which absorbs microwave energy. As when grilling and frying, the dish must be preheated according to the manufacturer's instructions and must be reheated in between cooking batches of food. Do not place browning dishes on work surfaces and always wear oven gloves when handling them as they get very hot.

## MICROWAVE THERMOMETERS

Ordinary meat and sugar thermometers cannot be used in a microwave, as the mercury in them is adversely affected by microwave energy. These specially designed thermometers should be inserted into the thickest part of the food to obtain a reading (if the food is meat, the thermometer should not touch any bone).

## ROASTING RACKS

These are used to raise meat and poultry above their own juices during cooking, to thaw large, solid items such as turkeys, or to reheat rolls, pastries, cakes and breads. They are usually made of a hard plastic or ceramic material.

# COOKING TECHNIQUES

Because of the particular way that microwave cookers work, special cooking techniques have to be used to achieve the best results.

## ARRANGEMENT OF FOOD

Arranging the food in the container correctly is necessary to make sure that it cooks, reheats or thaws evenly. Place the thicker parts of the food outermost, and thinner, more delicate areas near the centre, overlapping them where necessary or covering them with a very small piece of foil, shiny side in. When cooking several items, such as small cakes, jacket potatoes or baked apples, arrange them in a circle on a plate or directly on the oven shelf to allow the microwaves to penetrate from the centre as well as the outside. If this is not possible, rearrange the items during the cooking, thawing or reheating, placing the outer items in the centre and vice versa, and removing items as soon as they are cooked, warm or thawed.

The more surface area that can be exposed to the microwaves, the quicker and more even the cooking, reheating or thawing will be. Arrange items such as peas in a single layer rather than piled in the centre.

## BROWNING

Many foods cooked in a microwave cooker do not brown as they would when cooked conventionally. This can be overcome in several ways. Meats and poultry can be browned in a browning dish, under a grill or in a frying pan. They can also be sprinkled with paprika pepper, or browned breadcrumbs or brushed with sauces such as tomato, brown sauce, Tabasco, soy or Worcestershire sauce, or glazed with honey, marmalade or apricot jam.

## COVERING

Covering will prevent the surface of moist foods such as vegetables from drying out, and will also speed up the cooking of foods by trapping moisture underneath the cover. The covering you use can be of any material that is suitable for use in a microwave cooker (see p. 10). If using cling film or plastic bags, remember to make a hole in them to prevent ballooning and bursting, by allowing steam to escape. Fold back one corner of a cling film covering so that the food can easily be stirred if necessary. Fatty items that are likely to spatter, such as bacon, can be covered with absorbent kitchen paper as this will soak up the fat. Unevenly shaped foods such as chicken joints will have to be partially covered during cooking to prevent thinner areas from becoming overcooked. Do this with a very small piece of foil wrapped closely over the food, shiny side in. Breads and pastries will not need covering as they do not need to be kept moist during cooking.

## LINING

Cake containers other than plastic ones should be lined with greaseproof paper. Remove the paper as soon as the cake has been turned out, to prevent sticking.

## SEASONING

Salt will have a toughening effect on meats, fish and vegetables so do not add it directly to foods without any liquid until cooking is complete.

## STANDING TIME

All food continues to cook after being removed from the microwave cooker (or when the power is switched off) because of the conduction of heat. The period during which this happens is known as the 'standing time', and must always be taken into account when estimating cooking times. The time taken will generally depend on the size and density of the foods. If in doubt, always undercook rather than overcook, and test the food at the end of the standing time. It can always be cooked for a few extra seconds.

## TURNING AND STIRRING

Turning and stirring are, of course, important in conventional cooking to ensure that food is evenly cooked, but they are even more important in microwave cooking, where the food cooks from the outer edges inwards. Denser foods, such as meat and poultry (or other foods that are cooked whole, such as jacket potatoes), should be turned over during the cooking period. With solid foods such as cakes the container should be turned several times during cooking. Even if the cooker has a turntable it is advisable to turn cakes to ensure even cooking. Foods that can be stirred should be stirred from the outside to the inside.

# FACTORS AFFECTING COOKING

Several factors will affect the timings and results of foods cooked in a microwave.

## AMOUNT

The larger the amount of food being cooked, the longer it will take to cook. As a general guildeline, allow about one third to one half extra cooking time when doubling the ingredients. When cooking quantities are halved, decrease the cooking time by slightly more than half the time allowed for the full quantity of that food. Always underestimate rather than overestimate cooking time in the microwave – food which is undercooked can always be returned to the oven for further cooking.

## COMPOSITION

Foods with a high moisture content will take longer to cook or reheat than drier foods, and foods which are high in fat or sugar will cook or reheat more quickly than those which are low in these ingredients. Jams, marmalades and sugary coatings on cakes, puddings or tarts will heat up much more quickly than the dough or pastry in these foods and can become extremely hot so do not attempt to eat them straight from the microwave. Some foods, such as cheese, eggs, cream, soured cream, mushrooms and seafood are easily overcooked. These should always be cooked for the minimum time recommended and must be watched carefully during the cooking period just in case they start to overheat. If possible, microwave on LOW for more gentle cooking.

### CONTAINER TYPE

Food cooking times are also affected by the size, shape and material of the container used to cook them in (see p. 9).

### DENSITY AND TEXTURE

Light, open-textured foods such as breads, cakes and puddings cook and reheat more quickly than denser foods such as meat. Meat which must be thoroughly cooked, such as pork and poultry, may have to stand after cooking to allow the heat to be conducted to the centre of the food.

### SIZE AND SHAPE

Several small pieces of food cook more quickly than the same amount of food cooked in one piece. For example pieces of meat cut into small cubes for stews and casseroles will cook more quickly than the same quantity of meat cooked in a joint, but it is important to make sure that all the pieces are cut to the same size so that they cook at the same speed. Whole poultry will cook more evenly if it is well trussed and joints of meat if boned and rolled.

### TEMPERATURE

The colder the starting temperature of the food, the longer it will take to heat up. Ideally, chilled food should be allowed to stand at room temperature for about an hour before being cooked or reheated to keep cooking time to a minimum. Alternatively, a little extra should be added to the cooking times, although there is the risk of overcooking with this method.

## THE DOS AND DON'TS OF MICROWAVE COOKING

### DON'TS

The following should never be attempted in a microwave:
◆ Deep fat frying (it is not possible to control the temperature of oil used).
◆ Cooking eggs in their shells (microwaving causes pressure to build up under the shell, causing it to explode.)
◆ Cooking double crust pastries, crusty bread, pizzas, batter recipes such as pancakes and Yorkshire pudding, souffles, meringues, meringue toppings and roast potatoes.
◆ Cooking and reheating puddings containing alcohol because it reaches too high a temperature and can easily burn.

### DOS

◆ Freshen up stale coffee beans by microwaving for a minute on low.
◆ Take the chill off vinegar and oil before making mayonnaise.
◆ Melt chocolate for cakes and icing; soften butter before creaming with other ingredients (but be sure to only put it in the microwave for a few seconds – it must not melt).
◆ Warming up sugar before jam-making.
◆ Heating milk before adding to a roux.

## FREEZING AND THAWING

Pack food to be frozen in containers that are suitable for both the freezer and the microwave. Freezer-to-oven microware, designed especially for freezing conventionally cooked foods to be reheated in a microwave, is now increasingly available. Cardboard is ideal for pies, flans and non-liquid dishes which need microwaving only for a short time, but it can only be used once. Boil-in-the-bags and roasting bags, which are ideal for freezing casseroles, vegetables and small joints, can both be put directly into the microwave.

Thawing the food evenly is very important. When food is thawed, smaller ice crystals will melt first. If thawing is too rapid, therefore, parts of the food will start to cook before the areas of larger ice crystals have thawed. For thawing to take place evenly it must be done gently. Microwave on LOW or DEFROST settings. Some cookers will thaw food by automatically switching on and off at a high setting to allow rest periods inbetween short bursts of microwaving, (see p. 12). If your oven has no LOW or DEFROST settings, you can thaw manually by turning off the oven every 30 seconds and allowing the food to stand for 1½ minutes before turning the oven on again for another 30 seconds. The number of heating and rest periods will depend on the size and amount of the food being thawed – the larger the item the longer the periods of heating and rest. (Some foods, such as joints, also need to be given a standing time at the end of the thawing cycle, as they will continue to thaw during this time.)

If the food begins to thaw unevenly, cover the area that is beginning to cook with a small piece of foil, shiny side inwards. Turn foods over during thawing and if possible separate items such as chops and steaks. Break up liquid and semi-liquid foods such as casseroles with a fork at the beginning of thawing, and shake or fork small fruit and vegetables apart. Cover foods such as cakes, breads and pastries with kitchen paper to absorb the moisture.

Foods should be put into containers of an appropriate size and shape when being thawed: stews, casseroles, sauces and other liquid foods, for example, will thaw more evenly if put into a deep dish that keeps their contents together. If the dish is too large, the liquid will start to heat before the rest of the food has begun to thaw.

If food has been frozen in polythene bags with metal ties, replace the ties with string or elastic bands before putting in the microwave; similarly, transfer food from aluminium foil trays into more suitable containers. Open cartons and any other containers with lids and slit or pierce polythene bags or packets. Foods with skins should also be pierced.

## REHEATING

Foods can be reheated in a microwave with no loss of nutrients or flavour. Follow the same procedure as when reheating foods conventionally and cover foods such as casseroles to prevent them drying out. Stir the food occasionally for even heating; items that cannot be stirred should be turned or re-arranged.

Reheating in a microwave is extremely quick so special attention should be given to small items of food to avoid overcooking. Special attention must be paid to cooked pastry and breads. Place these on absorbent kitchen paper to absorb moisture during reheating and prevent the bottom from becoming soggy. Microwaves are attracted to the moist fillings in pies and pasties, so that the liquid will heat up quickly. The steam produced by this is often absorbed into the pastry covering which may not leave it as crisp as that reheated in a conventional oven.

To test whether the food is ready, feel the container beneath it – if it feels warm the food will be hot. With pastry foods such as fruit pies, the outer pastry should feel just warm. The temperature of pastry and filling will equalise if given a few minutes standing time.

# ADAPTING RECIPES TO THE MICROWAVE

With an understanding of microwave cooking methods, it is not difficult to adapt your favourite recipes to the microwave.

## ROASTING

Conventional roasting recipes are very simple to adapt to the microwave. Often it is simply a matter of consulting a microwave cooking chart to determine microwave time and setting. Remember that during the standing time, cooking will be completed by the conduction of heat. Cover or wrap the meat in foil and leave to stand for 15-20 minutes.

Small joints, less than 1.4 kg (3 lb), do not have time to brown during microwaving. If you do not like the paler appearance of microwaved meats, use a browning dish or glaze the meat by basting with juices that include paprika, turmeric, brown sugar, honey or other dark-coloured flavouring to give the meat a browned appearance.

## GRILLING AND FRYING

Recipes for grilling and stir-frying food (though not shallow and deep frying) can be successfully adapted to the microwave cooker. Cook the food quickly in the microwave and then brown under the grill. Alternatively use a browning dish.

Many conventional recipes call for an initial frying to brown or sear meat before cooking. If you do not have a browning dish, brown conventionally and then cook the food in the microwave.

## STEWING AND BRAISING

Conventionally cooked stews and casseroles depend on long, slow cooking to tenderise tough cuts of meat and to allow the flavours of the vegetables and herbs to combine. For this reason, there is little point in using the microwave for stews other than those with ingredients which do not need tenderising such as most poultry and vegetable stews.

When adapting conventional stew or casserole recipes to the microwave, it is usually necessary to reduce the amount of liquid as there is less evaporation when microwaving because of the reduced cooking time. Start with about one-quarter less liquid and add more during cooking if necessary. Herbs and spices do not have time to mellow, so use half the amount stated in conventional recipes.

## POACHING, STEAMING AND BOILING

When cooking conventionally, these cooking methods require added liquid to help tenderise food and retain its moisture, to rehydrate it (as with rice) or simply to prevent food from sticking to the pan. Because microwaved food cooks in its own moisture and there is no risk of sticking, the amount of liquid added is minimal, often much less than the liquid indicated in a conventional recipe. When steaming foods, added liquid is eliminated altogether and most fresh vegetables can be microwaved in less than 90 ml (6 tbsp) water. Very moist vegetables, such as spinach, require no added water. Fish is successfully cooked in its own moisture. With all these forms of cooking, the container should be three-quarters covered to allow steam to escape. The exceptions are steamed puddings which should be completely, but loosely, covered.

In most cases, cooking times are greatly reduced. The exceptions are rice and dried pasta because they need to rehydrate before they start cooking. Therefore, they require the same cooking time as a conventional recipe. If you require more than 300 ml (½ pint) water then it is more economical and quicker to use an electric kettle to boil the water.

## BAKING

Follow recipe instructions for greasing and lining but do not grease and flour containers as this produces a soggy coating to the cake. Instead, use greased greaseproof paper. As most conventional baking equipment is made of metal, choose from the wide range of containers which can be placed in the microwave cooker such as ovenproof glass or plastic containers (which do not need to be greased). For large cakes, cook in a ring mould or the centre will not be cooked.

Cakes cooked in a microwave cooker do not brown because the sugar in them does not caramelise and form a crust on the surface. For this reason, use dark ingredients such as dark brown sugar, molasses, treacle, chocolate or cocoa powder. Alternatively, disguise the cake's surface with icing or whipped cream.

Microwaved cakes will rise higher during cooking than those baked conventionally. To avoid possible spillage, never fill a container more than half-full.

Make sure the cake is given quarter turns to ensure even cooking. When cooked, a cake will still look moist on the top (normally it would be considered slightly underdone). Leave cakes to stand in the container for 5-10 minutes to complete the cooking.

# SOUPS

—— LENTIL AND BACON SOUP ——

*A healthy, filling and nutritious soup, ideal for cold winter days*

SEE PAGE 17

# Cooking Tips

◆

*When making a soup in a microwave oven, use a deep, round container that allows plenty of room for the expansion of the liquid as it comes to the boil and for it to be stirred.*

◆

*Although freshly microwaved soups are tasty, they will actually improve in flavour if made in advance, refrigerated for several hours and then reheated.*

◆

*Soups can be reheated in individual bowls, so saving on washing up.*

◆

*Reheat soups on a LOW setting if they contain cream, seafood, mushrooms or pulses but use a HIGH setting for all others.*

◆

*Pour soup that is to be frozen into single-portion containers so that it can be thawed in the microwave more quickly than a large quantity.*

◆

*When reheating soups it is important to stir the soup to ensure even heating.*

◆

## HEATING CANNED SOUP

Pour the soup into a large jug, individual soup bowls or a soup tureen, diluting if recommended by the manufacturer, eg. condensed soups. Cover with cling film, pulling back one corner to allow the steam to escape. Microwave on HIGH until hot. (A 435 g (15 oz) can will require 3-4 minutes.) Stir the soup and leave to stand, covered, for a few minutes before serving.

## COOKING DEHYDRATED SOUP MIXES

Reconstitute according to the packet instructions in a large jug or bowl which should be no more than two thirds full. Cover with cling film, pulling back one corner to allow the steam to escape. Microwave on HIGH to bring to the boil. (600-750 ml (1-1¼ pints) takes 6-8 minutes; 1 litre (1¾ pints) takes 8-10 minutes.) Stir and leave to stand, covered, for a few minutes before serving.

## LENTIL AND BACON SOUP

SERVES 6

| 100 g (4 oz) streaky bacon, rinded and chopped |
| 25 g (1 oz) butter or margarine |
| 100 g (4 oz) red lentils |
| 2 leeks, trimmed and finely chopped |
| 2 carrots, peeled and finely chopped |
| 1 litre (1¾ pints) chicken stock |
| 30 ml (2 tbsp) chopped fresh parsley |
| salt and pepper |
| orange shreds, to garnish |

◆ Place the bacon and butter in a large bowl and microwave on HIGH for 2 minutes. Add the lentils and toss to coat them in the fat, then add the leeks, carrots and stock.
◆ Cover and microwave on HIGH for 18 minutes or until the lentils are cooked. Stir two or three times during the cooking time.
◆ Cool slightly, then liquidise the soup in a blender or food processor until smooth. Add the parsley, season and microwave on HIGH for 2-3 minutes or until the soup is hot. Garnish with orange shreds and serve.

## CREAM OF MUSHROOM SOUP

SERVES 4-6

| 50 g (2 oz) butter or margarine |
| 1 small onion, skinned and chopped |
| 1 chicken stock cube |
| 225 g (8 oz) button mushrooms, sliced |
| 1 bouquet garni |
| 25 g (1 oz) cornflour |
| 330 ml (½ pint) milk |
| salt and pepper |
| 50 ml (2 fl oz) single cream |

◆ Put the butter and chopped onion in a large bowl. Cover with cling film, pulling back one corner to allow the steam to escape. Microwave on HIGH for 5-7 minutes or until softened.
◆ Dissolve the stock cube in 600 ml (1 pint) boiling water and add to the onion with the sliced mushrooms and bouquet garni. Re-cover and microwave on HIGH for 15-20 minutes.
◆ Remove the bouquet garni and either sieve the soup or liquidise it in a blender or food processor until smooth.
◆ Blend the cornflour with a little of the milk, then stir in the remaining milk. Stir into the mushroom mixture and re-cover.
◆ Microwave on HIGH for about 10 minutes, stirring frequently. Season with salt and pepper, pour into a serving dish and swirl the cream on top.

## QUICK ONION SOUP

SERVES 6

| 25 g (1 oz) butter or margarine |
| 2 large onions, skinned and finely sliced |
| 298 ml (10½ oz) can condensed consommé |
| salt and pepper |
| six 2.5 cm (1 inch) slices French bread |
| 50 g (2 oz) Gruyère or Cheddar cheese, grated |

◆ Put the butter in a large bowl and microwave on HIGH for 45 seconds or until the butter melts.
◆ Add the onions, cover with cling film, pulling back one corner to allow the steam to escape and microwave on HIGH for 8-10 minutes or until the onions are very soft, stirring occasionally.
◆ Stir in the consommé and 450 ml (¾ pint) water. Season well with salt and pepper. Re-cover with cling film, pulling

back one corner to allow the steam to escape and microwave on HIGH for 10 minutes or until very hot, stirring occasionally. Leave to stand, covered.

◆ Arrange the French bread in a circle on a large flat plate and sprinkle with the cheese. Microwave on HIGH for 1 minute or until the cheese melts.

◆ Transfer the soup to a warmed soup tureen or individual bowls and float bread on top. Serve immediately.

## QUICK TOMATO AND PEPPER SOUP

### SERVES 4

| |
|---|
| 397 g (14 oz) can tomatoes |
| 200 g (7 oz) can pimentos, drained |
| 15 ml (1 tbsp) vegetable oil |
| 1 garlic clove, skinned and crushed |
| 1 small onion, skinned and finely chopped |
| 15 ml (1 level tbsp) plain flour |
| 450 ml (¾ pint) chicken stock |
| salt and pepper |
| snipped fresh chives and croûtons, to garnish |

◆ Liquidise the tomatoes and pimentos in a blender or food processor until smooth, then sieve to remove the seeds.

◆ Place the oil, garlic and onion in a large bowl and microwave on HIGH for 5 minutes or until slightly softened.

◆ Stir in the flour then gradually stir in the stock. Add the tomato, pimento purée and salt and pepper.

◆ Microwave on HIGH for 8-10 minutes or until the soup has thickened, stirring frequently. Serve, garnished with chives and croûtons.

## MINTED COURGETTE SOUP

### SERVES 6

| |
|---|
| 450 g (1 lb) courgettes, trimmed and thinly sliced |
| 1 bunch spring onions, trimmed and thinly sliced |
| 25 g (1 oz) butter or margarine |
| 900 ml (1½ pints) chicken stock |
| 45 ml (3 tbsp) chopped fresh mint |
| salt and pepper |
| 150 ml (¼ pint) natural yogurt |
| yogurt and mint sprigs, to garnish |

◆ Place the butter in a large bowl and microwave on HIGH for 45 seconds or until the butter melts. Add the courgettes and onions. Cover and microwave on HIGH for 6 minutes or until the courgettes are beginning to soften.

◆ Stir in the stock and mint and season to taste with salt and pepper. Microwave on HIGH for 8 minutes or until the vegetables are soft.

◆ Liquidise the soup in a blender or food processor and leave to cool. Add the yogurt and stir well. Check seasoning and chill.

◆ Ladle the soup into individual chilled bowls. Garnish each bowl with a swirl of yogurt and a mint sprig. Serve immediately.

## CHILLED PEA AND MINT SOUP

### SERVES 4-6

| |
|---|
| 50 g (2 oz) butter or margarine |
| 1 medium onion, skinned and coarsely chopped |
| 450 g (1 lb) peas |
| 568 ml (1 pint) milk |
| 600 ml (1 pint) chicken stock |
| 2 large mint sprigs |
| pinch of caster sugar |
| salt and pepper |
| 150 ml (¼ pint) natural yogurt |
| mint sprigs, to garnish |

◆ Put the butter into a 2.8 litre (5 pint) ovenproof glass bowl and microwave on HIGH for 45 seconds or until the butter melts.

◆ Add the onion and cover the bowl with cling film, pulling back one corner to allow the steam to escape, and microwave on HIGH for 5-7 minutes or until the onion is soft.

◆ Add the peas, milk, stock, 2 mint sprigs and sugar. Three-quarters cover with cling film and microwave on HIGH for about 8 minutes or until the liquid is boiling. Reduce the setting and microwave on LOW for 15 minutes or until the peas are really tender. Season well with salt and pepper and cool slightly.

◆ Remove about 45 ml (3 level tbsp) peas from the soup and put them aside for the garnish. Rub the remaining peas through a sieve, or liquidise them in a blender or food processor until quite smooth.

◆ Pour the purée into a large serving bowl. Adjust the seasoning and leave to cool for 30 minutes. Stir in the yogurt and cover and chill for 2-3 hours before serving.

◆ Serve garnished with the reserved peas and mint sprigs.

## CHILLED PEA AND MINT SOUP

*A delicately coloured, chilled soup with a subtle taste of mint*

SEE OPPOSITE

## CELERY AND STILTON SOUP

### SERVES 6

25 g (1 oz) butter or margarine

4 celery sticks, trimmed and finely chopped

30 ml (2 level tbsp) plain flour

300 ml (½ pint) milk

600 ml (1 pint) chicken stock

225 g (8 oz) Stilton cheese, crumbled

salt and pepper

◆ Place the butter in a large serving bowl and microwave on HIGH for 45 seconds or until the butter melts. Stir in the celery, cover, and microwave on HIGH for 5 minutes or until the celery begins to soften.

◆ Stir in the flour and microwave on HIGH for 30 seconds. Gradually stir in the milk and stock. Cover and microwave on HIGH for 8 minutes or until the celery is tender. Stir occasionally during cooking.

◆ Gradually add the Stilton and stir until well blended with the liquid. Season to taste, adding salt carefully as Stilton can be rather salty.

◆ Heat through in the microwave on HIGH for 1-2 minutes. Serve immediately.

## CHILLED CUCUMBER AND MUSHROOM SOUP

### SERVES 4-6

15 ml (1 tbsp) vegetable oil

1 small onion, skinned and finely chopped

1 garlic clove, skinned and crushed

1 cucumber, peeled and finely chopped

750 ml (1¼ pints) vegetable or chicken stock

salt and pepper

75 g (3 oz) mushrooms, chopped

150 ml (¼ pint) single cream

15 ml (1 tbsp) chopped fresh mint

a few drops of green food colouring (optional)

mushroom slices, to garnish

◆ Place the oil, onion and garlic in a large ovenproof bowl, three-quarters cover with cling film and microwave on HIGH for 5-7 minutes or until softened.

◆ Add the cucumber and microwave on HIGH for 5 minutes or until the cucumber is slightly softened.

◆ Stir in the stock and season well with salt and pepper.

Three-quarters cover with cling film and microwave on HIGH for 6-7 minutes or until the cucumber is tender.

◆ Leave for 5-10 minutes to cool slightly, then stir in the mushrooms. Liquidise the soup in a blender or food processor until smooth, then leave for 1-2 hours until cool.

◆ Stir in the cream, mint, and food colouring, if using, adjust the seasoning and chill.

◆ Ladle the soup into individual chilled bowls and serve garnished with mushroom slices.

## CREAM OF CELERY SOUP

### SERVES 4

25 g (1 oz) butter or margarine

1 large head celery, trimmed and thinly sliced

1 medium onion, skinned and chopped

900 ml (1½ pints) chicken stock

300 ml (½ pint) milk

salt and pepper

1 bouquet garni

60 ml (4 tbsp) single cream

celery leaves or parsley, to garnish

◆ Put the butter into a 2.8 litre (5 pint) ovenproof glass bowl and microwave on HIGH for 45 seconds or until the butter melts. Add the celery and onion and stir well to coat evenly with the butter. Cover with cling film, pulling back one corner to allow the steam to escape. Microwave on HIGH for 6-8 minutes or until the celery softens, stirring frequently.

◆ Add the chicken stock, milk, salt, pepper and bouquet garni to the celery. Three-quarters cover the bowl with cling film and microwave on HIGH for 18-20 minutes or until the celery is very soft.

◆ Cool the soup slightly, remove the bouquet garni and then liquidise in a blender or food processor until smooth, or rub through a sieve.

◆ Return the soup to a clean, ovenproof serving bowl and reheat on HIGH for 2 minutes.

◆ Stir the cream into the soup. Serve garnished with chopped celery leaves or parsley.

## VICHYSSOISE

### SERVES 4

| |
|---|
| 25 g (1 oz) butter or margarine |
| 2 medium leeks, white parts only, thinly sliced |
| 1 small onion, skinned and finely chopped |
| 350 g (12 oz) potatoes, peeled and thinly sliced |
| 600 ml (1 pint) chicken stock |
| salt and pepper |
| 1 blade mace |
| 300 ml (½ pint) double cream |
| 30 ml (2 tbsp) snipped fresh chives or finely chopped watercress, to garnish |

◆ Put the butter into a 1.7 litre (3 pint) ovenproof glass bowl and microwave on HIGH for 45 seconds or until the butter melts.

◆ Add the leeks and onion and mix together. Cover with cling film, pulling back one corner to allow the steam to escape, and microwave on HIGH for 5-7 minutes or until the leeks and onion are softened.

◆ Add the potatoes, stock, salt, pepper and mace and stir well. Three-quarters cover with cling film and microwave on HIGH for 15-17 minutes or until the vegetables are very soft, stirring frequently.

◆ Allow the soup to cool a little. Remove the blade of mace, then rub through a fine sieve, or liquidise in a blender or food processor until smooth. Pour the soup into a clean bowl, cover and refrigerate for 3-4 hours, or overnight, until well chilled.

◆ Just before serving, stir in the cream. Serve sprinkled with chives or watercress.

## TOMATO AND CARROT SOUP

### SERVES 6

| |
|---|
| 25 g (1 oz) butter or margarine |
| 1 large onion, skinned and finely chopped |
| 1 garlic clove, skinned and crushed |
| 225 g (8 oz) carrots, peeled and finely chopped |
| 450 g (1 lb) ripe tomatoes, skinned and chopped |
| 2 eating apples, peeled, cored and diced |
| 1 bouquet garni |
| 1.1 litres (2 pints) chicken stock |
| salt and pepper |
| double cream and snipped chives, to garnish |

◆ Place the butter in a large bowl and microwave on HIGH for 45 seconds or until the butter melts. Stir in the onion and garlic. Cover and microwave on HIGH for 3 minutes or until the onion begins to soften.

◆ Add the carrots, tomatoes, apples, bouquet garni and stock. Season to taste, cover and microwave on HIGH for 21 minutes or until the vegetables are tender.

◆ Discard the bouquet garni and liquidise the mixture in a blender or food processor until smooth. Pour the soup back into the bowl and microwave on HIGH for 2 minutes or until hot.

◆ Ladle the soup into warmed bowls and swirl the tops with double cream. Sprinkle with chives and serve.

## BORSCH (BEETROOT SOUP)

### SERVES 4

| |
|---|
| 6 small raw beetroot, total weight about 1 kg (2¼ lb), peeled |
| 2 medium onions, skinned and chopped |
| 1.1 litres (2 pints) beef stock |
| salt and pepper |
| 30 ml (2 tbsp) lemon juice |
| 90 ml (6 tbsp) dry sherry |
| 150 ml (¼ pint) soured cream |
| snipped fresh chives, to garnish |

◆ Grate the beetroot directly into a 2.8 litre (5 pint) ovenproof glass bowl. Add the onions, stock, salt and pepper. Three-quarters cover the bowl with cling film and microwave on HIGH for 20-25 minutes until the beetroot and onions are very tender, stirring frequently.

◆ Strain, discard the vegetables and add the lemon juice and sherry to the liquid. Adjust the seasoning. Serve hot or chill in the refrigerator for at least 2 hours and serve cold. Serve garnished with a whirl of soured cream and a sprinkling of snipped chives.

## WATERCRESS AND ORANGE SOUP

### SERVES 6

50 g (2 oz) butter or margarine

1 large onion, skinned and chopped

2 large bunches watercress, trimmed and chopped

45 ml (3 level tbsp) plain flour

salt and pepper

1.1 litres (2 pints) chicken stock

grated rind and juice of 1 medium orange

3 slices white bread

150 ml (¼ pint) single cream

◆ Put the butter into a 2.8 litre (5 pint) ovenproof glass bowl and microwave on HIGH for 45 seconds or until the butter melts. Add the onions, cover with cling film, pulling back one corner to allow the steam to escape, and microwave on HIGH for 5-6 minutes or until the onions soften.
◆ Add the watercress to the onions, cover and microwave on HIGH for 1-2 minutes. Stir in the flour, salt, pepper and stock. Three-quarters cover with cling film and microwave on HIGH for 8 minutes, stirring frequently.
◆ Add the orange rind and 45 ml (3 tbsp) orange juice to the soup. Allow to cool for about 5 minutes, then liquidise in a blender or food processor until smooth.
◆ Cut the bread into small cubes and grill until golden.
◆ Return the soup to a clean ovenproof glass bowl and stir in the cream. Microwave on LOW for 6-7 minutes, stirring frequently, until the soup is hot but not boiling.
◆ Serve the soup either hot or well chilled, garnished with the toasted croûtons.

## CORN CHOWDER

### SERVES 4-6

50 g (2 oz) butter or margarine

2 medium onions, skinned and sliced

100 g (4 oz) streaky bacon, rinded and diced

45 ml (3 level tbsp) plain flour

1.1 litres (2 pints) chicken stock

225 g (8 oz) potatoes, peeled and cut into 1 cm (½ inch) dice

175 g (6 oz) carrots, peeled and coarsely grated

335 g (11.8 oz) can sweetcorn, drained

150 ml (¼ pint) single cream

salt and pepper

chopped fresh parsley, to garnish

◆ Put the butter into a 2.8 litre (5 pint) ovenproof glass bowl and microwave on HIGH for 45 seconds or until the butter melts. Add the onions and the bacon. Cover with cling film, pulling back one corner to allow the steam to escape, and microwave on HIGH for 5-6 minutes or until the onions are softened.
◆ Stir in the flour and microwave on HIGH for 1 minute, then gradually stir in the stock, potatoes and carrots. Three-quarters cover with cling film and microwave on HIGH for about 8 minutes until boiling, stirring frequently. Microwave on HIGH for a further 10-12 minutes or until the potatoes are tender.
◆ Add the sweetcorn and stir in the cream. Microwave on LOW for 3-4 minutes until heated through but do not boil.
◆ Season the soup to taste with salt and pepper. Serve garnished with chopped parsley.

## MINESTRONE

### SERVES 6

2 small leeks, trimmed and thinly sliced

1 carrot, peeled and cut into 0.5 cm (¼ inch) dice

2 celery sticks, trimmed and thinly sliced

3 streaky bacon rashers, rinded and chopped

25 g (1 oz) butter or margarine

1 garlic clove, skinned and crushed

5 ml (1 tsp) chopped fresh basil or 2.5 ml (½ level tsp)

900 ml (1½) pints boiling chicken stock

226 g (8 oz) can tomatoes

213 g (7.5 oz) can red kidney beans, drained

salt and pepper

50 g (2 oz) long grain rice

50 g (2 oz) shelled fresh or frozen peas

30 ml (2 tbsp) chopped fresh parsley

25 g (1 oz) freshly grated Parmesan cheese

◆ Put the leeks, carrot, celery and bacon into a large ovenproof glass bowl and add the butter, garlic and basil. Three-quarters cover with cling film and microwave on HIGH for 15 minutes or until the carrot begins to soften. Stir the ingredients two or three times during cooking.
◆ Stir in the stock, the tomatoes with their juice and the beans and season with salt and pepper. Microwave on HIGH for 10 minutes or until the vegetables are soft, stirring once during cooking.
◆ Add the rice, peas and parsley. Stir well and microwave on HIGH for 5 minutes or until the pasta is tender. Stir the soup once during cooking. Leave it to stand for 5 minutes, then serve sprinkled with the cheese.

# CAULIFLOWER SOUP

### SERVES 4-6

*50 g (2 oz) butter or margarine*

*1 medium onion, skinned and finely chopped*

*30 ml (2 level tbsp) plain flour*

*750 ml (1¼ pints) chicken stock*

*1 small cauliflower, broken into florets*

*salt and pepper*

*30 ml (2 tbsp) single cream*

*chopped fresh parsley, to garnish*

◆ Place the butter in a large ovenproof glass bowl and microwave on HIGH for 45 seconds or until the butter melts. Stir in the onion, cover with cling film, pulling back one corner to allow the steam to escape, and microwave on HIGH for 5-7 minutes or until the onion is softened.

◆ Stir in the flour and microwave on HIGH for 1 minute. Gradually stir in the stock and microwave on HIGH for 3-4 minutes, stirring occasionally, until the liquid is boiling and thickened.

◆ Place the cauliflower in an ovenproof glass bowl, cover with cling film, pulling back one corner to allow the steam to escape, and microwave on HIGH for 7-8 minutes, stirring occasionally, until the cauliflower is softened.

◆ Add the cauliflower to the sauce and microwave on HIGH for 4 minutes. Allow the soup to cool for about 5 minutes, then pour it into a food processor or blender and liquidise until smooth. Season well with salt and pepper.

◆ Return the soup to a clean ovenproof glass bowl. Microwave on HIGH for 2-3 minutes to reheat the soup. Stir in the cream. Serve garnished with parsley.

# ALMOND SOUP

### SERVES 6

*100 g (4 oz) ground almonds*

*2 celery sticks, trimmed and finely chopped*

*1 small onion, skinned and finely chopped*

*600 ml (1 pint) chicken stock*

*25 g (1 oz) butter or margarine*

*25 g (1 oz) plain flour*

*300 ml (½ pint) milk*

*45 ml (3 tbsp) double cream*

*1 egg yolk*

*salt and pepper*

*toasted flaked almonds, to garnish*

◆ Mix the almonds, celery and onion together in a large bowl and pour in the stock. Cover and microwave on HIGH for 10 minutes or until the liquid is boiling, then microwave for a further 4 minutes.

◆ Strain the liquid through a sieve and rub the almond paste through using a wooden spoon.

◆ Place the butter in the rinsed-out bowl and microwave on HIGH for 45 seconds or until the butter melts. Stir in the flour and microwave on HIGH for 30 seconds. Gradually whisk in the milk and almond liquid and microwave on HIGH for 3 minutes or until boiling.

◆ Blend the cream and egg yolk together and slowly add to the soup, stirring until well blended. Season to taste with salt and pepper. Garnish with the toasted almonds and serve.

# BUTTERMILK AND DILL SOUP

### SERVES 2

*2 small leeks, white part only, finely chopped*

*25 g (1 oz) butter or margarine*

*1 medium potatoes, each weighing about 100 g (4 oz), peeled*

*300 ml (½ pint) hot chicken stock*

*30 ml (2 tbsp) chopped fresh dill*

*salt and pepper*

*300 ml (½ pint) buttermilk*

◆ Put the chopped leek into a medium bowl with the butter. Grate in the potato.

◆ Cover with cling film, pulling back one corner to allow the steam to escape, and microwave on HIGH for 4-5 minutes or until the vegetables have softened, stirring occasionally.

◆ Stir in the chicken stock and half of the dill, cover again and microwave on HIGH for 10-12 minutes or until the potato is very soft. Season well with salt and pepper.

◆ Allow to cool a little, then liquidise in a blender or food processor until smooth. Stir in the buttermilk and pour into a serving bowl. Chill for at least 2 hours before serving.

◆ To serve, sprinkle the remaining chopped dill on top. Serve with wholemeal bread, if liked.

## VEGETABLE SOUP

### SERVES 4

*50 g (2 oz) butter or margarine*

*225 g (8 oz) carrots, peeled and finely diced*

*175 g (6 oz) swede, peeled and finely diced*

*2 small leeks, trimmed and thinly sliced*

*25 g (1 oz) plain flour*

*450 ml (¾ pint) chicken stock*

*300 ml (½ pint) milk*

*salt and pepper*

*chopped fresh parsley, to garnish*

◆ Put the butter into a 1.7 litre (3 pint) ovenproof glass bowl and microwave on HIGH for 45 seconds or until the butter melts.

◆ Add the vegetables and lightly mix together. Three-quarters cover with cling film and microwave on HIGH for 8-10 minutes or until the vegetables begin to soften, stirring two or three times.

◆ Stir in the flour and stock. Microwave on HIGH for 10-15 minutes or until the vegetables are very soft. Stir in the milk and season well with salt and pepper. Microwave on HIGH for 2-3 minutes or until the soup is hot but not boiling. Serve sprinkled with chopped parsley.

## PEPPER AND GINGER WITH SESAME BREAD

### SERVES 2

*40 g (1½ oz) butter or margarine*

*1 large red pepper, seeded and coarsely chopped*

*1 small onion, skinned and finely chopped*

*1 cm (½ inch) piece of fresh ginger, peeled and grated*

*7.5 ml (1½ level tsp) paprika*

*pinch sugar*

*300 ml (½ pint) chicken stock*

*salt and pepper*

*150 ml (¼ pint) natural yogurt*

*15 ml (1 level tbsp) sesame seeds*

*3 slices bread, crusts removed*

*thin slices red pepper, to garnish (optional)*

◆ Put 15 g (½ oz) butter into a medium bowl with the chopped pepper, onion and ginger. Cover with cling film, pulling back one corner to allow the steam to escape, and microwave on HIGH for 7-8 minutes or until the vegetables have softened, stirring occasionally.

◆ Stir in 2.5 ml (½ level tsp) paprika and microwave on HIGH for 1 minute, uncovered.

◆ Stir in the sugar, chicken stock, salt and pepper. Re-cover and microwave on HIGH for 5-6 minutes or until the pepper is soft.

◆ Allow to cool a little, then liquidise in a blender or food processor until smooth and pour into 2 serving bowls.

◆ Put the remaining butter in a small bowl and microwave on HIGH for 10-15 seconds or until the butter is just soft enough to beat. Beat in the remaining paprika, the sesame seeds and salt and pepper to taste.

◆ Cut each slice of bread into 4 triangles and spread the sesame butter on both sides.

◆ Arrange the bread in a circle on a sheet of greaseproof paper and microwave on HIGH for 1 minute. Turn the bread over and microwave on HIGH for a further 1 minute or until the bread is firm. Leave to stand for 2 minutes.

◆ Meanwhile, microwave the soup on LOW for 2-3 minutes or until it is warmed through.

◆ Garnish the soup with thin slices of red pepper, and serve with the sesame bread.

# SMOKED HADDOCK CHOWDER

### SERVES 4

450 g (1 lb) smoked haddock fillet

1 bay leaf

450 ml (¾ pint) milk

25 g (1 oz) butter or margarine

1 large floury potato, peeled and finely diced

10 ml (2 tsp) lemon juice

chopped fresh parsley, to garnish

◆ Place the fish in a shallow dish with the bay leaf. Pour over the milk. Cover with cling film, pulling back one corner to allow the steam to escape and microwave on HIGH for 7 minutes or until cooked, turning the dish once.
◆ Drain, reserving the cooking liquid. Flake the fish, discarding the skin and any bones. Set aside.
◆ Place the butter or margarine and diced potato in a large bowl. Cover and microwave on HIGH for 5 minutes or until the potato begins to soften.
◆ Add the fish, reserved cooking liquid, lemon juice, and 150 ml (¼ pint) water. Stir gently and microwave on HIGH for 2 minutes or until heated through. Garnish with parsley and serve.

# LEMON SOUP

### SERVES 4-6

25 g (1 oz) butter or margarine

1 medium onion, skinned and thinly sliced

1 large carrot, peeled and thinly sliced

2 celery sticks, washed, trimmed and thinly sliced

2 lemons

1.1 litres (2 pints) chicken stock

2 bay leaves

salt and pepper

150 ml (¼ pint) single cream

snipped chives and lemon slices, to garnish

◆ Put the butter into a large bowl. Microwave on HIGH for 45 seconds until the butter melts. Add the onions, carrot and celery and mix well. Cover with cling film, pulling back one corner to let steam escape and microwave on HIGH for 8 minutes until the vegetables soften.
◆ Meanwhile, thinly pare the lemons using a potato peeler. Put the rinds in a small bowl and pour over 300 ml (½ pint) boiling water. Cover with cling film, pulling back one corner to let steam escape and microwave on HIGH for 1½ minutes.

Drain. Squeeze the juice from the lemons to give 75-90 ml (5-6 tbsp).
◆ Add the blanched lemon rind and the juice, stock and bay leaves to the softened vegetables; season well. Cover as before and microwave on HIGH for about 8 minutes until boiling. Stir and microwave on HIGH for a further 10 minutes until the vegetables are very soft.
◆ Cool the soup a little, remove the bay leaves and then purée in a blender or food processor until quite smooth.
◆ Return the soup to a clean bowl and stir in the cream. Microwave on LOW for about 5-6 minutes until hot but not boiling, stirring frequently. Adjust the seasoning to taste. Serve the soup hot or chilled, garnished with snipped chives and lemon slices.

# POTATO AND ONION SOUP

### SERVES 6

40 g (1½ oz) butter or margarine

1 bunch of spring onions, trimmed and chopped

450 g (1 lb) potatoes, peeled and diced

1 bay leaf

600 ml (1 pint) chicken stock

salt and pepper

150 ml (¼ pint) milk

90 ml (6 tbsp) double cream

strips of spring onion, to garnish

◆ Place the butter or margarine in a large bowl and microwave on HIGH for 45 seconds or until melted. Add the spring onions, cover with cling film, pulling back one corner to let steam escape and microwave on HIGH for 5-7 minutes or until softened.
◆ Add the potatoes, bay leaf, stock, salt and pepper and microwave on HIGH for 15 minutes or until the vegetables are tender. Discard the bay leaf.
◆ Leave to cool slightly, then purée in a blender or food processor.
◆ Pour the soup back into the bowl, add the milk and reheat on HIGH for 4 minutes. Add the cream and whisk thoroughly. Check seasoning. Garnish with strips of spring onion.

# STARTERS

───── SEAFOOD SCALLOPS ─────

*An elegant starter combining firm white fish and shellfish in a
creamy sauce*

SEE PAGE 29

# Cooking Tips

◆

*Use your microwave to prepare starters in advance or to serve hot starters. Prepare in individual dishes then reheat in the microwave.*

◆

*Remember that bread can be warmed in the microwave. Place 4 rolls in a wicker serving basket and microwave on HIGH for 20-30 seconds.*

◆

*Butter for spreading can be softened in the microwave on LOW for 1 minute.*

◆

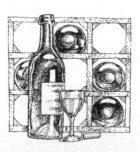

## SEAFOOD SCALLOPS

### SERVES 4

| |
|---|
| 225 g (8 oz) haddock fillet |
| 150 ml (¼ pint) dry white wine |
| small piece of onion |
| 1 parsley sprig |
| 1 bay leaf |
| 450 g (1 lb) potatoes, peeled and coarsely chopped |
| 75 g (3 oz) butter or margarine |
| 225 ml (8 fl oz) milk |
| salt and pepper |
| 50 g (2 oz) button mushrooms, thinly sliced |
| 45 ml (3 level tbsp) plain flour |
| 50 g (2 oz) peeled prawns |
| chopped fresh parsley, to garnish |

◆ Place the haddock in a shallow ovenproof dish, pour over the wine and add the onion, parsley and bay leaf. Cover the dish with cling film, pulling back one corner to allow the steam to escape. Microwave on HIGH for 4-5 minutes until the fish is tender enough to flake easily.

◆ Drain the haddock juices into a measuring jug and make the liquid up to 150 ml (¼ pint) with water, if necessary. Skin and flake the fish. Set the fish and the cooking liquid aside.

◆ Put the potatoes into a 1.7 litre (3 pint) ovenproof glass bowl and add 175 ml (6 fl oz) water. Three-quarters cover the bowl with cling film and microwave on HIGH for 6-8 minutes until the potatoes are cooked, stirring twice during the cooking time. Drain the potatoes well, then mash them with 40 g (1½ oz) butter, 25 ml (1 fl oz) milk and salt and pepper. Beat the potatoes until they are smooth and creamy.

◆ Put 15 g (½ oz) of the remaining butter in a small ovenproof glass bowl, microwave on HIGH for 30 seconds until the butter melts, then stir in the mushrooms. Cover with cling film, pulling back one corner to allow the steam to escape, and microwave on HIGH for 2-3 minutes until the mushrooms are cooked, shaking the bowl two or three times during the cooking time.

◆ Put the remaining butter into an ovenproof glass bowl and microwave on HIGH for 45 seconds until the butter melts. Stir in the flour and microwave on HIGH for 30 seconds, then gradually whisk in the remaining milk and the reserved fish liquid. Microwave on HIGH for 45 seconds, then whisk well. Microwave on HIGH for 2 minutes, whisking every 30 seconds until the sauce thickens. Season it well with salt and pepper. Stir in the flaked haddock, the mushrooms and the prawns.

◆ Spoon the fish mixture into 4 scallop shells or small gratin dishes. Put the potato in a large piping bag fitted with a large star nozzle and pipe a neat potato border around each scallop shell or gratin dish. Microwave on HIGH for about 5 minutes until the scallops are well heated through, changing the position of the scallops twice during the cooking time.

◆ Garnish the scallops with parsley and serve them immediately. If wished, the scallops may be quickly browned under a hot grill just before serving.

## HOT AVOCADO AND PRAWNS

### SERVES 2

| |
|---|
| 1 shallot or ½ small onion, skinned and finely chopped |
| 15 ml (1 tbsp) vegetable oil |
| 1 ripe avocado |
| 10 ml (2 tsp) lime or lemon juice |
| 30 ml (2 tbsp) natural yogurt |
| 30 ml (2 tbsp) mayonnaise |
| 1.25 ml (¼ level tsp) prepared mustard |
| salt and pepper |
| 75 g (3 oz) peeled prawns |
| 15 ml (1 tbsp) snipped fresh chives |
| lime or lemon twists and unpeeled prawns, to garnish |

◆ Put the shallot and oil in a medium bowl and cover with cling film, pulling back one corner to allow the steam to escape. Microwave on HIGH for 3-4 minutes or until the shallot is soft, stirring occasionally.

◆ Meanwhile, halve and stone the avocado. Using a teaspoon, scoop out most of the flesh into a bowl, leaving a 1 cm (½ inch) shell. Rub the inside of the avocado shell with half of the lime juice.

◆ Mash the scooped-out avocado with a fork to a smooth pulp. Gradually mix in the yogurt, mayonnaise, mustard and remaining lime juice. Season well with salt and pepper.

◆ Stir the prawns into the cooked shallot and microwave on HIGH for 1 minute, stirring occasionally.

◆ Strain the prawns, stir into the avocado and yogurt mixture, and mix together well.

◆ Microwave on HIGH for 1-2 minutes or until just heated through, stirring occasionally. Stir in the chives.

◆ Put the avocado shells on to a small ovenproof serving plate and fill with the prawn mixture. Microwave on HIGH for a further 1-2 minutes or until warmed through. Transfer one of the avocados to a second serving plate. Garnish with the lime and prawns and serve immediately.

## MUSHROOMS IN GARLIC BUTTER

### SERVES 4

| |
|---|
| 225 g (8 oz) medium mushrooms |
| 50 g (2 oz) butter or margarine |
| 2 garlic cloves, skinned and crushed |
| 1 small onion, skinned and finely chopped |
| 15 g (½ oz) fresh brown breadcrumbs |
| 30 ml (2 tbsp) chopped fresh parsley |
| salt and pepper |
| French bread, to serve |

◆ Remove the mushroom stems and finely chop them. Set the mushroom caps aside.
◆ Place the butter in a medium bowl and microwave on HIGH for 45 seconds or until the butter melts. Add the garlic, onion and chopped mushroom stems. Cover and microwave on HIGH for 5-7 minutes or until soft. Stir in the breadcrumbs, parsley and seasoning.
◆ Stuff each mushroom cap with a little of the mixture, pressing down lightly. Arrange the mushrooms in a circle on a plate and microwave on HIGH for 2-3 minutes, or until hot. Serve with French bread.

## MUSHROOM COCOTTES

### SERVES 4

| |
|---|
| 25 g (1 oz) butter or margarine |
| 100 g (4 oz) button mushrooms, sliced |
| 2.5 ml (½ level tsp) cornflour |
| salt and pepper |
| 4 eggs |
| 60 ml (4 tbsp) double cream |
| 50 g (2 oz) Gruyère cheese, thinly sliced |
| hot buttered toast, to serve |

◆ Place the butter in a medium bowl and microwave on HIGH for 45 seconds or until the butter melts. Stir in the mushrooms and microwave on HIGH for 2 minutes.
◆ Blend the cornflour with about 5 ml (1 tsp) water. Add to the bowl of mushrooms and microwave on HIGH for 1 minute. Season to taste with salt and pepper.
◆ Spoon the mixture into 4 ramekin dishes and break an egg into each dish. Gently prick each egg yolk. Spoon over the cream and top with the cheese. Microwave on HIGH for 4 minutes or until the eggs are just set. Serve with hot buttered toast.

## CRABMEAT-FILLED COURGETTE SLICES

### SERVES 4

| |
|---|
| 4 medium courgettes, trimmed |
| 150 g (5 oz) can crabmeat, drained and flaked |
| 50 g (2 oz) fresh breadcrumbs |
| 10 ml (2 tsp) lemon juice |
| 60 ml (4 tbsp) soured cream or mayonnaise |
| 15 ml (1 tbsp) snipped fresh chives |
| 60 ml (4 level tbsp) freshly grated Parmesan cheese |
| salt and pepper |
| fresh chives, to garnish |

◆ Cut the courgettes in half lengthways. Using a teaspoon, scoop out centres to make a small hollow. Discard centres.
◆ Put the courgette halves into a shallow flameproof dish with 45 ml (3 tbsp) water. Cover and microwave on HIGH for 5 minutes.
◆ Meanwhile, mix the crabmeat, breadcrumbs, lemon juice, soured cream, chives and half the Parmesan cheese together. Season to taste with salt and pepper.
◆ Pour off the liquid from the dish of courgettes. Divide the crabmeat mixture between each courgette, neatly stuffing along centres. Sprinkle with remaining cheese. Cover and microwave on HIGH for 4 minutes or until courgettes are hot.
◆ Brown the cheese topping under a hot grill. Garnish with fresh chives and serve.

## CORN ON THE COB WITH HERB BUTTER

### SERVES 4

| |
|---|
| 4 corn on the cob |
| 100 g (4 oz) butter, softened |
| salt and pepper |
| 5 ml (1 tsp) lemon juice |
| 45 ml (3 tbsp) finely chopped fresh mixed herbs, such as mint, parsley, lemon thyme and marjoram |

◆ Peel back the husks from the corn and remove the silk.
◆ Beat the butter with the remaining ingredients. Spread the herb butter all over the ears of corn, then re-cover them with the green husks. If the cobs are without husks, wrap each one in greaseproof paper.
◆ Place the corn cobs side by side in a shallow ovenproof dish and microwave on HIGH for about 8-9 minutes or until the corn is tender, turning and repositioning the cobs two or three times during the cooking time.

## — CRABMEAT-FILLED COURGETTE SLICES —

*The texture of the crab, Parmesan and breadcrumb mix contrasts well
with the courgette in this starter dish*

SEE OPPOSITE

### ——— VEGETABLE AND CHEESE TERRINE ———
*The texture of the beans, carrots and peppercorns contrasts well with the*
*smooth cheese layers in this terrine*

SEE OPPOSITE

# VEGETABLE & CHEESE TERRINE

### SERVES 8

| |
|---|
| *100 g (4 oz) carrots, peeled and cut into matchsticks* |
| *100 g (4 oz) French beans, trimmed* |
| *10 large fresh spinach leaves* |
| *500 g (1 lb) full fat soft cheese* |
| *3 egg yolks* |
| *15 ml (1 tbsp) lemon juice* |
| *salt and pepper* |
| *100 g (4 oz) green peppercorns* |

◆ Place the carrots and beans in separate roasting bags. Add 45 ml (3 tbsp) water to each and pierce the bags. Microwave on HIGH for 3 minutes or until the vegetables are just tender, then drain and set aside.

◆ Wash the spinach in several changes of water, drain well and place in a bowl. Cover and microwave on HIGH for 1 minute. Drain and rinse under cold running water.

◆ Mix the cheese, egg yolks and lemon juice together and season with salt and pepper.

◆ Line a 20.5 cm (8 inch) microwave loaf dish with half the spinach leaves. Spread one quarter of the cheese mixture in the base of the dish and cover with the carrots. Top with one third of the remaining cheese and arrange the beans on top. Spread over half the remaining cheese and top with the green peppercorns. Finish with the rest of the cheese and cover with the reserved spinach leaves.

◆ Cover with cling film and microwave on MEDIUM for 5 minutes. Give the dish a half turn, then microwave on HIGH for 3-4 minutes or until set. Leave to cool in the pan, then chill before serving.

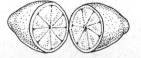

# FARMHOUSE PATE

### SERVES 8

| |
|---|
| *225 g (8 oz) lamb's liver, coarsely chopped* |
| *700 g (1½ lb) belly of pork, rinded and coarsely chopped* |
| *1 large onion, skinned and chopped* |
| *1 garlic clove, skinned and crushed* |
| *60 ml (4 tbsp) tomato purée* |
| *30 ml (2 tbsp) brandy* |
| *50 g (2 oz) stuffed green olives, sliced* |
| *5 ml (1 tsp) chopped fresh mixed herbs or 2.5 ml (½ level tsp) dried* |
| *salt and pepper* |
| *225 g (8 oz) streaky bacon, rinded* |
| *hot buttered toast, to serve* |

◆ Mince the liver, pork, onion and garlic together in a mincer or food processor.

◆ Place in a bowl and mix in the tomato purée, brandy, olives and herbs. Season to taste with salt and pepper.

◆ Line a terrine dish with the streaky bacon rashers and spoon in the liver mixture.

◆ Cover and microwave on LOW for 25 minutes. Cool in the dish, then refrigerate overnight.

◆ Turn out, and serve, cut in slices, with hot buttered toast.

# HADDOCK PATE

### SERVES 4-6

| |
|---|
| *225 g (8 oz) smoked haddock fillet* |
| *25 ml (5 tsp) lemon juice* |
| *225 g (8 oz) full fat soft cheese* |
| *15 ml (1 tbsp) chopped fresh parsley* |
| *salt and pepper* |

◆ Place the haddock fillet in a buttered shallow ovenproof dish and sprinkle with 10 ml (2 tsp) lemon juice. Cover the top of the dish with cling film, pulling back one corner to allow the steam to escape. Microwave the fish on HIGH for 4-5 minutes or until the haddock is cooked and the flesh flakes easily.

◆ Drain the haddock well. Remove any skin, membrane and bones. Allow the fish to cool, then flake it finely.

◆ Beat the cheese in a small mixing bowl until it is soft and creamy. Beat in the remaining lemon juice, the chopped parsley and the flaked haddock. Season the mixture liberally with salt and pepper.

## FENNEL A LA GRECQUE

SERVES 4

2 large heads Florence fennel

45 ml (3 tbsp) vegetable oil

1 large onion, skinned and chopped

150 ml (¼ pint) red wine

30 ml (2 tbsp) tomato purée

30 ml (2 tbsp) lemon juice

1 bay leaf

2.5 ml (½ tsp) chopped fresh basil or 1.25 ml (¼ level tsp) dried

5 ml (1 level tsp) sugar

French bread, to serve

◆ Trim the root and stalk ends of the fennel and reserve the leaves for garnish. Quarter the bulb and cut into thin slices.
◆ Put the oil and onion into a large casserole and cover with cling film, pulling back one corner to allow the steam to escape. Microwave on HIGH for 7 minutes or until the onion is softened.
◆ Add the sliced fennel and all the remaining ingredients except the fennel leaves to the onion and stir well. Three-quarters cover the top of the dish with cling film and microwave on HIGH for 6-8 minutes until boiling, then stir. Reduce the setting to LOW and microwave for 12-14 minutes, stirring occasionally, until the fennel is just tender.
◆ Garnish with the reserved fennel leaves and serve warm with French bread.

## LEEKS A LA GRECQUE

SERVES 6

6 medium leeks, trimmed and sliced into 5 cm (2 inch) lengths

1 small onion, skinned and finely chopped

2 large tomatoes, skinned, seeded and chopped

100 ml (4 fl oz) dry white wine

75 ml (3 tbsp) olive oil

1 garlic clove, skinned and crushed

salt and pepper

chopped fresh basil or parsley, to garnish

hot crusty bread and butter, to serve

◆ Place the leeks in a shallow dish in a single layer. Sprinkle over the onion and tomatoes. Add the wine, oil and garlic. Season to taste with salt and pepper. Cover and microwave on HIGH for 13-16 minutes or until the leeks are tender.
◆ Leave until cold. Serve on side plates, garnished with the basil or parsley, and with hot crusty bread and butter.

## MUSSEL BISQUE

SERVES 6

25 g (1 oz) butter or margarine

30 ml (2 level tbsp) plain flour

900 ml (1½ pints) milk

60 ml (4 tbsp) dry sherry

450 g (1 lb) frozen mussels, thawed

150 ml (¼ pint) single cream

salt and pepper

chopped fresh parsley, to garnish

◆ Place the butter in a large serving bowl and microwave on HIGH for 45 seconds or until the butter melts.
◆ Stir in the flour and microwave on HIGH for 30 seconds. Gradually whisk in the milk and the sherry. Microwave on HIGH for 4 minutes, whisking after every minute, until the sauce is boiling and has thickened.
◆ Add the mussels and microwave on HIGH for 2-4 minutes or until the mussels are heated through. Stir in the single cream and season. Serve, garnished with chopped parsley.

## CURRIED EGGS

SERVES 6

1 medium onion, skinned and finely chopped

15 ml (1 tbsp) vegetable oil

10 ml (2 level tsp) curry powder

5 ml (1 level tsp) paprika

10 ml (2 tsp) tomato purée

150 ml (¼ pint) mayonnaise

150 ml (¼ pint) natural yogurt

6 hard-boiled eggs, shelled and halved lengthways

watercress, to garnish

thinly sliced brown bread and butter, to serve

◆ Mix the onion and oil together in a small bowl and microwave on HIGH for 5-7 minutes or until the onion has softened.
◆ Stir in the curry powder, paprika and tomato purée. Microwave on HIGH for 2 minutes. Cool slightly, then add the mayonnaise and yogurt.
◆ Arrange the halved eggs cut side down on individual serving plates. Pour over the curry sauce and garnish with watercress. Serve with thinly sliced brown bread and butter.

# SPINACH TARTS WITH TOMATO AND BASIL SALAD

### SERVES 2

| |
|---|
| 50 g (2 oz) plain wholemeal flour |
| salt and pepper |
| 50 g (2 oz) butter or margarine |
| 2 egg yolks |
| 1 small onion, skinned and finely chopped |
| 1 small garlic clove, skinned and crushed |
| 300 g (10.6 oz) packet frozen leaf spinach |
| 75 ml (5 level tbsp) freshly grated Parmesan cheese |
| 60 ml (4 tbsp) double cream |
| freshly grated nutmeg |
| 3 large tomatoes |
| 15 ml (1 tbsp) chopped fresh basil |
| 15 ml (1 tbsp) olive or vegetable oil |

◆ Mix the flour and a pinch of salt in a bowl. Cut half of the butter into small pieces and add it to the flour.

◆ Rub the butter in until the mixture resembles fine breadcrumbs, then make a well in the centre and stir in one of the egg yolks and 15-30 ml (1-2 tbsp) water. Mix together using a round bladed knife. Knead lightly to give a firm, smooth dough.

◆ Roll out the dough thinly. Invert two 10 cm (4 inch) shallow glass flan dishes and cover the base and sides with the dough. Cover with cling film and chill while making the filling.

◆ Put the remaining butter in a large bowl and microwave on HIGH for 1 minute or until the butter melts.

◆ Stir in the onion and garlic and cover with a cling film, pulling back one corner to allow the steam to escape. Microwave on HIGH for 4-5 minutes or until the onion is softened.

◆ Add the spinach, cover again and microwave on HIGH for 8-9 minutes or until it is thawed, stirring frequently.

◆ Stir in 60 ml (4 tbsp) Parmesan cheese, the cream and season well with salt, pepper and nutmeg.

◆ Remove the cling film from the pastry cases and prick all over, with a fork. Microwave on HIGH, pastry side uppermost, for 2-2½ minutes or until the pastry is firm to the touch. Leave to stand for 4-5 minutes, then carefully invert the pastry cases on to a wire rack. Remove the flan dishes and leave the pastry cases to crisp.

◆ Meanwhile, thinly slice the tomatoes and arrange on 2 large serving plates. Sprinkle with the basil and drizzle over the olive oil. Season with salt and pepper.

◆ Microwave spinach filling on HIGH for 2-3 minutes, stirring occasionally. Stir in remaining egg yolk and microwave on HIGH for 1-1½ minutes or until slightly thickened.

◆ Transfer the pastry cases to the serving plates and carefully spoon the spinach filling into the centres. Sprinkle the tarts with remaining Parmesan cheese and serve immediately.

# CHILLED COURGETTE MOUSSE WITH SAFFRON SAUCE

### SERVES 2

| |
|---|
| 275 g (10 oz) small courgettes, trimmed |
| 15 g (½ oz) butter or margarine |
| 7.5 ml (1½ tsp) lemon juice |
| 100 g (4 oz) low fat soft cheese |
| salt and pepper |
| 5 ml (1 level tsp) gelatine |
| 45 ml (3 tbsp) natural yogurt |
| pinch of saffron strands |
| 1 egg yolk |
| fresh herb sprigs, to garnish |

◆ Cut one of the courgettes into very thin slices lengthways, using a potato peeler or sharp knife. Put the slices into a medium bowl with 30 ml (2 tbsp) water.

◆ Cover with cling film, pulling back one corner to allow the steam to escape, and microwave on HIGH for 2-3 minutes or until the slices are just tender, stirring once. Drain and dry with absorbent kitchen paper.

◆ Use the courgettes slices to line 2 oiled 150 ml (¼ pint) ramekin dishes. Set aside while making the filling.

◆ Finely chop the remaining courgettes and put into a medium bowl with half of the butter and the lemon juice.

◆ Cover with cling film, pulling back one corner to allow the steam to escape, and microwave on HIGH for 5-6 minutes or until tender, stirring occasionally.

◆ Allow to cool slightly, then liquidise in a blender or food processor with the remaining butter and the cheese until smooth. Season well with salt and pepper.

◆ Put the gelatine and 15 ml (1 tbsp) water into a small bowl or cup and microwave on LOW for 1-1½ minutes or until the gelatine has dissolved, stirring occasionally. Add to the courgette purée and mix together thoroughly.

◆ Pour into the lined dishes and leave to cool. Chill for at least 1 hour or until set.

◆ Meanwhile, make the sauce. Put the yogurt, saffron, egg yolk, salt and pepper into a small bowl and microwave on LOW for 1-1½ minutes, or until slightly thickened, stirring frequently. Strain, then leave to cool.

◆ To serve, loosen the courgette moulds with a palette knife then turn out on to two individual serving plates. Pour over the sauce, garnish with a herb sprig and serve immediately.

## CHILLED COURGETTE MOUSSE
### —— WITH SAFFRON SAUCE ——

*This delicate light green mousse is served on a delicious
yogurt-based sauce*

SEE PAGE 35

### SPINACH TARTS WITH
### TOMATO AND BASIL SALAD
*Delightful, thinly rolled wholemeal tarts served with a refreshing salad*

SEE PAGE 35

## SEAFOOD SALAD

SERVES 4

225 g (8 oz) firm white fish fillets, such as cod or haddock

100 g (4 oz) peeled prawns

½ small green pepper, finely diced

5 ml (1 tsp) lemon juice

salt and pepper

shredded lettuce, to serve

black olives and paprika, to garnish

◆ Place the fish on a plate and cover with cling film, pulling back one corner to allow the steam to escape.
◆ Microwave on HIGH for about 3 minutes or until the flesh is just tender. If the fish is thick, turn it over after about 1½ minutes. Leave the fish to stand, covered, until cool.
◆ Cut the fish into cubes. Add the prawns and green pepper and mix together with the lemon juice and mayonnaise. Season with salt and pepper.
◆ Line 4 scallop shells or individual dishes with shredded lettuce. Arrange fish mixture on top and garnish with olives and paprika.

## CHICKEN LIVER PATE

SERVES 6

225 g (8 oz) chicken livers, finely chopped

100 g (4 oz) streaky bacon, rinded and finely chopped

1 medium onion, skinned and thinly sliced

15 ml (1 level tbsp) wholegrain mustard

15 ml (1 tbsp) brandy or sherry

1 garlic clove, skinned and crushed

salt and pepper

125 g (4 oz) butter or margarine

lemon slices and parsley sprigs, to garnish

◆ Place the liver, bacon and onion in a 1.7 litre (3 pint) microwave dish with the mustard, brandy, garlic and seasonings.
◆ Cover and microwave on HIGH for 4 minutes and stir well. Re-cover and microwave on HIGH for a further 4 minutes or until the liver and bacon are tender. Leave to cool.
◆ Liquidise the mixture in a blender or food processor with the butter until smooth. Adjust seasoning.
◆ Spoon into a serving dish, cover and chill in the refrigerator before serving. Garnish the pâté with lemon slices and parsley sprigs.

## KIPPER PATE

SERVES 3 - 4

225 g (8 oz) frozen kipper fillets

75 g (3 oz) butter or margarine, diced

30 ml (2 tbsp) single cream

few drops anchovy essence

salt and pepper

hot buttered toast, to serve

◆ Put the kippers in their wrapping on a plate. Cut a cross in the wrapping with a pair of scissors.
◆ Microwave on LOW for about 8 minutes to thaw.
◆ Put the butter into a small bowl. Microwave on HIGH for 45-60 seconds until melted.
◆ Place the kippers in a blender or food processor with the cream, anchovy essence, pepper and a little salt and two thirds of the butter. Blend until smooth.
◆ Turn the pâté into a small dish or individual ramekin dishes and cover with the remaining melted butter. Chill in the refrigerator. Serve with hot buttered toast.

# PARMESAN MUSHROOMS

## SERVES 2

50 g (2 oz) butter or margarine

8 medium flat mushrooms

1 small garlic clove, skinned and crushed

75 g (3 oz) fresh brown breadcrumbs

100 ml (4 level tbsp) freshly grated Parmesan cheese

20 ml (4 tsp) lemon juice

salt and pepper

grated nutmeg

30 ml (2 tbsp) chopped fresh parsley

lemon twists and fresh parsley, to garnish

French bread, to serve

◆ Put half of the butter in a small bowl and microwave on HIGH for 45 seconds or until melted.

◆ Finely chop the mushroom stalks and one of the mushrooms and stir into the melted butter with the garlic. Microwave on HIGH for 1½ minutes or until softened, stirring once.

◆ Stir in the breadcrumbs, half of the Parmesan and the lemon juice. Mix together well and season with salt, pepper and nutmeg. Stir in half of the parsley.

◆ Arrange the mushroom caps on an ovenproof serving plate and spoon on the stuffing mixture.

◆ Sprinkle with the remaining Parmesan and parsley and dot with the remaining butter.

◆ Microwave on HIGH for 3-5 minutes or until the mushrooms are cooked. Garnish with lemon twists and parsley and serve with French bread.

# AUBERGINE DIP

## SERVES 6

900 g (2 lb) aubergines

salt and pepper

3 garlic cloves, skinned and crushed

60 ml (4 tbsp) olive oil

juice of ½ a lemon

chopped fresh parsley or 1 anchovy fillet, to garnish

celery, carrot and pepper sticks, to serve

◆ Peel and dice the aubergines and place them in a colander or sieve. Sprinkle with salt and leave them to stand for 30 minutes, then rinse and drain them well on absorbent kitchen paper. Place the aubergines in a large bowl and add 60 ml (4 tbsp) water and 1.25 ml (¼ level tsp) salt.

◆ Cover with cling film, pulling back one corner to let steam escape and microwave on HIGH for 12-15 minutes until the aubergines are soft, stirring two or three times during the cooking time. Drain the aubergines and leave them to cool slightly.

◆ Place the cooked aubergines in a blender, food processor or mortar, with the garlic. Blend them together, then slowly add the oil, drop by drop. Add the lemon juice and season with salt and pepper.

◆ Turn the aubergine dip into a small serving bowl and chill before serving. Garnish with parsley or a rolled anchovy fillet. Place the bowl in the centre of a large plate and surround it with raw vegetables (crudités) neatly trimmed, for dipping.

# LUNCHES, SUPPERS & SNACKS

## Ratatouille

*A Mediterranean classic, cooked in a fraction of the time traditionally recommended for it*

SEE PAGE 43

# Cooking Tips

◆

*Take care when cooking recipes containing eggs and cheese as they are easy to overcook and will become tough and rubbery.*

◆

*Cheese will cook more evenly if grated rather than sliced or diced. To melt cheese, add it just before the end of cooking.*

◆

*Poach eggs in ramekins or teacups. Prick the yolk with the point of a sharp knife, before cooking, to prevent it exploding.*

◆

*Do not boil eggs in their shells in the microwave oven. Pressure builds up and they explode.*

◆

## RATATOUILLE

### SERVES 4

| |
|---|
| 2 aubergines, sliced |
| salt and pepper |
| 30 ml (2 tbsp) vegetable oil |
| 2 onions, skinned and sliced |
| 2 courgettes, sliced |
| 1 small green pepper, seeded and sliced |
| 4 tomatoes, skinned, seeded and quartered |
| 10 ml (2 tsp) chopped fresh basil or 5 ml (1 level tsp) dried |
| 1 garlic clove, skinned and crushed |
| basil sprigs, to garnish |
| garlic bread (see p. 167) to serve |

◆ Put the aubergine slices into a colander or sieve and sprinkle them with salt. Leave them to stand for 30 minutes, then rinse and drain the slices well on absorbent kitchen paper.

◆ Put the oil and onions into a 2.8 litre (5 pint) ovenproof glass bowl. Cover them with cling film, pulling back one corner to allow the steam to escape, and microwave on HIGH for 5-7 minutes, stirring occasionally, until the onions soften.

◆ Add the remaining vegetables, basil and garlic to the onions and mix well. Three-quarters cover with cling film and microwave on HIGH for 20-22 minutes until the vegetables are very soft, stirring two or three times during the cooking time.

◆ Season the ratatouille well with salt and pepper. Allow it to cool, then cover it and refrigerate it for 3-4 hours, or overnight, until well chilled.

◆ Serve the ratatouille in individual bowls, garnished with sprigs of basil, with hot garlic bread.

## GRANARY LEEK TOASTS

### SERVES 2

| |
|---|
| 25 g (1 oz) butter or margarine |
| 4 medium leeks, trimmed and finely chopped |
| salt and pepper |
| 10 ml (2 level tsp) plain flour |
| 65 g (2½ oz) full fat soft cheese with garlic and herbs |
| 5 ml (1 tsp) lemon juice |
| 1 egg yolk |
| 3 slices granary bread, toasted |
| chopped fresh parsley, to garnish |

◆ Put the butter into a medium bowl and microwave on HIGH for 45 seconds or until the butter melts.

◆ Stir the chopped leeks into the melted butter. Cover with cling film, pulling back one corner to allow the steam to escape, and microwave on HIGH for 7-8 minutes or until the leeks are very soft, stirring occasionally. Season with salt and pepper.

◆ Stir in the flour and microwave on HIGH for 2 minutes, stirring frequently. Then gradually stir in the cheese and lemon juice and beat together well. Stir in the egg yolk. Microwave on HIGH for 1-2 minutes or until the mixture is warmed through and slightly thickened.

◆ Cut the toast in half diagonally and arrange on 2 serving plates. Spoon on the leek mixture, garnish with parsley and serve immediately.

## EGGS BENEDICT

### SERVES 3

| |
|---|
| 3 English muffins, split |
| 150 g (5 oz) unsalted butter |
| 3 thin slices cooked ham, halved |
| 6 eggs |
| 3 egg yolks |
| 30 ml (2 tbsp) lemon juice |
| salt and pepper |

◆ Grill the muffins on the split sides until golden brown. Spread with 25 g (1 oz) of the butter. Top each muffin with half a slice of ham and keep warm.

◆ Break the eggs into a microwave muffin pan or bun tray. Gently prick each yolk and microwave on HIGH for 2½ minutes or until the eggs are just set.

◆ To make the sauce, beat the egg yolks, lemon juice, salt and pepper together in a small bowl.

◆ Cut the remaining butter into quarters and place in a medium bowl. Microwave on HIGH for 45 seconds or until the butter melts. Stir in the egg yolk mixture and whisk thoroughly with a balloon whisk. Microwave on HIGH for 45 seconds or until the sauce is just thick enough to coat the back of a spoon, whisking every 15 seconds during cooking.

◆ Remove from the oven and continue to whisk the sauce for about 20 seconds to thicken further.

◆ To serve, place an egg on top of each ham-topped muffin and spoon over the sauce.

*Note:* the sauce can be made in advance and kept in the refrigerator; cover the surface with cling film to prevent a skin forming. Reheat on LOW and whisk often, otherwise the sauce may curdle. If the sauce starts to curdle, quickly open the oven door and whisk the sauce vigorously.

## CREAMY SCRAMBLED EGG WITH SMOKED SALMON

### SERVES 1

25 g (1 oz) smoked salmon trimmings

2 eggs, size 2

30 ml (2 tbsp) double cream or milk

25 g (1 oz) butter

salt and pepper

buttered toast, to serve

chopped fresh parsley, to garnish

◆ Cut the salmon into small pieces and set aside. Then put the eggs, cream and butter into a medium bowl and season with a little salt and lots of pepper. Whisk together well.

◆ Microwave on HIGH for 1 minute or until the mixture just begins to set around the edge of the bowl. Whisk vigorously to incorporate the set egg mixture.

◆ Add the smoked salmon and microwave on HIGH for 1½-2 minutes, whisking every 30 seconds and taking care not to break up the salmon, until the eggs are just set but still very soft.

◆ Check the seasoning, and spoon on to the toast. Garnish with chopped parsley and serve immediately.

To serve 2: double all the ingredients and follow the recipe as above, but in point 2 microwave on HIGH for 2 minutes; in point 3 microwave on HIGH for 2 minutes.

## BROCCOLI AND EGGS

### SERVES 4

225 g (8 oz) broccoli, trimmed

50 g (2 oz) butter or margarine

6 eggs, size 2

75 ml (5 tbsp) milk

salt and pepper

4 slices hot toast, crusts removed

◆ Cut the broccoli into neat, even-sized sprigs. Carefully peel off the tough outer skin from the stalks, peeling right up to the flower heads.

◆ Place the broccoli sprigs in a shallow ovenproof dish and add 60 ml (4 tbsp) water. Cover the top with cling film, pulling back one corner to allow the steam to escape. Microwave the broccoli on HIGH for 4-5 minutes until the sprigs are just tender, rearranging them halfway through the cooking time.

◆ Remove the cooked broccoli from the oven and keep it hot while cooking the eggs.

◆ Put the butter into a medium ovenproof glass bowl and microwave on HIGH for 45 seconds or until the butter melts. Add the eggs, milk, salt and pepper and lightly beat the ingredients together. Microwave them on HIGH for 3-4 minutes, stirring every 30 seconds and drawing the edges to the middle, until the eggs are only just set and are quite moist. Leave them to stand for 1-2 minutes. The eggs for this dish need to be very soft and creamy — if they are overcooked and dry, the dish will be spoilt.

◆ Place the slices of toast on to individual serving plates. Reheat the broccoli on HIGH for ½-1 minute.

◆ Divide the scrambled eggs evenly among the toast, spooning it on neatly. Garnish the eggs with the hot sprigs of broccoli and serve immediately.

## EGGS FLORENTINE

### SERVES 4

900 g (2 lb) fresh spinach, trimmed and coarsely chopped

25 g (1 oz) butter or margarine

45 ml (3 level tbsp) plain flour

1.25 ml (¼ level tsp) mustard powder

300 ml (½ pint) milk

100 g (4 oz) Cheddar cheese, finely grated

salt and pepper

4 eggs

brown bread and butter, to serve

◆ Put the spinach in a large bowl. Cover and microwave on HIGH for 4 minutes or until the spinach is just tender. Leave to stand, covered.

◆ Put the butter in a medium bowl and microwave on HIGH for 45 seconds or until the butter melts. Stir in the flour and mustard and microwave on HIGH for 30 seconds.

◆ Gradually whisk in the milk. Microwave on HIGH for 5 minutes until the milk boils and thickens, whisking after every minute. Stir in two thirds of the cheese. Season with salt and pepper.

◆ Break the eggs into a microwave muffin pan or bun tray. Gently prick the yolks with a fine skewer or needle and microwave on HIGH for 2 minutes or until the eggs are just set.

◆ Drain the spinach thoroughly, place in a flame-proof dish, put the eggs on top and spoon the sauce over. Sprinkle with the reserved cheese and brown under a hot grill. Serve with brown bread and butter.

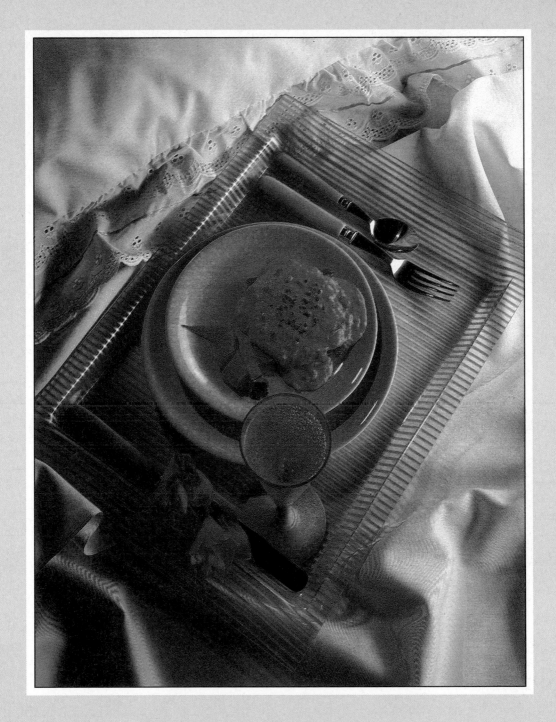

## Creamy Scrambled Egg with
### Smoked Salmon

*A perfect celebration breakfast, especially when served with a glass of champagne*

SEE OPPOSITE

## EGG FRICASSEE

### SERVES 4

| |
|---|
| 200 ml (7 fl oz) milk |
| small slice of onion |
| half a small carrot, peeled and sliced |
| 1 bay leaf |
| 6 black peppercorns |
| 6 eggs |
| 25 g (1 oz) butter or margarine |
| 30 ml (2 level tbsp) plain flour |
| 142 ml (5 fl oz) soured cream |
| 30 ml (2 tbsp) snipped fresh chives or finely chopped fresh tarragon |
| salt and pepper |
| cooked rice, to serve |

◆ Pour the milk into a measuring jug and add the onion, carrot, bay leaf and peppercorns. Microwave on HIGH for 3 minutes or until the milk boils. Leave to stand, covered, for 15 minutes.
◆ Meanwhile, conventionally boil the eggs for 10 minutes starting with cold water. Rinse under cold running water, shell and cut into slices. Keep the eggs warm.
◆ Strain the milk, discarding the vegetables, bay leaf and peppercorns.
◆ Place the butter in a medium bowl and microwave on HIGH for 45 seconds or until the butter melts. Stir in the flour and microwave on HIGH for 30 seconds. Gradually whisk in the milk and microwave on HIGH for 5 minutes or until the milk boils and thickens, whisking occasionally. Whisk in the soured cream and chives. Season to taste.
◆ Reserve a few egg slices and add the rest to the sauce. Garnish with the egg slices and serve at once with rice.

*Note:* the sauce can be made in advance and reheated, but do not allow it to boil. Add eggs just before serving; do not reheat them with the sauce or they may become rubbery.

## POACHED EGGS ON A MUFFIN

### SERVES 2

| |
|---|
| salt and pepper |
| 2 eggs |
| 1 muffin |
| 40 g (1½ oz) Cheddar cheese, grated |
| toasted muffins and butter, to serve |

◆ Put 30 ml (2 tbsp) water into each of two 150 ml (¼ pint) ramekin dishes. Add a large pinch of salt to each ramekin. Microwave on HIGH for 1 minute or until the water boils.
◆ Break an egg into each dish and prick the yolks carefully with a cocktail stick or fine skewer.
◆ Cover loosely with cling film or a double thickness of greaseproof paper and microwave on MEDIUM for 1½-2 minutes or until the white is nearly set. Leave to stand.
◆ Cut the muffin in half and put on a serving plate. Sprinkle with the cheese and microwave on HIGH for 30 seconds or until the cheese has almost melted. Transfer one muffin half to another serving plate.
◆ Drain the eggs and spoon one egg on to each muffin half. Season with salt and pepper and serve immediately with toasted, buttered muffins.

## POACHED EGGS

### SERVES 2

| |
|---|
| 2.5 ml (½ tsp) white vinegar |
| 2 eggs |
| hot buttered toast, to serve |

◆ Pour 450 ml (¾ pint) boiling salted water and the vinegar into a large shallow dish and microwave on HIGH for 1-2 minutes until the water returns to the boil.
◆ Carefully break each egg on to a saucer, prick the yolk with a fine skewer or needle and slide one at a time into the water.
◆ Cover the dish with cling film and microwave on HIGH for 1 minute.
◆ Pierce the cling film and leave the eggs to stand, covered, for 1-2 minutes to set. Using a slotted spoon, transfer the eggs to the hot buttered toast.

*To poach 4 eggs:* use 600 ml (1 pint) boiling salted water with 5 ml (1 tsp) vinegar and proceed as above. After adding the eggs, cover and cook for 1½-2 minutes.

## SCRAMBLED EGGS

SERVES 2

*4 eggs*

*60 ml (4 tbsp) milk*

*25 g (1 oz) butter or margarine (optional)*

*salt and pepper*

*hot buttered toast, to serve*

◆ Put all the ingredients in a medium mixing bowl and whisk together with a balloon whisk.
◆ Microwave on HIGH for 1½ minutes until the mixture just begins to set around the egg of the bowl.
◆ Whisk vigorously to incorporate the set egg mixture. Microwave on HIGH for a further 1½-2 minutes, whisking every 30 seconds, until the eggs are just set. Remember that the mixture will continue to cook a little after it has been removed from the oven. Serve on hot buttered toast.

## STUFFED PEPPERS AND TOMATOES

SERVES 2

*1 green pepper*

*4 medium tomatoes*

*15 ml (1 tbsp) vegetable oil*

*1 small onion, skinned and chopped*

*1 garlic clove, skinned and crushed*

*10 ml (2 level tsp) tomato purée*

*5 ml (1 level tsp) paprika*

*100 g (4 oz) lean minced beef*

*30 ml (2 tbsp) chopped fresh mint*

*50 ml (2 fl oz) hot beef stock*

*salt and pepper*

*fresh mint, to garnish*

◆ Cut the pepper in half lengthways and remove the seeds. Cut a slice off the top of each tomato and scoop out the pulp. Roughly chop the pulp and the lids.
◆ Put the oil, onion and garlic into a medium bowl and cover with cling film, pulling back one corner to let steam escape. Microwave on HIGH for 4-5 minutes or until softened.
◆ Stir in the tomato purée, paprika, minced beef, chopped tomato, mint, stock, salt and pepper. Microwave on HIGH for 8-10 minutes or until the beef is cooked and the sauce is slightly reduced.
◆ Put the pepper into a shallow dish with 30 ml (2 tbsp)

water. Cover with cling film, pulling back one corner to let steam escape. Microwave on HIGH for 3-5 minutes or until tender. Drain.
◆ Stuff the pepper halves and the tomatoes with the mince mixture and return to the shallow dish.
◆ Microwave on HIGH for 3-5 minutes or until the peppers are really tender and the filling reheated. Serve each person with one pepper half and two tomatoes. Garnish with mint and serve hot.

## HOT BAGUETTE SANDWICH WITH SALAMI AND RED PEPPER SAUCE

SERVES 2

*15 ml (1 tbsp) olive or vegetable oil*

*1 small onion, skinned and chopped*

*5 ml (1 level tsp) paprika*

*2.5 ml (½ level tsp) sugar*

*pinch of cayenne pepper*

*1 small red pepper, cored, seeded and chopped*

*15 ml (1 level tbsp) plain flour*

*150 ml (¼ pint) chicken stock*

*225 g (8 oz) Mozzarella cheese*

*4 thin slices Danish salami*

*1 small baguette, about 30.5 cm (12 inches) long*

*salt and pepper*

*a few black olives, stoned (optional)*

◆ Put the oil, onion, paprika, sugar, cayenne pepper and chopped red pepper in a medium bowl. Cover with cling film, pulling back one corner to allow the steam to escape, and microwave on HIGH for 5-7 minutes or until the vegetables soften, stirring occasionally.
◆ Stir in the flour and microwave on HIGH for 30 seconds. Then gradually stir in the chicken stock and microwave on HIGH for 5-6 minutes, stirring frequently, until the pepper is soft and the sauce has thickened.
◆ Meanwhile, cut the Mozzarella into thin slices and remove the rind from the salami. Cut the baguette in half widthways, then cut each half in half lengthways. Arrange a layer of Mozzarella on 2 halves. Top with a layer of salami. Season with pepper.
◆ When the sauce is cooked, let it cool a little then liquidise in a blender or food processor until smooth. Spoon on top of the salami. Top with a few olives, if using. Put the other half of the baguette on top of each half to make 2 sandwiches.
◆ Wrap each sandwich in greaseproof paper and microwave on HIGH for 1-1½ minutes or until the sandwiches are just warmed through. Serve immediately.

## HOT BAGUETTE SANDWICH WITH SALAMI
### AND RED PEPPER SAUCE

*An excellent light meal, with its meat and cheese stuffing and tangy sauce*

SEE PAGE 47

## FRENCH BREAD PIZZA

*An excellent, easily prepared alternative to the traditional Italian dish*

SEE PAGE 52

## QUICK PIZZA

### SERVES 2

*226 g (8 oz) can tomatoes, well drained*

*10 ml (2 tsp) tomato purée*

*5 ml (1 tsp) chopped fresh mixed herbs or oregano, or 2.5 ml (½ level tsp) dried*

*salt and pepper*

*225 g (8 oz) self raising flour*

*60 ml (4 tbsp) vegetable oil*

*100 g (4 oz) Cheddar cheese, grated*

*a few anchovy fillets and stuffed green or black olives, to garnish*

◆ Put the tomatoes into a small bowl with the tomato purée, herbs, salt and pepper and mash well with a fork.
◆ Put the flour and a pinch of salt into a mixing bowl, make a well in the centre, add the oil and 75-90 ml (5-6 tbsp) water and mix together to form a soft dough. Knead it lightly on a floured surface until it is smooth.
◆ Roll out the dough to two 20 cm (8 inch) rounds. Lightly oil 2 large, flat ovenproof plates and place a round of dough on each plate. Microwave the dough, one piece at a time, on HIGH for 2-3 minutes or until the surface looks puffy.
◆ Spread the mashed tomatoes over the two pieces of dough, then sprinkle them with the cheese. Garnish with anchovy fillets and olives.
◆ Microwave the pizzas, one at a time, on HIGH for 4-5 minutes. Remote from the oven and leave to stand for 3-4 minutes before serving.

## BAKED BEANS OR SPAGHETTI ON TOAST

### SERVES 1

*1 slice bread, toasted*

*140 g (5 oz) can baked beans or spaghetti in tomato sauce*

◆ Place the hot toast on a serving plate, then spoon the beans or spaghetti on to the toast.
◆ Microwave on HIGH for 1-1½ minutes and serve immediately.

*Note:* Beans may 'pop' during the heating period, so do not overheat them.

## EGG AND BACON

### SERVES 1

*2 streaky bacon rashers, rinded*

*1 egg*

◆ Snip the bacon fat at intervals. Place the bacon slices on a serving plate or in a shallow dish and cover with absorbent kitchen paper. Microwave on HIGH for 1-1½ minutes until cooked.
◆ Remove from the plate or dish and add the egg. Prick the egg yolk with a fine skewer or needle and cover with cling film.
◆ Microwave on HIGH for about 30 seconds then leave to stand, covered, for 1 minute.
◆ Return the bacon to the plate or dish and cook, covered, for 15-30 seconds.

## CRISPY CHEESE AND HAM SANDWICHES

### MAKES 2

*4 slices bread*

*10 ml (2 tsp) Dijon mustard*

*2 slices cooked ham*

*50 g (2 oz) Cheddar cheese, grated*

*15 g (½ oz) butter or margarine*

◆ Preheat a browning dish to maximum according to the manufacturer's instructions.
◆ Meanwhile, spread the bread with the mustard. Top two slices with the ham and then the cheese. Place the remaining slices of bread on top to make the sandwiches. Then spread the butter on the outside of each sandwich.
◆ As soon as the browning dish is ready and without removing the dish from the oven, put in the sandwiches. Microwave on HIGH for 15 seconds, then quickly turn the sandwiches over and microwave on HIGH for 15-20 seconds or until the cheese has almost settled. Cut in half and serve immediately.

# BACON AND EGG SCRAMBLE

### SERVES 2

*4 streaky bacon rashers, rinded*

*4 eggs, beaten*

*30 ml (2 tbsp) double cream (optional)*

*25 g (1 oz) butter, cut into small pieces*

*salt and pepper*

*4 slices bread, toasted*

*15 ml (1 tbsp) chopped fresh parsley, to garnish*

◆ Snip the bacon fat at intervals to prevent curling. Place on an ovenproof plate and cover with absorbent kitchen paper.

◆ Microwave on HIGH for 2-2½ minutes or until the bacon is cooked. Chop roughly.

◆ Place the eggs, cream, if using, and butter in a medium ovenproof glass bowl and season well with salt and pepper.

◆ Microwave on HIGH for 1 minute, stirring well after 30 seconds. Add the bacon and microwave on HIGH for 1-1½ minutes or until the eggs are just cooked, stirring frequently.

◆ Spoon the bacon and egg scramble on to toast, garnish with parsley and serve immediately.

# BEEF BURGERS

### SERVES 4

*450 g (1 lb) lean minced beef*

*1 large onion, skinned and grated*

*5ml (1 level tsp) salt*

*1.25 ml (¼ level tsp) cayenne pepper*

*30 ml (2 tbsp) vegetable oil*

*4 plain or toasted hamburger buns, to serve*

◆ Mix the beef and onion together and season with salt and cayenne pepper.

◆ Divide the mixture into 4 and shape each piece into a neat burger about 2.5 cm (1 inch) thick.

◆ Preheat a large browning dish to maximum according to the manufacturer's instructions, adding the oil for the last 30 seconds. (Alternatively, put the oil into a large shallow dish and microwave on HIGH for 1-2 minutes until hot.)

◆ Without removing the dish from the oven, press 2 beef burgers flat on to the hot surface and microwave on HIGH for 2-3 minutes. Turn the burgers over, reposition them and microwave on HIGH for 2-3 minutes until cooked. Repeat with the remaining burgers. Serve in plain or toasted hamburger buns.

# DEVILLED KIDNEYS

### SERVES 2

*225 g (8 oz) lamb's kidneys*

*15 g (½ oz) butter or margarine*

*1 medium onion, skinned and chopped*

*1 garlic clove, skinned and crushed (optional)*

*2 streaky bacon rashers, chopped*

*5 ml (1 level tsp) cornflour*

*226 g (8 oz) can tomatoes*

*5 ml (1 level tsp) French mustard*

*5 ml (1 tsp) tomato purée*

*2.5 ml (½ tsp) Worcestershire sauce*

*2.5 ml (½ level tsp) cayenne pepper*

*salt and pepper*

*French bread, to serve*

◆ Skin the kidneys and cut them in half. Remove the core with scissors or a sharp knife.

◆ Put the butter in a large ovenproof glass bowl and microwave on HIGH for 30 seconds or until the butter melts. Stir in the onion, garlic, if using, and bacon and microwave on HIGH for 5-7 minutes or until the onion and bacon are softened.

◆ Blend the cornflour to a smooth paste with a little of the tomato juice. Add to the onion and garlic mixture with the tomatoes and remaining juice, mustard, tomato purée, Worcestershire sauce, cayenne pepper and seasoning.

◆ Microwave on HIGH for 5-7 minutes until the liquid boils and thickens, stirring occasionally.

◆ Add the kidneys, cover with cling film and microwave on HIGH for 3½-4½ minutes or until the kidneys are cooked, stirring occasionally. Serve hot with French bread.

## WELSH RAREBIT

### SERVES 2

| |
|---|
| 25 g (1 oz) butter or margarine |
| 5 ml (1 level tsp) mustard powder |
| pinch of salt |
| pinch of cayenne pepper |
| dash of Worcestershire sauce |
| 75 g (3 oz) mature Cheddar cheese, grated |
| 30 ml (2 tbsp) brown ale or milk |
| 2 slices bread, toasted |

◆ Put the butter in a medium bowl and microwave on HIGH for 20 seconds or until the butter is soft.
◆ Stir in the mustard, salt, cayenne pepper, Worcestershire sauce, grated cheese and ale. Microwave on HIGH for about 30 seconds or until the mixture is hot and bubbling.
◆ Beat the cheese mixture well then spread it over the toast. Place on serving plates and microwave on HIGH for 20-30 seconds or until it is heated through. Serve immediately.

VARIATION
*Onion Rarebit:* Thinly slice one small onion and arrange on the bread before pouring the cheese mixture over.

## FRENCH BREAD PIZZA

### SERVES 2

| |
|---|
| 397 g (14 oz) can tomatoes, drained |
| 15 ml (1 tbsp) tomato purée |
| 1 small onion, skinned and chopped |
| 1 garlic clove, skinned and crushed |
| 10 ml (2 tsp) chopped fresh mixed herbs or 5 ml (1 level tsp) dried |
| salt and pepper |
| 1 small French loaf |
| 100 g (4 oz) Mozzarella or Cheddar cheese, grated |
| a few olives and anchovy fillets (optional) |

◆ Put the tomatoes, tomato purée, onion, garlic, herbs and salt and pepper in a medium bowl and microwave on HIGH for 5 minutes or until the mixture is hot and slightly reduced.
◆ Cut the French bread in half horizontally then cut each length in half. Place crust side down, side by side, on a large flat serving plate.
◆ Spoon the tomato topping on to the bread and cover with the grated cheese. Arrange the olives and anchovies, if using, on top of the cheese. Microwave on HIGH for 1 minute until the pizza is heated through. Serve immediately.

## PIZZA FLAN

### SERVES 4

| |
|---|
| 20.5 cm (8 inch) flan case (see p. 184) |
| For the filling: |
| 45 ml (3 tbsp) vegetable oil |
| 450 g (1 lb) onions, skinned and thinly sliced |
| 2 garlic cloves, skinned and crushed |
| 1 medium green pepper, cored, seeded and thinly sliced |
| 397 g (14 oz) can chopped tomatoes, drained |
| 30 ml (2 tbsp) tomato purée |
| 2.5 ml (½ tsp) mixed herbs |
| salt and pepper |
| 200 g (7 oz) Mozzarella cheese, thinly sliced |
| 50 g (2 oz) can anchovies, drained |
| 8 black olives, stoned |

◆ Mix the oil, onions, garlic and green pepper together in a large bowl and microwave on HIGH for 5-7 minutes or until the vegetables are soft.
◆ Stir in the tomatoes, tomato purée, herbs and seasoning and microwave on HIGH for 5 minutes.
◆ Place the flan case on a serving plate and spoon in the filling. Arrange the cheese, anchovies and olives on top. Microwave on HIGH for 5 minutes or until the topping is bubbling and the cheese is melted. Serve with a green salad, if liked.

## PIZZA FLAN

*A light but filling meal for four, based on the traditional Italian dish*

SEE OPPOSITE

## CHEESE SOUFFLE

### SERVES 4

| |
|---|
| *40 g (1½ oz) butter or margarine* |
| *25 g (1 oz) plain flour* |
| *150 ml (¼ pint) milk* |
| *2.5 ml (½ level tsp) mustard powder* |
| *salt and pepper* |
| *3 eggs, separated* |
| *75 g (3 oz) mature Cheddar cheese, finely grated* |

◆ Rub the inside of a 1.4 litre (2½ pint) soufflé dish with 15 g (½ oz) of the butter.
◆ Place the remaining butter in a medium bowl and microwave on HIGH for 45 seconds or until the butter melts. Stir in the flour and microwave on HIGH for 30 seconds. Using a balloon whisk, gradually whisk in the milk, mustard and salt and pepper. Return to the oven and microwave on HIGH for 2½ minutes, stirring after every minute, until the mixture is thick and smooth. Leave to cool slightly.
◆ Beat the egg yolks into the sauce, one at a time. Reserve 15 ml (1 tbsp) cheese and add the rest to the sauce. Stir until well blended.
◆ Whisk the egg whites until stiff and fold into the sauce.
◆ Spoon the mixture into the buttered dish. Smooth the top and sprinkle with the reserved cheese.
◆ Place in the oven and microwave on LOW for 10 minutes until the soufflé has risen. Serve at once, with a green salad and hot crusty bread and butter if liked.

## CHEESE AND MUSHROOM OMELETTE

### SERVES 2

| |
|---|
| *15 g (½ oz) butter or margarine* |
| *1 small onion, skinned and thinly sliced* |
| *50 g (2 oz) mushrooms, sliced* |
| *75 g (3 oz) Gruyère or Cheddar cheese, grated* |
| *3 eggs* |
| *30 ml (2 tbsp) milk* |
| *15 ml (1 tbsp) chopped fresh parsley* |
| *salt and pepper* |

◆ Put the butter in a 20.5 cm (8 inch) shallow dish and microwave on HIGH for 30 seconds or until the butter melts.
◆ Add the onion and mushrooms, cover with cling film and microwave on HIGH for 3 minutes or until the vegetables are softened, stirring once.

◆ Beat half of the cheese, the eggs, milk, parsley and salt and pepper together and pour into the dish. Cover loosely with cling film and microwave on LOW for a further 3 minutes or until the omelette is set.
◆ Carefully remove the cling film and sprinkle with the remaining cheese.

## CHEESE AND SALAMI PIE

### SERVES 1

| |
|---|
| *100 g (4 oz) potatoes, peeled and thinly sliced* |
| *½ small onion, skinned and very thinly sliced* |
| *50 g (2 oz) Gruyère cheese, grated* |
| *25 g (1 oz) salami, rinded, thinly sliced and cut into strips* |
| *salt and pepper* |
| *grated nutmeg to taste* |
| *30 ml (2 level tbsp) fresh breadcrumbs* |
| *10 ml (2 level tsp) freshly grated Parmesan cheese* |
| *chopped fresh parsley, to garnish* |

◆ Layer the sliced potatoes in an individual round oven-proof gratin dish with the onion, Gruyère cheese and salami. Season with salt, pepper and nutmeg.
◆ Cover with cling film, pulling back one corner to allow the steam to escape, and microwave on HIGH for 4 minutes or until the potato is almost tender.
◆ Uncover, mix the breadcrumbs and cheese together and sprinkle evenly on the top. Microwave on HIGH for 2 minutes. Leave to stand for 5 minutes, garnish with parsley, then serve with a green salad, if liked.

## CHEESE AND POTATO PIE

### SERVES 4

900 g (2 lb) potatoes, peeled and coarsely grated

1 medium onion, skinned and finely chopped

275 g (10 oz) Cheddar cheese, coarsely grated

225 g (8 oz) ham, cut into 1 cm (½ inch) cubes

pinch of grated nutmeg

salt and pepper

25 g (1 oz) butter or margarine, diced

50 g (2 oz) fresh breadcrumbs

30 ml (2 tbsp) chopped fresh parsley

◆ Pat the potatoes dry with absorbent kitchen paper and mix with the onion, cheese and ham. Season well with nutmeg and salt and pepper.

◆ Spoon the mixture into a 26.5 cm (10½ inch) shallow round dish and dot with the butter. Cover and microwave on HIGH for 20-25 minutes or until the potato is cooked.

◆ Mix the breadcrumbs and parsley together and sprinkle evenly over the top. Place under a hot grill until golden brown. Serve hot with a green salad if liked.

## MUSHROOMS ON TOAST

### SERVES 1

15 g (½ oz) butter or margarine

100 g (4 oz) button mushrooms, halved

pinch of dried thyme

2.5 ml (½ tsp) lemon juice

5 ml (1 level tsp) plain flour

5 ml (1 tsp) mushroom ketchup

5 ml (1 tsp) chopped fresh parsley, to garnish

salt and pepper

1 slice buttered toast, to serve

◆ Put the butter into a medium bowl and microwave on HIGH for 30 seconds or until the butter melts.

◆ Stir in the mushrooms, thyme, lemon juice and 15 ml (1 tbsp) water, and microwave on HIGH for 2-3 minutes or until the mushrooms are cooked, stirring occasionally.

◆ Sprinkle in the flour and mix together well. Microwave on HIGH for 1 minute or until the mixture thickens, stirring occasionally.

◆ Stir in the mushroom ketchup and season to taste with salt and pepper. Microwave on HIGH for 2 minutes to develop the flavour. Spoon on to the toast, garnish with parsley and serve immediately.

*To serve 2:* double all the ingredients and follow the recipe as above, but in point 1 microwave on HIGH for 30 seconds; in point 2 microwave on HIGH for 3-4 minutes; in point 4 microwave on HIGH for 2-3 minutes.

## DEVILLED CHICKEN LIVERS

### SERVES 2

25 g (1 oz) butter or margarine

1 small onion, skinned and finely chopped

1 garlic clove, skinned and crushed

5 ml (1 level tsp) curry powder

100 g (4 oz) chicken livers, trimmed and cut into bite-sized pieces

pinch of cayenne pepper

salt and pepper

dash of Worcestershire sauce

10 ml (2 tsp) tomato purée

4 thick slices bread, toasted

◆ Put the butter in a large shallow bowl and microwave on HIGH for 45 seconds or until the butter melts. Stir in the onion, garlic and curry powder and microwave on HIGH for 3-4 minutes or until the onion is slightly softened.

◆ Stir in the chicken livers and cayenne pepper and season with salt and pepper. Stir in the Worcestershire sauce and tomato purée and 15-30 ml (1-2 tbsp) water to make a moist consistency.

◆ Cover with cling film and microwave on HIGH for 3 minutes or until the livers are just cooked, shaking the bowl occasionally.

◆ Place the toast on 2 serving plates and spoon the chicken mixture over.

◆ Microwave one plate at a time on HIGH for 30 seconds. Serve immediately.

## SPICY NUT BURGERS WITH
### —— CORIANDER RAITA ——

*Delightfully spiced with coriander, cumin and ginger, these burgers are
served with a refreshing yogurt sauce*

SEE PAGE 58

### — VEGETABLE AND CHICK-PEA CASSEROLE —

*A wholesome, satisfying dish with a pleasing range of textures and colours*

SEE PAGE 58

## SPICY NUT BURGERS WITH CORIANDER RAITA

### SERVES 2

45 ml (3 tbsp) vegetable oil

1 small onion, skinned and chopped

1 medium carrot, peeled and finely grated

1 garlic clove, skinned and crushed

1 cm (½ inch) piece fresh ginger, peeled and chopped

2.5 ml (½ level tsp) coriander seeds, finely crushed

2.5 ml (½ level tsp) cumin seeds

100 g (4 oz) mixed nuts, finely chopped

25 g (1 oz) Cheddar cheese, finely grated

50 g (2 oz) brown breadcrumbs

salt and pepper

1 egg, size 6, beaten

30 ml (2 tbsp) chopped fresh coriander

150 ml (¼ pint) natural yogurt

lemon wedges and fresh coriander, to garnish

◆ Put 15 ml (1 tbsp) oil, the onion, carrot, garlic and ginger in a medium bowl. Cover with cling film, pulling back one corner to allow the steam to escape, and microwave on HIGH for 5-7 minutes or until the vegetables have softened, stirring occasionally.

◆ Stir in the coriander and cumin seeds and microwave on HIGH for 1 minute, stirring occasionally. Stir in the nuts and microwave on HIGH for 2 minutes, stirring once.

◆ Stir in the cheese and breadcrumbs and season with salt and pepper. Mix thoroughly and bind together with the egg.

◆ Preheat a browning dish to maximum, according to the manufacturer's instructions.

◆ Meanwhile, divide the mixture into 6 and shape into burgers. When the browning dish is hot, add the remaining oil and microwave on HIGH for 30 seconds.

◆ Quickly put the burgers in the dish and microwave on HIGH for 1½ minutes, then turn over and microwave on HIGH for a further minute or until browned. Leave to stand for 1 minute.

◆ Meanwhile, make the coriander raita. Beat the chopped coriander into the yogurt and season with salt and pepper.

◆ Garnish the burgers with lemon wedges and coriander and serve hot with the coriander raita.

## VEGETABLE AND CHICK-PEA CASSEROLE

### SERVES 6 AS A MAIN DISH

4 courgettes, trimmed and cut into 1 cm (½ inch) lengths

1 red pepper, cored, seeded and chopped

1 green pepper, cored, seeded and chopped

2 medium onions, skinned and coarsely chopped

2 carrots, peeled and thinly sliced

225 g (8 oz) turnips, peeled and thinly sliced

1 small cauliflower, trimmed and cut into florets

4 large tomatoes, skinned, seeded and chopped

100 g (4 oz) dried apricots, cut into quarters

2 garlic cloves, skinned and crushed

425 g (15 oz) can chick-peas, drained

25 g (1 oz) almonds, blanched

5 ml (1 level tsp) ground turmeric

10 ml (2 level tsp) paprika

2.5 ml (½ level tsp) ground coriander

salt and pepper

600 ml (1 pint) vegetable stock

chopped fresh coriander or parsley, to garnish

◆ Place all of the prepared vegetables, the apricots, the garlic, chick-peas and almonds in a large casserole dish and stir in the spices, the salt, pepper and stock. Cover the dish with a lid or with cling film, pulling back one corner to allow the steam to escape.

◆ Microwave on HIGH for 8-10 minutes or until the vegetables come to the boil, then microwave for a further 30-40 minutes until the vegetables are well cooked. Stir two or three times during cooking. Serve garnished with coriander or parsley.

## JACKET POTATOES

### SERVES 4

*4 large potatoes, each weighing about 225 g (8 oz)*

◆ Wash and scrub the potatoes. Prick the skin all over with a fork. Arrange in the oven in a circle with a space in the centre, on absorbent kitchen paper.
◆ Microwave on HIGH for 6 minutes then turn the potatoes over and cook for a further 6-8 minutes or until the potatoes feel soft when gently squeezed. (As a general guideline, one potato will take 4 minutes, two potatoes will take 6-7 minutes.)

## STUFFED BAKED POTATOES

### SERVES 2

*2 large potatoes, each weighing about 225 g (8 oz)*

*25 g (1 oz) butter or margarine*

*1 small onion, skinned and finely chopped*

*30 ml (2 tbsp) milk*

*75 g (3 oz) Cheddar cheese, grated*

*30 ml (2 tbsp) chopped fresh parsley*

*salt and pepper*

◆ Scrub the potatoes thoroughly, then prick them all over using a fork. Microwave on HIGH for 10 minutes or until the potatoes are soft.
◆ Place the butter in a medium ovenproof glass bowl and microwave on HIGH for 30 seconds or until the butter melts. Add the onion and mix thoroughly. Three-quarters cover with cling film and microwave on HIGH for 5-7 minutes or until the onion is soft.
◆ Halve the potatoes and scoop out the insides, leaving a thin shell. Add the potato flesh to the onion and mash well together.
◆ Add the milk, half of the cheese and the parsley. Season to taste. Mix well together.
◆ Pile the mixture back into the potato shells and place them on a large ovenproof serving dish. Sprinkle with the remaining cheese and microwave on HIGH for 2 minutes or until the potatoes are heated through. Brown under a preheated grill if desired.

## HAM AND LEEKS AU GRATIN

### SERVES 4

*8 medium leeks, trimmed*

*salt and pepper*

*8 slices cooked ham*

*50 g (2 oz) butter or margarine*

*50 g (2 oz) plain flour*

*300 ml (½ pint) milk*

*100 g (4 oz) Gruyère or Cheddar cheese, grated*

*grated nutmeg to taste*

*25 g (1 oz) fresh breadcrumbs*

*chopped fresh parsley, to garnish*

◆ Put the leeks in a shallow ovenproof dish, add 150 ml (¼ pint) water and season with a little salt and pepper. Cover the dish with cling film, pulling back one corner to allow the steam to escape and microwave on HIGH for about 10-12 minutes or until the leeks are very soft, turning them over and repositioning them two or three times during the cooking time.
◆ Drain the liquid from the leeks into a measuring jug and make up the amount to 300 ml (½ pint) with stock or water, if necessary. Leave the leeks to cool slightly.
◆ When cool enough to handle, wrap each leek in a slice of ham and arrange them neatly in a shallow ovenproof dish.
◆ Put the butter into a 1.1 litre (2 pint) ovenproof glass bowl, and microwave on HIGH for 45 seconds or until the butter melts. Stir in the flour and microwave on HIGH for 45 seconds. Gradually whisk in the milk and the reserved cooking liquid. Microwave on HIGH for 1 minute, then whisk the mixture thoroughly. Continue to microwave on HIGH for about 5 minutes, whisking every 30 seconds until the sauce thickens.
◆ Stir half of the cheese into the sauce and then season it with salt, pepper and a little grated nutmeg. Stir the sauce until the cheese melts.
◆ Pour the sauce over the leeks and ham and sprinkle it with the breadcrumbs and the remaining cheese. Microwave on HIGH for 4-5 minutes or until the leeks and ham are well heated through and the cheese has melted. Garnish with parsley just before serving.

## SPICED WHEAT PEPPERS

### SERVES 4

| |
|---|
| 75 g (3 oz) bulgar wheat |
| 2 medium green peppers |
| 1 medium yellow or red pepper |
| 50 g (2 oz) butter or margarine |
| 2 medium onions, skinned and chopped |
| 5 ml (1 level tsp) chilli powder |
| 5 ml (1 level tsp) ground cumin |
| 300 ml (½ pint) natural yogurt |
| 75 g (3 oz) cucumber, peeled, halved, seeded and finely chopped |
| chopped fresh parsley, to garnish |
| salt and pepper |

◆ Place the wheat in a mixing bowl and cover it with cold water. Cover the bowl and leave the wheat to stand for 1 hour.

◆ Cut each pepper in half vertically and remove the seeds. Finely chop one of the green peppers.

◆ Alternating the colours, place the halved peppers side by side in a shallow ovenproof dish and add 60 ml (4 tbsp) water. Cover the dish with a lid or with cling film, pulling back one corner to allow the steam to escape. Microwave on HIGH for 6 minutes, repositioning the peppers 3 times during the cooking time. Remove them from the oven and leave them to stand while preparing the filling.

◆ Put the butter into an ovenproof dish and microwave on HIGH for 1 minute or until the butter melts, then stir in the chopped pepper, onions, chilli powder and cumin.

◆ Cover the dish with cling film, pulling back one corner to allow the steam to escape, and microwave on HIGH for 5-7 minutes or until the onions and pepper are soft. Add the well-drained bulgar wheat and microwave on HIGH for 1 minute, stirring twice during the cooking time.

◆ Drain almost all of the water from the peppers. Fill the peppers with the wheat filling and cover with a lid or with cling film, pulling back one corner to allow the steam to escape. Microwave on HIGH for 10 minutes, giving the dish a quarter turn 3 times during the cooking time.

◆ Put the yogurt and cucumber into a small ovenproof glass bowl and microwave on HIGH for 30-45 seconds until they are hot but not boiling, then season well with salt and pepper.

◆ Sprinkle the peppers with the chopped parsley, season well with salt and pepper, and serve them with the cucumber and yogurt sauce served separately.

## VEGETABLE MOUSSAKA

### SERVES 4-6

| |
|---|
| 2 large aubergines, cut into 0.5 cm (¼ inch) slices |
| salt and pepper |
| 15 ml (1 tbsp) vegetable oil |
| 1 large onion, skinned and chopped |
| 2 garlic cloves, skinned and crushed |
| 397 g (14 oz) can tomatoes |
| 15 ml (1 level tbsp) tomato purée |
| 5 ml (1 level tsp) sugar |
| 10 ml (2 tsp) chopped fresh basil or 5 ml (1 level tsp) dried |
| 450 g (1 lb) courgettes, trimmed and coarsely chopped |
| 150 ml (¼ pint) natural yogurt |
| 5 ml (1 level tsp) cornflour |
| 100 g (4 oz) Cheddar cheese, grated |

◆ Put the aubergines into a colander, sprinkle with salt and leave for about 30 minutes to extract any bitter juices. Rinse in cold, running water and dry thoroughly with absorbent kitchen paper.

◆ Put the oil, onion, garlic, tomatoes and their juice, tomato purée, sugar, basil and courgettes in a large bowl and microwave on HIGH for 12-15 minutes or until the courgettes are softened and the liquid has slightly reduced. Season well with salt and pepper

◆ Spread half of the tomato mixture in the bottom of a shallow flameproof dish.

◆ Arrange half of the aubergine slices in a single layer on top of the tomato mixture. Repeat the layers ending with a layer of aubergines. Microwave on HIGH for 10 minutes or until the aubergine is tender.

◆ Meanwhile, blend the yogurt into the cornflour then stir in the cheese and season well with salt and pepper.

◆ Spread the yogurt mixture in an even layer on top of the moussaka and microwave for a further 1-2 minutes or until hot. Brown under a hot grill, if desired. Leave to stand for 5 minutes before serving.

## Vegetable Moussaka

*No one will miss the meat in this substantial and tasty vegetarian recipe*

SEE OPPOSITE

## TUNA FISH CAKES

### SERVES 4

| |
|---|
| 2 large potatoes, total weight about 350 g (12 oz) |
| 25 g (1 oz) butter or margarine |
| 1 small onion, skinned and finely chopped |
| 198 g (7 oz) can tuna, drained and flaked |
| 1 hard-boiled egg, shelled and chopped (optional) |
| 30 ml (2 tbsp) chopped fresh parsley |
| 10 ml (2 tsp) lemon juice |
| salt and pepper |
| 1 egg, beaten |
| 100 g (4 oz) dried breadcrumbs |
| 30 ml (2 tbsp) vegetable oil |
| lemon wedges, to serve |

◆ Wash the potatoes thoroughly, but do not peel them, then prick them all over with a fork and microwave on HIGH for 8-10 minutes or until the potatoes are cooked.
◆ Put the butter in a large bowl and microwave on HIGH for 45 seconds or until the butter melts. Stir in the onion and microwave on HIGH for 5-7 minutes or until the onion is softened.
◆ Cut the potatoes in half horizontally and scoop out the insides. Mash with the onion and butter. Stir in the tuna, egg, if using, parsley and lemon juice and season well with salt and pepper.
◆ Preheat a browning dish to maximum according to the manufacturer's instructions.
◆ Meanwhile, shape the potato mixture into 8 cakes and coat in the beaten egg and breadcrumbs; season with salt and pepper.
◆ Add the oil to the browning dish then, without removing the dish from the oven, quickly add the fish cakes and microwave on HIGH for 2 minutes.
◆ Turn the cakes over and microwave on HIGH for 2 minutes. Serve with lemon wedges.

## KIDNEYS CURRIED IN PITTA BREAD

### SERVES 2

| |
|---|
| 6 lamb's kidneys |
| 30 ml (2 tbsp) vegetable oil |
| 1 medium onion, skinned and finely sliced |
| 5 ml (1 level tsp) curry powder |
| 5 ml (1 level tsp) ground cumin |
| 5 ml (1 level tsp) ground turmeric |
| 10 ml (2 tsp) lemon juice |
| 150 ml (¼ pint) chicken stock |
| 10 ml (2 level tsp) tomato purée |
| salt and pepper |
| 2 pitta bread |
| 30 ml (2 level tbsp) mango chutney |
| 1 medium carrot, peeled and coarsely grated |
| few lettuce leaves, shredded |

◆ Skin the kidneys and cut into small pieces, discarding the cores.
◆ Put the oil and half of the sliced onion into a medium bowl. Cover with cling film, pulling back one corner to let steam escape, and microwave on HIGH for 3-5 minutes or until softened.
◆ Stir in the curry powder, ground cumin and turmeric. Microwave on HIGH for 1 minute.
◆ Stir in the kidneys and microwave on HIGH for 3-5 minutes or until just changing colour, stirring occasionally.
◆ Stir in the lemon juice, stock, tomato purée, salt and pepper. Re-cover and microwave on HIGH for 4-5 minutes or until the kidneys are cooked.
◆ Microwave the pitta bread on HIGH for 15 seconds or until warm. Cut in half widthways and split each bread open to make two 'pockets'. Spread with mango chutney.
◆ Mix the remaining onion with the carrot and lettuce and use to fill the pitta bread. Spoon the kidney mixture on top of the salad and serve immediately.

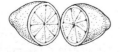

# Melted Cheese and Ham Sandwich

### SERVES 1

2 large slices bread

5 ml (1 level tsp) wholegrain mustard

40 g (1½ oz) Gruyère cheese

50 g (2 oz) ham

salt and pepper

15 g (½ oz) butter or margarine

◆ Preheat a browning dish on HIGH for 4-5 minutes.
◆ Meanwhile, spread the bread slices with the mustard. Cut the cheese into thin slivers and pile on top of one slice. Cut the ham into strips and arrange evenly on top of the cheese. Season with salt and pepper.
◆ Put the second slice of bread on top, mustard side down, and spread with half of the butter. Turn the sandwich over and spread with the remaining butter.
◆ Quickly put the sandwich into the browning dish and microwave on HIGH for 30 seconds, then turn over and microwave on HIGH for 20–30 seconds or until the cheese melts.

# SOUSED HERRINGS

### SERVES 4

4 herrings, cleaned and boned

salt and pepper

150 ml (¼ pint) malt vinegar

3-4 black peppercorns

1 small onion, skinned and sliced

green salad, to serve

◆ Trim the heads, tails and fins from the fish. Remove any remaining bones and sprinkle the inside of the fish with salt and pepper.
◆ Roll the fish up, skin side out, from the head end. Secure with wooden cocktail sticks. Arrange in a single layer in a shallow dish.
◆ Mix the vinegar with 150 ml (¼ pint) water, add the peppercorns and pour over the fish. Arrange the onion slices on top.
◆ Cover with cling film, pulling back one corner to allow the steam to escape, and microwave on HIGH for 6-8 minutes, turning the dish after 3 minutes.
◆ Leave the fish to cool in the liquid then chill. Serve with a green salad.

# Onion Cocottes

### SERVES 4

25 g (1 oz) butter or margarine

2 medium onions, skinned and finely chopped

2.5 ml (½ level tsp) cornflour

salt and pepper

4 eggs

60 ml (4 tbsp) double cream

50 g (2 oz) Cheddar cheese, thinly sliced

hot buttered toast, to serve

◆ Put the butter in a medium bowl and microwave on HIGH for 45 seconds until melted. Stir in the onions and microwave on HIGH for 5–7 minutes until softened.
◆ Blend the cornflour with about 5 ml (1 tbsp) water. Stir into the onions and microwave on HIGH for 1 minute. Season with salt and pepper.
◆ Divide the mixture between four ramekin dishes and break an egg into each dish. Gently prick each egg yolk with a needle, fine skewer or wooden cocktail stick. Spoon the cream over and top with the cheese. Microwave on HIGH for 4 minutes or until the eggs are just set. Leave to stand for 1-2 minutes.
◆ Serve with hot buttered toast.

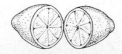

# FISH & SHELLFISH

PRAWNS AND LETTUCE
—— COOKED IN BRANDY AND CREAM ——
*An unusual but delicious combination of ingredients, tastes and textures*

SEE PAGE 67

# Cooking Tips

◆

*To prevent fish drying out, brush skin with melted butter or margarine.*

◆

*Cover the dish with cling film to help keep fish moist during cooking. Pierce the cling film in several places.*

◆

*Remember that fish cooks very quickly so take care not to let it overcook. Shellfish is particularly critical. Take into account the standing time, as during this time the heat will equalise throughout the food.*

◆

*Slash the skin of whole fish in one or two places to prevent it from bursting during cooking.*

◆

*If cooking more than one fish, overlap the thin parts, keeping them separate with a small piece of cling film.*

◆

*Fillets of fish may be cooked flat or rolled up. Reposition during cooking.*

◆

*Large fish should be cooked in a single layer and turned over once during cooking.*

◆

*All fish with the exception of breadcrumbed pieces, should be covered with pierced cling film.*

◆

*Season fish with salt after it has cooked to prevent it toughening and drying out the flesh.*

◆

*Arrange small whole fish in a cartwheel, the tails towards the centre, for more even cooking.*

◆

*Thaw frozen cutlets and fillets in their original wrappings, which should first be slashed.*

◆

## PRAWNS AND LETTUCE COOKED IN BRANDY AND CREAM

### SERVES 1

| |
|---|
| 175 g (6 oz) medium raw prawns, in the shell |
| 15 g (½ oz) butter or margarine |
| salt and pepper |
| 25 ml (1½ tbsp) brandy |
| 45 ml (3 tbsp) double cream |
| 4 green Cos lettuce leaves, shredded |
| lemon twists, to garnish |

◆ Prepare the prawns. Remove the shells, leaving the tail shells intact. Then, with kitchen scissors, split the prawns along the inner curve, stopping at the tail shell, and cutting deep enough to expose the dark vein. Spread each prawn wide open, remove the dark vein then rinse under cold running water. Dry thoroughly on kitchen paper.
◆ Put the butter into a medium bowl and microwave on HIGH for 45 seconds or until the butter melts. Stir in the prawns and microwave on HIGH for 1½-2½ minutes, or until the prawns just turn pink, stirring frequently. Remove with a slotted spoon and set aside.
◆ Season with salt and pepper and quickly stir in the brandy and the cream. Microwave on HIGH for 4-4½ minutes or until the mixture is thickened and reduced.
◆ Stir in the prawns and lettuce and mix together carefully. Microwave on HIGH for 30-45 seconds or until the prawns are just heated through. Garnish with lemon twists and serve immediately.

*Note:* if you find it difficult to buy raw prawns, buy the best quality cooked prawns in the shell and omit point 1.

## POACHED FISH

### SERVES 4

| |
|---|
| 700 g (1½ lb) white fish fillets or cutlets |
| salt and pepper |
| 50 ml (2 fl oz) milk |
| 15 g (½ oz) butter or margarine |

◆ Place the fish in a single layer in a shallow dish. Mix the seasoning with the milk and pour over the fish. Flake the butter on top.
◆ Cover the dish with cling film, pulling back one corner to allow the steam to escape, and microwave on HIGH for 5-6 minutes or until the fish flakes when tested with a fork. Leave to stand, covered, for 5 minutes before serving.

## WHOLE FISH COOKED WITH GARLIC AND SPICES

### SERVES 2

| |
|---|
| 1 fish such as sea bass, sea bream or grey mullet, weighing about 700 g (1½ lb), cleaned and scaled if necessary |
| 2 garlic cloves, skinned |
| finely grated rind and juice of 1 lemon |
| 1 green chilli, seeded (optional) |
| 2.5 cm (1 inch) piece of fresh root ginger, peeled and finely grated |
| 15 ml (1 level tbsp) ground coriander |
| 30 ml (2 tbsp) chopped fresh coriander |
| 5 ml (1 level tsp) garam masala |
| 2.5 ml (½ level tsp) ground cardamom |
| 15 ml (1 level tbsp) ground almonds |
| 1 medium onion, skinned and chopped |
| 30 ml (2 tbsp) vegetable oil |
| salt and pepper |
| chopped fresh coriander, to garnish |

◆ Pierce the fish eyes with a sharp knife to prevent them popping during cooking then slash the fish 3 times on each side. Set aside.
◆ Put the garlic, lemon rind and juice, chilli, ginger, ground and fresh coriander, garam masala, cardamom, almonds and onion in a blender or food processor and liquidise until smooth.
◆ Put half of the oil in a medium bowl and stir in the purée. Microwave on HIGH for 2-3 minutes until thickened, stirring occasionally. Spoon the mixture into the 6 slashes and the inside of the fish.
◆ Place the fish on a large ovenproof serving plate, pour over the remaining oil and season with salt and pepper. Cover loosely with cling film, pulling back one corner to allow the steam to escape, and microwave on HIGH for 4 minutes per 450 g (1 lb) or until tender, turning the fish over once during cooking. Garnish with coriander and serve hot straight from the plate.

# HADDOCK MOUSSE

### SERVES 4

| |
|---|
| 450 g (1 lb) haddock fillet |
| 15 ml (1 level tbsp) gelatine |
| 50 ml (2 fl oz) white wine vinegar |
| 4 hard-boiled eggs, shelled |
| 450 ml (¾ pint) mayonnaise |
| 10 ml (2 tsp) tomato purée |
| 5 ml (1 tsp) anchovy essence |
| salt and pepper |
| 2 egg whites |
| 1 small bunch watercress, trimmed and finely chopped |
| dill sprig, to garnish |

◆ Arrange the fish in a single layer in a shallow dish. Cover and microwave on HIGH for 6 minutes or until tender. Flake the fish, discarding skin and bones.

◆ Sprinkle the gelatine over the vinegar in a small bowl. Leave to soften slightly then add 225 ml (8 fl oz) hot water. Microwave on HIGH for 30 seconds or until the gelatine is dissolved.

◆ Place the hard-boiled eggs, 150 ml (¼ pint) mayonnaise, tomato purée, anchovy essence, seasoning and fish in a blender or food processor and liquidise until smooth. Gradually stir in the gelatine. Tip into a bowl and refrigerate just until the mixture is thick enough to coat the back of a spoon.

◆ Whisk the egg whites until stiff and fold into the fish mixture. Spoon into a 1.7-2.3 litre (3-4 pint) ring mould and refrigerate for about 2 hours until set.

◆ Beat the finely chopped watercress into the remaining mayonnaise and set aside.

◆ Unmould the mousse on to a serving plate. Spoon over a little of the green mayonnaise and garnish with the dill sprig. Serve the remaining mayonnaise separately.

# HERRINGS IN OATMEAL

### SERVES 2

| |
|---|
| 2 small herrings, cleaned |
| salt and pepper |
| 30 ml (2 level tbsp) medium oatmeal |
| 15 g (½ oz) butter or margarine |
| 15 ml (1 tbsp) vegetable oil |
| 5 ml (1 tsp) lemon juice |
| lemon wedges and parsley, to garnish |

◆ Preheat a browning dish to maximum according to the manufacturer's instructions.

◆ Meanwhile, bone the herrings. With a sharp knife cut off the heads just behind the gills, then cut along the belly towards the tail so that the fish can be opened out.

◆ Place the fish flat on a board, skin side upwards, and, with the heel of your hand, press along the backbone to loosen it.

◆ Turn the fish over and lift out the backbone, using the tip of a knife if necessary to help pull the bone away cleanly.

◆ Discard the bone, then wash and dry the fish. Season the inside of each herring with salt and pepper then coat the fish in the oatmeal.

◆ Put the butter and oil in the browning dish, then quickly add the herrings. Microwave on HIGH for 1 minute, then turn them over and microwave on HIGH for 1-2 minutes or until the fish is tender.

◆ Sprinkle over the lemon juice. Serve immediately with a little of the butter spooned over and garnish with lemon wedges and parsley.

# MONKFISH IN WHITE WINE

### SERVES 4

| |
|---|
| 25 g (1 oz) butter or margarine |
| 1 large onion, skinned and chopped |
| 1 garlic clove, skinned and crushed |
| 450 g (1 lb) courgettes, trimmed and sliced |
| 30 ml (2 level tbsp) plain flour |
| 15 ml (1 level tbsp) paprika |
| 150 ml (¼ pint) dry white wine |
| 150 ml (¼ pint) fish or chicken stock |
| 225 g (8 oz) tomatoes, skinned, seeded and chopped |
| 15 ml (1 level tbsp) fresh basil or 5 ml (1 level tsp) dried |
| salt and pepper |
| 900 g (2 lb) monkfish, skinned, boned and cut into 5 cm (2 inch) pieces |

◆ Place the butter in a large bowl and microwave on HIGH for 45 seconds or until the butter melts. Add the onion and garlic and microwave on HIGH for 5-7 minutes or until the onion is softened, stirring once. Add the courgettes, cover and microwave on HIGH for 2 minutes.

◆ Stir in the flour, paprika, wine, stock, tomatoes, basil and seasoning. Microwave on HIGH for 5 minutes or until the liquid is boiling, then continue to microwave on HIGH for a further 5 minutes.

◆ Add the fish, cover and microwave on HIGH for 10 minutes or until the fish is tender, stirring once.

### ——— HADDOCK MOUSSE ———

*This delicate mousse is served with a delicious watercress mayonnaise.*
*Shown here with Monkfish in white wine (opposite).*

SEE OPPOSITE

# SCALLOPS IN CREAM SAUCE

### SERVES 4

| |
|---|
| 700 g (1½ lb) potatoes, peeled and cut into small pieces |
| salt and pepper |
| 1 egg, beaten |
| 450 g (1 lb) frozen scallops, thawed |
| 225 g (8 oz) button mushrooms, sliced |
| 150 ml (¼ pint) dry cider |
| 15 ml (1 tbsp) lemon juice |
| 25 g (1 oz) butter or margarine |
| 25 g (1 oz) plain flour |
| 150 ml (¼ pint) double cream |
| chopped fresh parsley, to garnish |

◆ Cook the potatoes in boiling salted water in the conventional way. Drain and mash with the egg and seasoning.

◆ Meanwhile, slice each scallop in half and place in a medium casserole together with the mushrooms, cider, lemon juice and 150 ml (¼ pint) water. Cover and microwave on HIGH for 10 minutes, stirring once. Strain, reserving 300 ml (½ pint) cooking liquid.

◆ Place the butter in a medium bowl and microwave on HIGH for 45 seconds or until the butter melts. Stir in the flour and microwave on HIGH for 30 seconds. Gradually whisk in the reserved cooking liquid and the cream. Microwave on HIGH for 3 minutes or until thickened, whisking frequently. Season to taste.

◆ Stir the scallops and mushrooms into the sauce. Spoon into 4 individual gratin dishes or scallop shells.

◆ Spoon the potatoes into a large piping bag fitted with a large star nozzle and pipe around the borders of the dishes. Microwave on HIGH for 5 minutes until the scallops are heated through.

◆ Grill under a hot grill until golden brown. Garnish with parsley and serve.

# BAKED MACKEREL

### SERVES 4

| |
|---|
| 50 g (2 oz) butter or margarine |
| 1 small onion, skinned and finely chopped |
| 1 eating apple, peeled and coarsely grated |
| 50 g (2 oz) Cheddar cheese, grated |
| 25 g (1 oz) fresh breadcrumbs |
| finely grated rind of ½ an orange |
| salt and pepper |
| 4 mackerel, cleaned and heads removed |
| 60 ml (4 tbsp) fresh orange juice |
| orange wedges and chopped fresh parsley, to garnish |

◆ Put 25 g (1 oz) of the butter into an ovenproof bowl and microwave on HIGH for 30 seconds until the butter melts. Add the onion. Cover with cling film, pulling back one corner to allow the steam to escape, and microwave on HIGH for 3-4 minutes or until the onion softens.

◆ Stir the apple, cheese, breadcrumbs and orange rind into the softened onion and season very well with salt and pepper.

◆ Fill each fish with the apple stuffing and secure the opening with wooden cocktail sticks. Slash the skin 3 times on each side.

◆ Put the remaining butter into a large shallow ovenproof dish large enough to take the fish in a single layer. Microwave on HIGH for 1 minute until melted. Stir in the orange juice.

◆ Place the fish in the dish side by side and cover with greaseproof paper. Microwave on HIGH for 3 minutes, turn over the mackerel and reposition them so that the outside fish are in the middle. Recover and microwave on HIGH for 3-4 minutes until the fish are cooked and the flesh flakes easily when tested with a fork. Remove the cocktail sticks.

◆ Garnish the mackerel with orange wedges and parsley and serve immediately.

## SCAMPI AND BACON KEBABS

### SERVES 2

| |
|---|
| 40 g (1½ oz) butter or margarine, cut into small pieces |
| 1 garlic clove, skinned and crushed |
| 15 ml (1 tbsp) chopped fresh parsley |
| 5 ml (1 tsp) lemon juice |
| salt and pepper |
| 4 smoked streaky bacon rashers, rinded |
| 175 g (6 oz) scampi |
| chopped fresh parsley, to garnish |

◆ Put the butter and garlic in a shallow rectangular dish and microwave on HIGH for 1 minute or until the butter melts.
◆ Stir in the parsley and lemon juice and season with salt and pepper. Microwave on HIGH for 1 minute, stirring once.
◆ Stretch the bacon rashers, using the back of a knife, and cut in half widthways.
◆ Thread the bacon and the scampi on to 8 wooden skewers, winding the bacon under and over the scampi.
◆ Dip the kebabs in the garlic butter and arrange in a single layer in the dish. Cover loosely with a double thickness of absorbent kitchen paper and microwave on HIGH for 4-5 minutes or until the bacon is cooked, repositioning once during cooking.
◆ Serve 4 kebabs each, with the garlic butter poured over and garnished with parsley.

## SWEET AND SOUR FISH CASSEROLE

### SERVES 4

| |
|---|
| 75 g (3 oz) soft brown sugar |
| 75 ml (5 tbsp) cider vinegar |
| 45 ml (3 tbsp) soy sauce |
| 45 ml (3 level tbsp) cornflour |
| 1 green pepper, cored, seeded and thinly sliced |
| 237 g (8 oz) can crushed pineapple |
| 397 g (14 oz) can tomatoes |
| 450 g (1 lb) firm white fish, such as cod or haddock, cut into 5 cm (2 inch) pieces |
| 225 g (8 oz) peeled prawns |

◆ In a large casserole, blend the sugar, vinegar, soy sauce and cornflour together. Microwave on HIGH for 3 minutes or until the sauce is just boiling, stirring once.

◆ Stir in the green pepper and the canned pineapple and tomatoes with juices. Cover and microwave on HIGH for 5 minutes or until the sauce is boiling, then continue microwaving on HIGH for 10 minutes.
◆ Stir the fish into the sauce. Cover and microwave on HIGH for 6 minutes or until the fish is tender. Stir in the prawns, cover and microwave on HIGH for about 1 minute just to heat through. Serve at once, with rice, if liked.

## LEMON AND MUSTARD MACKEREL

### SERVES 1

| |
|---|
| 25 g (1 oz) butter or margarine |
| 1 small onion, skinned and finely chopped |
| 40 g (1½ oz) fresh white breadcrumbs |
| 10 ml (2 level tsp) black mustard seeds |
| finely grated rind and juice of 1 lemon |
| 5 ml (1 tsp) Dijon mustard |
| salt and pepper |
| 1 mackerel, weighing about 350 g (12 oz), cleaned |
| lemon slices, to garnish |

◆ Put half of the butter and the onion in a small bowl and microwave on HIGH for 3-4 minutes or until the onion has softened, stirring occasionally.
◆ Stir in the breadcrumbs, mustard seeds, the lemon rind, half of the lemon juice and the mustard. Season and set aside.
◆ Using a sharp knife, bone the mackerel. Cut off the head just behind the gills, then cut along the belly towards the tail so that the fish can be opened out.
◆ Place the fish flat on a board, skin side upwards, and with the heel of your hand press along the backbone to loosen it.
◆ Turn the fish right way up and lift out the backbone, using the tip of a knife to help pull the bone away cleanly.
◆ Discard the bone, then wash and dry the fish. Make 3 diagonal slashes about 0.5 cm (¼ inch) deep on each side.
◆ Stuff the fish with the lemon stuffing and put into a shallow dish. Pour over the remaining lemon juice and dot with the remaining butter. Season with salt and pepper.
◆ Cover with cling film, pulling back one corner to allow the steam to escape, and microwave on HIGH for 3-4 minutes or until the fish is tender.
◆ Serve immediately with a little of the cooking liquid poured over. Garnish with lemon slices.

To serve 2: double all the ingredients and follow the recipe as above, but in point 1 microwave on HIGH for 5-7 minutes; in point 8 microwave on HIGH for 5-6 minutes.

## PARCHMENT-BAKED SALMON
### — WITH CUCUMBER SAUCE —
*An elegant and nutritious dish, served with a refreshing
sharp mayonnaise*

SEE OPPOSITE

# PARCHMENT BAKED SALMON WITH CUCUMBER SAUCE

## SERVES 2

| |
|---|
| 25 g (1 oz) butter or margarine |
| ½ small cucumber, thinly sliced |
| 2 spring onions, trimmed and finely chopped |
| 60 ml (4 tbsp) dry white wine |
| 10 ml (2 tsp) chopped fresh dill |
| 1.25 ml (¼ level tsp) fennel seeds |
| salt and pepper |
| 2 salmon steaks, weighing about 175 g (6 oz) each |
| 45 ml (3 tbsp) mayonnaise |
| 30 ml (2 tbsp) natural yogurt |
| 1.25 ml (¼ tsp) lemon juice |
| fresh dill, to garnish |

◆ Put half the butter in a small bowl and microwave on HIGH for 30 seconds or until the butter melts. Stir in the cucumber slices, reserving 6 for cooking the salmon. Stir in the spring onions.

◆ Cover with cling film, pulling back one corner to allow the steam to escape, and microwave on HIGH for 4-5 minutes or until the vegetables are tender. Stir in half of the wine and half of the fresh dill, and microwave uncovered on HIGH for 2 minutes. Leave to cool.

◆ Put the remaining butter, the fennel seeds and the remaining wine in a small bowl and microwave on HIGH for 2 minutes or until the liquid is reduced by half. Season with salt and pepper.

◆ Cut two 28 cm (11 inch) squares of non-stick parchment or greaseproof paper and place a salmon steak on each. Arrange the reserved cucumber slices on top and pour over the butter, wine and fennel seeds. Fold 2 edges of each piece of paper together and twist the other 2 ends to seal and make parcels.

◆ Place the parcels on an ovenproof plate and microwave on HIGH for 4-5 minutes or until the fish is tender.

◆ While the fish is cooking, finish the sauce. Liquidise the cooled cucumber and onion mixture in a blender or food processor with the mayonnaise, yogurt, lemon juice, remaining dill, salt and pepper. Garnish the salmon with fresh dill and serve warm with the cucumber sauce.

# MUSSELS IN CREAM AND GARLIC SAUCE

## SERVES 1

| |
|---|
| 450 g (1 lb) live mussels |
| 75 ml (3 fl oz) dry white wine |
| ½ small onion, skinned and finely chopped |
| 1 garlic clove, skinned and crushed |
| 75 ml (3 fl oz) double cream |
| 5 ml (1 tsp) lemon juice |
| pinch of ground turmeric |
| salt and pepper |
| 1 egg yolk, size 6 |
| chopped fresh parsley, to garnish |

◆ Prepare the mussels. Put them in a sink or bowl and scrub thoroughly with a hard brush. Wash in several changes of water. Scrape off any 'beards' or tufts protruding from the shells, then leave the mussels to soak in a bowl of cold water for 20 minutes. Discard any mussels that are not tightly closed or do not close if tapped with a knife.

◆ Drain, and put into a large bowl with the wine and onion. Cover with cling film, pulling back one corner to allow the steam to escape, and microwave on HIGH for 4-6 minutes or until all the mussels have opened, stirring once. Discard any mussels which do not open.

◆ Strain the mussels through a sieve and return the cooking liquid to the bowl. Keep the mussels warm while making the sauce.

◆ For the sauce, stir the garlic into the reserved cooking liquid and microwave on HIGH for 4-5 minutes or until the liquid is reduced by half.

◆ Stir in the cream, lemon juice, turmeric, salt and pepper and microwave on HIGH for 2 minutes or until the cream is hot.

◆ Stir in the egg yolk and microwave on HIGH for 30 seconds or until the sauce thickens slightly, stirring occasionally.

◆ Pour the sauce over the mussels, sprinkle with chopped parsley and serve immediately.

*To serve 2:* double all the ingredients, using one size 2 egg yolk instead of size 6. Follow the recipe as above, but in point 4 cook the mussels in 3 batches so the timing remains the same; in point 3 pour the cooking liquids into one bowl; in point 4 microwave on HIGH for 5-6 minutes; in step 6 microwave on HIGH for 30 seconds-1 minute.

## HADDOCK AU GRATIN

SERVES 4

---

450 g (1 lb) haddock fillet

225 g (8 oz) smoked haddock fillet

60 ml (4 tbsp) dry white wine

6 black peppercorns

1 bay leaf

1 small onion, skinned and thinly sliced

50 g (2 oz) butter or margarine

100 g (4 oz) button mushrooms, sliced

45 ml (3 level tbsp) plain flour

pepper to taste

75 g (3 oz) Cheddar cheese, finely grated

25 g (1 oz) fresh breadcrumbs

25 g (1 oz) walnuts, finely chopped

---

◆ Place the fish in a shallow dish. Pour over the wine and 300 ml (½ pint) water. Add the peppercorns, bay leaf and onion. Cover and microwave on HIGH for 5 minutes, turning the dish once.

◆ Strain off the liquid and reserve. Flake the fish and discard the peppercorns, bay leaf and onion.

◆ Place the butter in a medium flameproof casserole and microwave on HIGH for 45 seconds or until the butter melts. Stir in the mushrooms and microwave on HIGH for 1 minute. Blend in the flour and microwave on HIGH for 30 seconds. Gradually stir in the cooking liquid and microwave on HIGH for 5-6 minutes, stirring after every minute, until boiling.

◆ Season to taste with pepper and stir in half the cheese and the fish. Microwave on HIGH for 2 minutes.

◆ Mix the breadcrumbs, remaining cheese and walnuts together. Spoon over the fish and brown under a hot grill.

## CURRIED COD STEAKS

SERVES 4

---

50 g (2 oz) butter or margarine

1 large onion, skinned and sliced

5 ml (1 level tsp) ground coriander

5 ml (1 level tsp) ground cumin

5 ml (1 level tsp) ground turmeric

4 cod steaks, each weighing 175 g (6 oz)

142 g (5 oz) natural yogurt

salt and pepper

chopped fresh parsley, to garnish

---

◆ Place the butter or margarine in a shallow dish and microwave on HIGH for 1 minute or until melted. Add the onion, stir well and microwave on HIGH for 5-7 minutes or until soft. Stir in the spices and microwave on HIGH for 2 minutes, stirring once.

◆ Arrange the fish on top of the onion and spices. Cover and microwave on HIGH for 5 minutes. Turn the fish over and microwave on HIGH for a further 5 minutes or until the fish flakes when tested with a fork.

◆ Remove the fish with a slotted spoon and arrange in a warmed serving dish. Keep hot.

◆ Stir the yogurt into the pan juices and season to taste with salt and pepper. Microwave on HIGH for 1 minute or until the sauce is heated through.

◆ Pour the sauce over the fish and sprinkle with chopped parsley. Serve at once, with rice, if liked.

## PAELLA

SERVES 6

---

1 small onion, skinned and finely chopped

2 garlic cloves, skinned and crushed

15 ml (1 tbsp) vegetable oil

350 g (12 oz) long grain rice

900 ml (1½ pints) boiling chicken stock

a few saffron strands

salt and pepper

6 chicken thighs

100 g (4 oz) frozen peas

1 red pepper, cored, seeded and sliced

100 g (4 oz) unpeeled prawns

225 g (8 oz) frozen mussels, thawed

---

◆ Mix the onion, garlic and oil together in a large serving bowl, and microwave on HIGH for 5-7 minutes or until the onion is softened, stirring once.

◆ Stir in the rice, stock and saffron. Season to taste with salt and pepper. Cover and microwave on HIGH for 13 minutes, stirring once. Leave to stand, covered.

◆ Place the chicken on a plate and microwave on HIGH for 5 minutes. Turn the chicken pieces over and microwave on HIGH for a further 5 minutes or until the chicken is tender. Grill under a hot grill until golden brown. Alternatively, heat a browning dish to maximum according to the manufacturer's instructions, brown the chicken, then microwave for 10 minutes, turning the chicken over once.

◆ Place the peas and pepper in a bowl and microwave on HIGH for 3 minutes. Stir in the prawns and mussels, cover and microwave on HIGH for 5 minutes.

◆ Lightly stir the rice with a fork and mix with the mussels, prawns and vegetables. Arrange the chicken on top. Cover and microwave on HIGH for 5 minutes or until the paella is heated through.

# FISH-STUFFED COURGETTES WITH TARRAGON SAUCE

## SERVES 2

| |
|---|
| 4 medium courgettes, trimmed |
| 225 g (8 oz) haddock or cod fillet |
| 45 ml (3 tbsp) milk |
| 1 small garlic clove, skinned and crushed |
| salt and pepper |
| 1 egg yolk, beaten |
| 15 ml (1 tbsp) vegetable oil |
| 10 ml (2 level tsp) plain flour |
| 150 ml (¼ pint) medium dry white wine |
| 15 ml (1 tbsp) chopped fresh tarragon or 5 ml (1 level tsp) dried |
| fresh tarragon, to garnish |

◆ Cut the courgettes in half lengthways and arrange in a single layer in a shallow dish.
◆ Pour over 60 ml (4 tbsp) water and cover with cling film, pulling back one corner to allow the steam to escape. Microwave on HIGH for 8-10 minutes or until the courgettes are just cooked.
◆ Drain the courgettes, reserving the cooking liquid. With a teaspoon, scoop out the flesh into a bowl, leaving a thin shell. Mash the flesh, pouring off any excess liquid.
◆ Put the fish in a shallow dish with the milk. Cover with cling film, pulling back one corner to allow the steam to escape, and microwave on HIGH for 2-3 minutes or until the fish is cooked. Drain, skin and flake the fish, reserving the cooking liquid.
◆ Mix the flaked fish with the courgette flesh, garlic, salt and pepper. Bind together with the egg yolk.
◆ Sandwich the courgette shells together with the stuffing and put on to 2 serving plates. Set aside.
◆ Put the oil and flour in a small bowl and microwave on HIGH for 1 minute. Gradually stir in the wine and the reserved cooking liquids. Stir in the tarragon, salt and pepper. Microwave on HIGH for 4-5 minutes, whisking frequently. Leave to stand.
◆ Meanwhile, microwave the stuffed courgettes, one plate at a time, for 2 minutes each or until hot. Cover to keep warm.
◆ Reheat the sauce on HIGH for 1 minute, if necessary. Garnish the stuffed courgettes with tarragon and serve immediately with the sauce.

# FISH TERRINE WITH BASIL SAUCE

## SERVES 2

| |
|---|
| 225 g (8 oz) whiting, sole or plaice fillet, skinned |
| 1 egg white, size 6, chilled |
| 5 ml (1 tsp) lemon juice |
| salt and pepper |
| 5 ml (1 tsp) chopped fresh dill or 2.5 ml (½ level tsp) dried |
| 25 ml (1½ tbsp) chopped fresh basil or 5 ml (1 level tsp) dried |
| 150 ml (¼ pint) soured cream, chilled |
| 100 g (4 oz) piece of fresh salmon tail fillet, skinned |
| a little milk |
| basil sprigs, to garnish |

◆ Grease two 11 × 7.5 cm (4½ × 3 inch), 350 ml (12 fl oz) ovenproof containers and line the base with greaseproof paper.
◆ Cut the whiting into small pieces, put in a blender or food processor and work until finely chopped.
◆ Gradually add the egg white, lemon juice, salt and pepper and blend until smooth.
◆ Turn into a bowl and stir in the dill and a third of the basil. Gradually beat in half of the soured cream. Cover and chill for 15 minutes.
◆ Cut the salmon into 1 cm (½ inch) cubes. Carefully stir into the fish mixture, then spoon into the lined container and carefully level the surface with a knife.
◆ Loosely cover with absorbent kitchen paper and microwave on LOW for 6½-7 minutes or until the mixture feels firm and shrinks slightly away from the edges of the containers. Leave to cool for about 30 minutes, then chill for at least 30 minutes.
◆ When ready to serve, make the sauce. Mix the remaining soured cream with a little milk to make a thin sauce. Stir in the remaining basil, salt and pepper.
◆ To serve, turn out the terrines and wipe with absorbent kitchen paper to remove any excess liquid. Coat 2 individual serving plates with the sauce and place a terrine in the centre of each. Garnish with basil and serve immediately.

## SCAMPI PROVENÇAL

### SERVES 2

25 g (1 oz) butter or margarine

1 garlic clove, skinned and crushed

2 large onions, skinned and chopped

227 g (8 oz) can tomatoes, drained and chopped

45 ml (3 tbsp) dry white wine

salt and pepper

450 g (1 lb) frozen scampi, thawed

30 ml (2 tbsp) chopped fresh parsley

◆ Place the butter in a medium bowl and microwave on HIGH for 45 seconds or until the butter melts. Stir in the garlic and onion and microwave on HIGH for 5-7 minutes or until the onion is soft, stirring once.
◆ Add the tomatoes, wine and seasoning and microwave on HIGH for 5 minutes.
◆ Stir in the scampi and parsley. Cover and microwave on HIGH for 5 minutes or until the fish is tender, stirring once. Serve with rice, if liked.

## STUFFED TROUT WITH CAPER SAUCE

### SERVES 4

150 g (5 oz) butter or margarine

1 small onion, skinned and finely chopped

50 g (2 oz) mushrooms, finely chopped

45 ml (3 tbsp) lemon juice

half a small head fennel, finely chopped

50 g (2 oz) fresh brown breadcrumbs

1 egg white, lightly beaten

salt and pepper

4 trout, weighing about 175 g (6 oz) each, cleaned and with heads removed

3 egg yolks

15 ml (1 level tbsp) capers

◆ Place 50 g (2 oz) butter in a medium bowl and microwave on HIGH for 45 seconds or until the butter melts. Stir in the onion, mushrooms, lemon juice and 15 ml (1 tbsp) chopped fennel. Cover and microwave on HIGH for 5-7 minutes or until the vegetables are soft, stirring once. Stir in the breadcrumbs and egg white and season.

◆ Stuff each trout with some of the mixture. Arrange the fish in a shallow oblong dish, head next to tail and stuffing pockets uppermost.
◆ Cover and microwave on HIGH for 5 minutes. Reposition the fish, cover and microwave for a further 5 minutes or until the fish is tender. Leave to stand, covered.
◆ Microwave the remaining butter in a medium bowl on HIGH until the butter melts.
◆ Whisk together the egg yolks and remaining lemon juice and season to taste. Gradually whisk into the butter or margarine. Microwave on HIGH for 45 seconds, whisking every 15 seconds, until the sauce is thick enough to coat the back of a spoon. Remove from the microwave and whisk for a further 20 seconds to cool slightly. Stir in the capers and serve with the trout.

## STUFFED TROUT

### SERVES 4

25 g (1 oz) butter or margarine

1 medium onion, skinned and finely chopped

75 g (3 oz) fresh breadcrumbs

30 ml (2 tbsp) chopped fresh parsley

finely grated rind and juice of 1 lemon

salt and pepper

4 whole trout, about 225 g (8 oz) each, cleaned

lemon wedges and chopped fresh parsley or tarragon, to garnish

cucumber sauce (see p. 214), to serve

◆ To make the stuffing, put the butter into a medium ovenproof glass bowl and microwave on HIGH for 1 minute or until the butter melts. Stir in the onion. Cover with cling film, pulling back one corner to allow the steam to escape, and microwave on HIGH for 5-7 minutes until the onion softens. Stir in the breadcrumbs, parsley, lemon rind and juice and the salt and pepper and mix together well.
◆ Fill each trout with the stuffing. Place the trout side by side in a large ovenproof dish.
◆ Cover with cling film, pulling back one corner to allow the steam to escape and microwave on HIGH for 8-10 minutes, turning the trout over and repositioning them halfway through cooking. Stand for 5 minutes before serving. Garnish with lemon wedges and parsley and serve with cucumber sauce.

## STUFFED TROUT

*Stuffed with a parsley, lemon and breadcrumb mix, the fish are served
with a delicate cucumber sauce*

SEE OPPOSITE

## POACHED TROUT WITH HORSERADISH CREAM

### SERVES 3

*3 trout, weighing about 225 g (8 oz) each, cleaned and with heads removed*

*45 ml (3 tbsp) cider vinegar*

*30 ml (2 tbsp) natural yogurt*

*60 ml (4 tbsp) mayonnaise*

*30 ml (2 tbsp) horseradish sauce*

*salt and pepper*

*curly endive or lettuce and cucumber, to garnish*

*thinly sliced brown bread and butter, to serve*

◆ In an oblong dish, arrange the trout with their backbones to the outside. Pour over the vinegar and 50 ml (2 fl oz) water. Cover and microwave on HIGH for 3 minutes. Turn the fish over and reposition it. Cover and microwave on HIGH for 3 minutes. Leave to stand until cold.

◆ When cold, drain the fish, cut in half along the backbones and remove the skin and bones. Arrange on a flat serving dish and keep cool.

◆ Mix the yogurt, mayonnaise and horseradish sauce together and season to taste. Pour the sauce over the fish. Garnish with the endive or lettuce and cucumber and serve.

## COD WITH TOMATOES AND PEPPERS

### SERVES 4

*2 medium onions, skinned and chopped*

*1 medium green pepper, cored, seeded and chopped*

*45 ml (3 tbsp) vegetable oil*

*30 ml (2 level tbsp) plain flour*

*150 ml (¼ pint) fish or chicken stock*

*5 ml (1 tsp) tomato purée*

*397 g (14 oz) can tomatoes*

*1 bay leaf*

*1 garlic clove, skinned and crushed*

*700 g (1½ lb) cod or haddock fillet, skinned and cut into 2.5 cm (1 inch) cubes*

*salt and pepper*

*30 ml (2 tbsp) chopped fresh parsley*

◆ Place the onion, pepper and vegetable oil in a large ovenproof casserole and mix well. Cover with cling film, pulling back one corner to allow the steam to escape, and microwave on HIGH for 5-7 minutes or until the vegetables have softened.

◆ Stir in the flour and microwave on HIGH for 1 minute. Gradually stir in the stock, tomato purée and tomatoes and microwave on HIGH for 2-3 minutes or until the liquid boils and thickens, stirring every minute.

◆ Add the bay leaf, garlic and fish, three-quarters cover with cling film and microwave on HIGH for 8-9 minutes or until the fish is cooked, stirring occasionally.

◆ Season well with salt and pepper and stir in the parsley. Serve hot.

## PAUPIETTES OF SOLE

### SERVES 6

*220 g (8 oz) can pink salmon*

*1 egg white*

*25 g (1 oz) fresh breadcrumbs*

*1 bunch watercress, trimmed*

*salt and pepper*

*6 sole or plaice fillets, skinned*

*50 ml (2 fl oz) dry white wine*

*50 ml (2 fl oz) double cream*

◆ To make the stuffing, drain the salmon, reserving the juice, and remove the skin and bones. Put into a blender or food processor along with the egg white, breadcrumbs and half the bunch of watercress. Season to taste and liquidise until very smooth.

◆ Cut the fish fillets in half lengthways. Season to taste and spread with the stuffing mixture. Roll up each fillet and secure with wooden cocktail sticks.

◆ Stand the fish roll-ups on their ends in a flan dish, packing them close together. Make up the salmon juice to 75 ml (3 fl oz) with water and add the wine. Pour the liquid over the fish. Cover and microwave on HIGH for 6 minutes or until tender, turning the dish once.

◆ Using a slotted spoon, transfer the roll-ups to a heated serving dish and keep hot.

◆ Add the cream to the pan juices and microwave on HIGH for 3 minutes or until the liquid is boiling, stirring occasionally, then continue microwaving for another 3-5 minutes until the sauce has reduced and is thickened. Season to taste and pour the sauce over the fish. Garnish with the remaining watercress and serve at once.

## KEDGEREE

### SERVES 4

225 g (8 oz) long grain rice

450 g (1 lb) smoked haddock fillet

50 g (2 oz) butter or margarine, cut into small pieces

1 large onion, skinned and chopped

10 ml (2 level tsp) curry powder

5 ml (1 level tsp) grated nutmeg

1 bunch watercress, trimmed

30 ml (2 tbsp) single cream

salt and pepper

2 hard-boiled eggs, shelled

◆ Place the rice and 600 ml (1 pint) boiling water in a large casserole. Stir once, then cover and microwave on HIGH for 12 minutes. Leave to stand, covered.
◆ Place the haddock in a large dish, cover and microwave on HIGH for 6 minutes, turning the dish once. Remove the skin and flake the fish, discarding any bones. Stir the fish into the rice.
◆ Place the butter or margarine in a medium bowl and microwave on HIGH for 45 seconds or until the butter melts. Stir in the onion, curry powder and nutmeg. Cover and microwave on HIGH for 5-7 minutes or until the onion is soft, stirring once. Stir it into the rice.
◆ Finely chop half the watercress and stir into the rice mixture along with the cream. Season to taste with pepper and add salt only if necessary. Cover and microwave on HIGH for 5 minutes to heat through.
◆ Cut each egg into quarters and arrange on the kedgeree. Garnish with the remaining watercress and serve immediately.

## HADDOCK AND SPINACH PIE

### SERVES 4

50 g (2 oz) butter or margarine

50 g (2 oz) plain flour

450 ml (¾ pint) milk

100 g (4 oz) Cheddar cheese, grated

salt and pepper

grated nutmeg to taste

454 g (1 lb) packet frozen leaf spinach

450 g (1 lb) smoked haddock fillet, skinned and cut into 2.5 cm (1 inch) strips

◆ Blend the butter, flour and milk together in a large bowl and microwave on HIGH for 4-5 minutes or until the sauce has thickened, whisking after every minute.
◆ Stir in half of the cheese and season well with salt, pepper and nutmeg. Set aside.
◆ Put the frozen spinach in a deep 20.5 cm (8 inch) square dish and microwave on HIGH for 6-7 minutes or until thawed.
◆ Turn into a sieve and drain thoroughly, then spread evenly over the base of the dish.
◆ Place the fish in a single layer on top of the spinach and microwave on HIGH for 4-5 minutes or until tender and the flesh flakes easily when tested with a fork.
◆ Pour the cheese sauce evenly over the fish to cover it completely. Microwave on HIGH for 5 minutes, then sprinkle the remaining cheese on top. Brown under a hot grill, if liked.

## FISH KEBABS

### SERVES 4

1 small onion, skinned and finely chopped

30 ml (2 tbsp) olive or vegetable oil

10 ml (2 tsp) lemon juice

15 ml (1 tbsp) chopped fresh mixed herbs or 5 ml (1 level tsp) dried

salt and pepper

450 g (1 lb) cod fillet, cut into 2.5 cm (1 inch) cubes

1 small green pepper, cored, seeded and cut into 2.5 cm (1 inch) cubes

8 button mushrooms

8 bay leaves

8 cherry tomatoes

◆ Mix together the onion, olive oil, lemon juice, herbs and seasoning in a large ovenproof glass bowl. Add the fish, pepper, mushrooms and bay leaves and leave to marinate for 1 hour.
◆ Remove the fish from the marinade with a slotted spoon and set aside.
◆ Cover the bowl of marinated vegetables with cling film and microwave on HIGH for 3 minutes, stirring once.
◆ Thread the cod, pepper, tomatoes, mushrooms and bay leaves on to 8 wooden skewers and brush with the marinade.
◆ Arrange the kebabs in a double layer on a roasting rack and microwave on HIGH for 4 minutes, then reposition them, brush with any remaining marinade and microwave on HIGH for 5-6 minutes or until the fish is tender. Serve with cooked rice, if liked.

## —— CEYLON PRAWN CURRY ——
*A delicious spicy, creamy dish, served with chutney on a bed of rice*

SEE OPPOSITE

# CEYLON PRAWN CURRY

### SERVES 4

| |
|---|
| 50 g (2 oz) butter or margarine |
| 1 large onion, skinned and finely chopped |
| 1 garlic clove, skinned and crushed |
| 15 ml (1 level tbsp) plain flour |
| 10 ml (2 level tsp) ground turmeric |
| 2.5 ml (½ level tsp) ground cloves |
| 5 ml (1 level tsp) ground cinnamon |
| 5 ml (1 level tsp) salt |
| 5 ml (1 level tsp) sugar |
| 50 g (2 oz) creamed coconut |
| 450 ml (¾ pint) chicken stock |
| 450 g (1 lb) peeled prawns or 12 Dublin Bay prawns, peeled |
| 5 ml (1 tsp) lemon juice |
| coriander sprigs, to garnish |
| cooked rice and chutney, to serve |

◆ Put the butter into a shallow ovenproof dish and microwave on HIGH for 1 minute until the butter melts; stir in the onion and garlic. Cover with cling film, pulling back one corner to allow the steam to escape, and microwave on HIGH for 5-7 minutes until the onion softens.
◆ Stir the flour, spices, salt and sugar into the onion. Microwave on HIGH for 2 minutes. Stir in the creamed coconut and stock. Microwave on HIGH for 6-8 minutes until boiling, stirring frequently.
◆ Add the prawns and lemon juice to the sauce and adjust the seasoning. Microwave on HIGH for 1-2 minutes until the prawns are heated through. Garnish with the coriander. Serve with rice and chutney.

# SKATE WITH ANCHOVIES AND CAPERS

### SERVES 2

| |
|---|
| 1 small skate wing, weighing about 450 g (1 lb) |
| 50 g (2 oz) butter or margarine |
| 50 g (2 oz) button mushrooms, thinly sliced |
| half a 50 g (1¾ oz) can anchovies, drained and finely chopped |
| 15 ml (1 level tbsp) capers |
| pepper |
| lemon wedges, to garnish |

◆ Cut the skate wing in half. Put 25 g (1 oz) of the butter in a large shallow dish and microwave on HIGH for 45 seconds or until the butter melts. Arrange the skate in the dish and cover with cling film, pulling back one corner to allow the steam to escape.
◆ Microwave on HIGH for 4 minutes per 450 g (1 lb). Turn the skate over and reposition the pieces halfway through cooking. Remove the skate and place on warmed serving plates.
◆ Add the remaining butter to the dish and microwave on HIGH, uncovered, for 45 seconds until the butter melts. Add the mushrooms and microwave on HIGH for 1 minute. Add the anchovies and capers and stir well. Microwave on HIGH for 1 minute until hot. Season with pepper. Pour over the stake and serve at once, garnished with lemon wedges.

# POACHED PLAICE IN CIDER

### SERVES 4

| |
|---|
| 50 g (2 oz) butter or margarine |
| 175 g (6 oz) carrots, peeled and thinly sliced |
| 3 celery sticks, trimmed and thinly sliced |
| 15 g (½ oz) plain flour |
| 200 ml (7 fl oz) dry cider |
| juice of ½ a lemon |
| 8 plaice fillets, skinned |
| 175 g (6 oz) button mushrooms, sliced |
| 226 g (8 oz) can tomatoes, drained |
| salt and pepper |

◆ Put the butter into a shallow ovenproof dish and microwave on HIGH for 45 seconds until the butter melts. Add the carrots and celery and mix well. Three-quarters cover with cling film and microwave on HIGH for 8-10 minutes until the carrots soften. Stir in the flour and microwave on HIGH for 1 minute. Gradually stir in the cider and lemon juice.
◆ Roll up the plaice fillets with the skin side inside, then place them on top of the vegetables. Scatter the mushrooms and tomatoes over the fish and season well with salt and pepper.
◆ Cover the dish with cling film, pulling back one corner to allow the steam to escape, and microwave on HIGH for 10-11 minutes until the fish and vegetables are cooked. Turn the dish two or three times during cooking. Uncover and microwave on HIGH for 2 minutes. Serve hot.

## SEAFOOD PANCAKES

### SERVES 4

| |
|---|
| 40 g (1½ oz) butter or margarine |
| 225 g (8 oz) piece of monkfish |
| 100 g (4 oz) wheatmeal flour |
| salt and pepper |
| 1 egg |
| 568 ml (1 pint) milk |
| vegetable oil, for frying |
| 25 g (1 oz) plain flour |
| 5 ml (1 tsp) lemon juice |
| 5 ml (1 level tsp) tomato purée |
| 100 g (4 oz) Cheddar cheese, grated |
| 100 g (4 oz) peeled shrimps |
| 50 g (2 oz) shelled cockles |
| 15 ml (1 tbsp) chopped fresh parsley |

◆ Beat 15 g (½ oz) of the butter in a bowl until soft, then spread it over the monkfish. Place in a shallow ovenproof dish and cover with cling film, pulling back one corner to allow the steam to escape. Microwave on HIGH for 5-6 minutes or until the fish is just cooked and flakes easily, turning over after 3 minutes. Cover and leave the fish to stand while making the pancakes.

◆ Put the wheatmeal flour and a good pinch of salt into a mixing bowl. Make a well in the centre of the flour and break in the egg. Gradually add 150 ml (¼ pint) of the milk, vigorously beating in the flour until a thick smooth batter is formed. Pour in a further 150 ml (¼ pint) milk and beat again.

◆ Heat a little oil in a frying-pan and when it is very hot pour in a small amount of batter. Tip the pan quickly so that the batter runs over the bottom of the pan to coat it thinly. Cook over a high heat for about 1 minute until the underside is golden brown, then turn the pancake over and cook the other side until golden brown. Remove it from the pan and keep it warm. Make 7 more pancakes in the same way.

◆ Remove any skin from the monkfish, flake the flesh and remove the bones. Put fish aside.

◆ Put the remaining 25 g (1 oz) butter into an ovenproof bowl and microwave on HIGH for 30 seconds or until the butter melts. Stir in the flour and microwave on HIGH for 1 minute. Gradually stir in the remaining milk. Microwave on HIGH for 45 seconds, then whisk well, Microwave on HIGH for 1½-2 minutes until the sauce boils, whisking every 30 seconds.

◆ Stir the lemon juice, tomato purée and half of the cheese into the hot sauce. Fold in the flaked monkfish, the shrimps and cockles. Season well with salt and pepper.

◆ Divide the fish mixture evenly among the pancakes and

neatly roll them up to enclose the filling. Place the pancakes side by side in a buttered shallow ovenproof dish. Sprinkle with the remaining cheese and the parsley. Cover with cling film, pulling back one corner to allow the steam to escape, and microwave on HIGH for 5-6 minutes until the pancakes are well heated through. Serve hot with a green salad, if liked.

## COD AND CUCUMBER MORNAY

### SERVES 4

| |
|---|
| 4 large cod cutlets |
| salt and pepper |
| 10 ml (2 tsp) chopped fresh parsley |
| 150 ml (¼ pint) dry cider |
| 15 g (½ oz) butter or margarine |
| 15 g (½ oz) plain flour |
| ½ a cucumber, peeled, cut in half lengthways, seeded and sliced |
| 150 ml (¼ pint) milk |
| 100 g (4 oz) Cheddar cheese, grated |
| slices of lemon and sprigs of watercress, to garnish |

◆ Place the cod cutlets in a shallow ovenproof serving dish or casserole, season with salt and pepper, add the parsley and pour the cider over them. Cover the dish with cling film, pulling back one corner to allow the steam to escape, and microwave on HIGH for 8-10 minutes or until the fish is almost cooked. Remove it from the oven, cover and leave to stand.

◆ Put the butter into an ovenproof glass bowl and microwave on HIGH for 45 seconds or until the butter melts. Stir in the flour and microwave on HIGH for 1 minute. Gradually stir in the milk and microwave on HIGH for 2-3 minutes until the sauce boils and thickens, whisking every minute. Stir in the cucumber, three-quarters cover with cling film and microwave on HIGH for 5-6 minutes until the cucumber is softened, stirring once or twice.

◆ Season with salt and pepper and pour the cucumber and milk over the cod cutlets. Sprinkle with the cheese. Microwave on HIGH for 5-6 minutes or until the cheese melts. Garnish with lemon slices and watercress. If wished this dish may be browned, after cooking, under a hot grill.

# COD STEAKS WITH PRAWNS AND CREAM

### SERVES 4

*40 g (1½ oz) butter or margarine*

*1 medium onion, skinned and chopped*

*40 g (1½ oz) plain flour*

*300 ml (½ pint) milk*

*150 ml (¼ pint) single cream*

*5 ml (1 tsp) prepared mustard*

*100 g (4 oz) peeled prawns*

*10 ml (2 tsp) lemon juice*

*salt and pepper*

*4 cod steaks, each weighing about 175 g (6 oz)*

*chopped fresh parsley, to garnish*

◆ Put the butter in a large bowl and microwave on HIGH for 45 seconds or until the butter melts.

◆ Stir in the onion and three-quarters cover with cling film or a lid. Microwave on HIGH for 5-7 minutes, stirring occasionally until the onion is softened.

◆ Stir in the flour, then the milk and microwave on HIGH for 2-3 minutes until the sauce thickens, whisking after every minute.

◆ Stir in the cream, mustard, prawns and lemon juice and season well with salt and pepper.

◆ Arrange the cod in a single layer in a round serving dish, with the thinnest parts of the fish towards the centre. Pour the sauce over and microwave on HIGH for 4 minutes per 450 g (1 lb) turning once, until the fish is tender and flakes when tested with a fork. Garnish with chopped parsley.

# LEMON-POACHED SALMON STEAKS

### SERVES 4-6

*100 g (4 oz) butter or margarine*

*30 ml (2 tbsp) finely chopped fresh mixed herbs*

*salt and pepper*

*200 ml (7½ fl oz) dry white wine*

*1 small carrot, peeled and very thinly sliced*

*1 celery stick, trimmed and very thinly sliced*

*1 small onion, skinned and very thinly sliced*

*1 bay leaf*

*6 white peppercorns, crushed*

*4 parsley sprigs*

*5 ml (1 level tsp) salt*

*thinly peeled rind and strained juice of 1 lemon*

*4-6 salmon steaks, about 2.5 cm (1 inch) thick*

◆ To make the herb butter, cream the butter until soft. If it is very hard, microwave on HIGH for 10 seconds until soft. Stir in the herbs, salt and pepper and beat together well. Shape the butter into a roll and wrap it in greaseproof paper or kitchen foil. Leave it in the refrigerator to harden while cooking the fish.

◆ Put the wine, vegetables, bay leaf, peppercorns, parsley, salt, lemon rind and juice into a deep ovenproof casserole and add 450 ml (¾ pint) water. Cover with the lid and microwave on HIGH for 8 minutes or until the liquid is boiling.

◆ Uncover the casserole and gently lower in the salmon steaks. Replace the lid and microwave on HIGH for 3 minutes or until the liquid starts to bubble.

◆ Microwave on HIGH for a further 2-3 minutes until the fish is tender. Give the dish a half turn halfway through cooking.

◆ Replace the lid after testing the fish and leave it to stand for 5 minutes. While the fish is standing, cut the butter into slices about 0.5 cm (¼ inch) thick. Remove the fish carefully with a slotted spoon. Serve hot with the herb butter.

## FISH PIE

SERVES 4

| |
|---|
| 700 g (1½ lb) cod fillet, even thickness |
| 75 g (3 oz) butter or margarine |
| about 300 ml (½ pint) milk |
| salt and pepper |
| 700 g (1½ lb) potatoes, peeled and sliced |
| 1 egg, beaten |
| 25 g (1 oz) plain flour |
| 3 eggs, hard-boiled and sliced |
| 50 g (2 oz) peeled prawns (optional) |
| chopped fresh parsley, to garnish |

◆ Place the cod in a shallow ovenproof dish, dot with 25 g (1 oz) of the butter, add 150 ml (¼ pint) of the milk and season well with salt and pepper. Cover with cling film, pulling back one corner to allow the steam to escape, and microwave on HIGH for 5-6 minutes until the cod is white and flakes easily when tested with a fork. Turn the dish two or three times during cooking. Stand for 5 minutes.
◆ Strain the juices from the cod into a measuring jug and make up to 300 ml (½ pint) with milk. Remove all the bones and skin from the cod, then flake the flesh. Set aside.
◆ Put the potatoes in a large ovenproof bowl with 90 ml (6 tbsp) water and three-quarters cover it with cling film. Microwave on HIGH for 12-15 minutes or until the potatoes are cooked, stirring two or three times during cooking.
◆ Drain any excess water from the potatoes. Mash and cream the potatoes with 25 g (1 oz) butter and the beaten egg.
◆ Put the remaining 25 g (1 oz) butter in an ovenproof bowl and microwave on HIGH for 30 seconds or until the butter melts, stir in the flour and microwave on HIGH for 30 seconds. Gradually stir in the measured milk. Microwave on HIGH for 30 seconds. Gradually stir in the measured milk. Microwave on HIGH for 45 seconds, then whisk well. Microwave on HIGH for 1¾-2 minutes until boiling, whisking every 30 seconds. Season well with salt and pepper.
◆ Fold the flaked cod, prawns and eggs into the sauce, then pour into a large ovenproof serving dish, or pie dish.
◆ Spoon or pipe the cooked potatoes over the fish mixture. Microwave on HIGH for 5-6 minutes until the pie is well heated through. Sprinkle with chopped parsley and serve immediately.

## SOUFFLE FISH RING

SERVES 4

| |
|---|
| 450 g (1 lb) firm white fish fillet, such as cod or haddock |
| 50 g (2 oz) fresh breadcrumbs |
| 3 eggs, separated |
| 50 g (2 oz) Cheddar cheese, grated |
| salt and pepper |
| 225 g (8 oz) carrots, peeled and cut into matchsticks |
| half a cucumber, cut into matchsticks |
| 75 g (3 oz) butter, cut into small pieces |
| finely grated rind and juice of 1 lemon |
| 45 ml (3 tbsp) finely chopped fresh parsley or snipped chives |

◆ Skin the fish and place the flesh in a blender or food processor together with the breadcrumbs, egg yolks and cheese. Season to taste and liquidise until very smooth.
◆ Whisk the egg whites until stiff and fold into the fish mixture.
◆ Spoon into a 1.7-2.3 litre (3-4 pint) ring mould and microwave on HIGH for 5-6 minutes or until the fish flakes, turning once. Leave to stand, covered.
◆ Place the carrots in a small bowl, cover and microwave on HIGH for 3 minutes. Add the cucumber and microwave on HIGH for 2 minutes. Set aside and keep hot.
◆ Place the butter in a small bowl and microwave on HIGH for 45 seconds or until the butter melts. Stir in the lemon rind, lemon juice, seasoning and parsley.
◆ Loosen the edges of the fish mould with a palette knife and unmould on to a serving plate. Fill the centre with some of the julienne vegetables. Spoon over some of the lemon butter. Serve with the remaining vegetables and pass the sauce separately.

# WHOLE FISH COOKED CHINESE STYLE

### SERVES 2

*2 whole fish, such as mullet, carp, bream, cleaned, total weight about 450 g (1 lb)*

*2.5 cm (1 inch) piece of root ginger, peeled*

*2 spring onions, trimmed*

*1 carrot, peeled*

*50 g (2 oz) ham*

*50 g (2 oz) mushrooms, thinly sliced*

*45 ml (3 tbsp) dry sherry*

*30 ml (2 tbsp) soy sauce*

*5 ml (1 level tsp) sugar*

*salt and pepper*

*spring onion tassels, to garnish*

◆ Slash the fish skin 3 times on each side to allow for even cooking and to prevent bursting. Place the fish in a shallow ovenproof dish.

◆ Thinly shred the ginger, onions, carrot and ham and sprinkle these over the fish, together with the mushrooms.

◆ Mix the remaining ingredients together, spoon them over the fish, then cover with cling film and microwave on HIGH for 3-4 minutes per 450 g (1 lb) or until the fish is tender, turning the fish over halfway through cooking. Serve garnished with spring onion tassels.

# HERRINGS WITH MUSTARD SAUCE

### SERVES 4

*90 g (3½ oz) butter or margarine.*

*45 ml (3 level tbsp) plain flour*

*450 ml (¾ pint) milk*

*30 ml (2 level tbsp) mustard powder*

*20 ml (4 tsp) malt vinegar*

*salt and pepper*

*30 ml (2 tbsp) single cream*

*4 large herrings, cleaned and heads removed*

*watercress, to garnish*

◆ To make the sauce, put 40 g (1½ oz) of the butter into a medium ovenproof glass bowl and microwave on HIGH for 45 seconds or until the butter melts. Stir in the flour and microwave on HIGH for 1 minute. Gradually stir in the milk. Microwave on HIGH for 45 seconds and whisk well. Microwave on HIGH for 2-3 minutes until the sauce boils, whisking every minute.

◆ Blend the mustard powder with the vinegar and stir into the sauce. Season with salt and pepper and stir in the cream. Cover the surface of the sauce closely with cling film to prevent a skin forming and set aside.

◆ Scrape the scales from the herrings with the back of a knife, and remove the fins. Slash the skin 3 times on each side of each herring, season well with salt and pepper. Beat the remaining butter in a bowl until soft and spread on both sides of the fish.

◆ Place the herrings in a shallow ovenproof serving dish. Loosely cover with cling film and microwave on HIGH for 2-3 minutes. Turn over the herrings and reposition. Loosely cover with cling film and microwave on HIGH for a further 2-3 minutes until the flesh flakes easily when tested with a fork. Remove the herrings from the oven and keep warm.

◆ Reheat the mustard sauce on HIGH for 2-3 minutes, whisking every minute. Pour some of the sauce over the fish and serve the rest separately. Garnish with watercress.

# POULTRY & GAME

## MARINATED CHICKEN
### —— WITH PEPPERS AND MARJORAM ——
*First marinated in lemon and garlic, the chicken is then steamed with peppers, onions and capers*

SEE PAGE 89

# Cooking Tips

◆

*Roasting bags are useful for cooking poultry without spattering. Use an elastic band to secure them, not metal twist ties which could cause arcing. Pierce the bags before cooking to allow steam to escape.*

◆

*Boned and rolled poultry cooks more evenly because the shape and thickness are consistent.*

◆

*Arrange portions of poultry so that the thinnest parts are pointing towards the centre of the dish.*

◆

*Salt toughens poultry and makes it dry out if added directly on the food without any liquid. It is best to add it after cooking has finished.*

◆

*Turn poultry portions over at least once during cooking to ensure even cooking.*

◆

*When cooking duck spoon off the fat during cooking to prevent a pool forming and spattering occuring.*

◆

*Poultry and game are cooked when a knife is inserted into the thickest part of the meat and the juices run clear.*

◆

# MARINATED CHICKEN WITH PEPPERS AND MARJORAM

## SERVES 2

| |
|---|
| 2 chicken breast fillets, skinned |
| 1 garlic clove, skinned and crushed |
| 10 ml (2 tsp) lemon juice |
| pinch of sugar |
| 45 ml (3 tbsp) olive or vegetable oil |
| 15 ml (1 tbsp) chopped fresh marjoram or 5 ml (1 level tsp) dried |
| 1 small onion, skinned and thinly sliced into rings |
| salt and pepper |
| 1 small red pepper, cored, seeded and coarsely chopped |
| 1 small yellow pepper, cored, seeded and coarsely chopped |
| 50 g (2 oz) black olives, halved and stoned |
| 15 ml (1 level tbsp) capers |
| fresh marjoram, to garnish |

◆ Cut the chicken breasts in half widthways, and put into a shallow dish just large enough to hold them in a single layer.
◆ Put the garlic, lemon juice and sugar in a small bowl and whisk together. Gradually whisk in the oil. Stir in the marjoram, onion rings, salt and pepper.
◆ Pour over the chicken, cover with cling film and leave to marinate for at least 30 minutes.
◆ Meanwhile, put the peppers into a shallow dish with 30 ml (2 tbsp) water, cover with cling film, pulling back one corner to allow the steam to escape, and microwave on HIGH for 5-6 minutes or until the peppers are just soft, stirring occasionally. Drain and set aside.
◆ To cook the chicken, pull back one corner of the cling film to allow the steam to escape, and microwave on HIGH for 5-6 minutes or until the chicken is tender, turning once.
◆ Add the peppers, olives and capers and microwave on HIGH for 1-2 minutes or until heated through, stirring once. Serve immediately, garnished with fresh marjoram.

# CHICKEN BREASTS STUFFED WITH STILTON

## SERVES 4

| |
|---|
| 125 g (4 oz) Stilton cheese, crumbled |
| 75 g (3 oz) unsalted butter, softened |
| 4 chicken breasts, skinned and boned |
| 8 smoked back bacon rashers, rinded |
| 45 ml (3 tbsp) vegetable oil |
| 100 ml (4 fl oz) red wine made up to 300 ml (½ pint) with chicken stock |
| 10 ml (2 level tsp) arrowroot |
| salt and pepper |
| watercress, to garnish |

◆ Cream the Stilton and unsalted butter together to make a smooth paste.
◆ Flatten the chicken breasts between 2 sheets of grease-proof paper. Make a horizontal slit in the centre of each breast to make a pocket and fill the pockets with the Stilton butter. Wind the bacon rashers around each breast.
◆ Preheat a browning dish to maximum according to the manufacturer's instructions, adding the oil for the last 30 seconds. (Or, put the oil into a shallow ovenproof dish and microwave on HIGH for 2 minutes until hot.)
◆ Without removing the browning dish from the oven, poach the chicken breasts in the dish rounded sides down. Microwave on HIGH for 5 minutes, turning the chicken over halfway during cooking.
◆ Pour the wine and stock into the dish, microwave on HIGH for about 5 minutes until the liquid is boiling. Cover the dish with a lid or with cling film, pulling back one corner to allow the steam to escape. Reduce the setting to LOW and microwave for about 10 minutes or until the chicken is very tender.
◆ Lift the chicken breasts from the dish, place on a hot serving dish, cover and keep warm.
◆ Blend the arrowroot with a little cold water to a smooth paste and stir this into the cooking juices. Microwave on HIGH for 4-5 minutes until the sauce thickens. Season well with salt and pepper.
◆ Pour the sauce over the chicken breasts, garnish with watercress and serve.

# CHICKEN AND COCONUT CURRY

### SERVES 4

| |
|---|
| 50 g (2 oz) desiccated coconut |
| 200 ml (7 fl oz) milk |
| 30 ml (2 tbsp) vegetable oil |
| 4 celery sticks, trimmed and sliced |
| 1 medium onion, skinned and sliced |
| 1 large red pepper, cored, seeded and sliced |
| 225 g (8 oz) cooking apples, peeled, cored and sliced |
| 2.5 ml (½ level tsp) chilli powder |
| 5 ml (1 level tsp) ground cinnamon |
| 60 ml (4 level tbsp) plain flour |
| 1.8 kg (4 lb) chicken, boned, skinned and the flesh cut into 2.5 cm (1 inch) cubes |
| 450 ml (¾ pint) chicken stock |
| salt and pepper |
| fresh coriander or parsley, to garnish |

◆ Put the coconut and milk into an ovenproof glass bowl and microwave on HIGH for 3-4 minutes or until the liquid boils. Remove this from the oven, cover and leave the milk to infuse for 30 minutes.

◆ Strain the milk through a fine sieve into another bowl, pressing the coconut to extract all the juices, then reserve.

◆ Put the oil into a large ovenproof casserole with the celery, onion, red pepper and apple and mix the ingredients together well. Cover the dish with a lid, or with cling film, pulling back one corner to allow the steam to escape. Microwave on HIGH for 5-6 minutes or until the vegetables soften.

◆ Uncover the dish and stir in the spices and the flour and microwave on HIGH for 2 minutes. Arrange the chicken pieces on top of the vegetables and microwave on HIGH for 4-5 minutes or until the pieces of chicken become opaque, turning over the pieces during the cooking time.

◆ Pour the stock and coconut milk over the chicken and season it with salt and pepper. Stir well, then cover with a lid, or with cling film, pulling back one corner to allow the steam to escape. Microwave on HIGH for 6-8 minutes or until the liquid boils. Reduce the setting and microwave on LOW for 20-30 minutes or until the chicken is very tender.

◆ Leave it to stand for 5 minutes and sprinkle with coriander leaves or parsley just before serving.

# MARINATED CHICKEN WITH PEANUT SAUCE

### SERVES 4

| |
|---|
| 60 ml (4 tbsp) olive oil |
| 30 ml (2 tbsp) herb vinegar |
| 10 ml (2 tsp) Dijon mustard |
| grated rind and juice of ½ a lemon |
| 15 ml (1 tbsp) soy sauce |
| 1 garlic clove, skinned and crushed |
| salt and pepper |
| 4 chicken breast fillets, skinned and the flesh cut into 2.5 cm (1 inch) cubes |
| For the sauce: |
| 1 small onion, skinned and chopped |
| 2 large tomatoes, skinned, seeded and chopped |
| 1 garlic clove, skinned and chopped |
| 15 ml (1 tbsp) tomato purée |
| 1.25-2.5 ml (¼-½ level tsp) cayenne pepper |
| 75 ml (3 fl oz) chicken stock |
| 15 ml (1 tbsp) soy sauce |
| 60 ml (4 tbsp) peanut butter |
| lemon and lime slices, to garnish |

◆ To make the marinade, whisk together the oil, vinegar, mustard, lemon rind and juice, soy sauce, garlic and seasonings until well blended.

◆ Thread the chicken cubes on to 8 wooden kebab sticks. Place these in a shallow ovenproof dish and pour the marinade over. Cover with cling film, pulling back one corner to allow the steam to escape. Leave to stand for 2 hours or overnight.

◆ In a blender or food processor liquidise all the ingredients for the sauce until smooth. Pour the sauce into an ovenproof glass bowl, cover and set aside until it is needed.

◆ Place the covered chicken in the oven and microwave on HIGH for 10-12 minutes or until the chicken is cooked, turning and repositioning at least twice during cooking time.

◆ Arrange the chicken in a serving dish. Reserve the cooking liquid and keep it hot while heating the sauce.

◆ Add the reserved cooking liquid to the sauce mixture, cover with cling film and microwave on HIGH for 5-6 minutes until the sauce boils, stirring frequently. Serve the chicken with the sauce handed separately.

## MARINATED CHICKEN WITH
### PEANUT SAUCE

*A classic Indonesian dish adapted for the microwave*

SEE OPPOSITE

## CHICKEN
## WITH VEGETABLE SAUCE

### SERVES 6

*50 g (2 oz) butter or margarine*

*3 carrots, peeled and finely chopped*

*2 leeks, white parts only, trimmed and thinly sliced*

*2 celery sticks, trimmed and thinly sliced*

*6 chicken breasts, skinned*

*600 ml (1 pint) boiling chicken stock*

*25 g (1 oz) plain flour*

*150 ml (¼ pint) double cream*

*1 egg yolk*

*5 ml (1 tsp) lemon juice*

*salt and pepper*

*grated nutmeg to taste*

*100 g (4 oz) Comté or Gruyère cheese, grated*

◆ Put 25 g (1 oz) of the butter into a large ovenproof casserole. Microwave on HIGH for 1 minute or until the butter melts. Add the carrots, leeks and celery, stir well and cover with a lid or cling film and microwave on HIGH for 10 minutes or until the vegetables are softened, stirring twice.
◆ Arrange the chicken on top of the vegetables. Pour in the boiling chicken stock. Cover and microwave on HIGH for 10-15 minutes or until the chicken is tender, giving the dish a quarter turn 3 times during cooking.
◆ Carefully lift the chicken from the casserole and place it in a large shallow ovenproof dish; cover and keep the chicken warm.
◆ Strain liquid from casserole, reserving 600 ml (1 pint), making it up to the right quantity with stock, if necessary.
◆ Liquidise the vegetables in a food processor or blender until smooth, then mix this with the reserved stock.
◆ Mix together the remaining butter and the flour to make a beurre manié.
◆ Microwave the vegetable and stock mixture on HIGH for about 5 minutes or until the liquid is hot but not boiling. Gradually whisk in the beurre manié, a few pieces at a time, until it is all incorporated. Microwave on HIGH for 4-5 minutes until boiling and whisk well.
◆ Stir the cream into the egg yolk and stir in the lemon juice to make a smooth sauce. Gradually whisk in cream and egg mixture. Add salt, pepper and a little grated nutmeg.
◆ Sprinkle half of the cheese over the chicken breasts and press it down firmly.
◆ Pour enough sauce to cover the chicken and sprinkle with the remaining cheese.
◆ Microwave on HIGH for 4-5 minutes or until the cheese melts and the sauce and chicken are hot. Brown under a hot grill and serve with the remaining sauce passed separately.

## CHICKEN ROULADES
## WITH MUSHROOMS IN CREAM

### SERVES 4

*350 g (12 oz) button mushrooms*

*1 medium onion, skinned and finely chopped*

*2 celery sticks, trimmed and finely chopped*

*1 garlic clove, skinned and crushed*

*30 ml (2 tbsp) vegetable oil*

*50 g (2 oz) walnuts, finely chopped*

*25 g (1 oz) fresh breadcrumbs*

*finely grated rind and juice of 1 lemon*

*10 ml (2 tsp) chopped fresh thyme or 5 ml (1 level tsp) dried*

*15 ml (1 tbsp) chopped fresh parsley*

*salt and pepper*

*4 chicken breasts, skinned and boned*

*25 g (1 oz) butter or margarine*

*15 ml (1 level tbsp) plain flour*

*150 ml (¼ pint) whipping cream*

*50 ml (2 fl oz) dry white wine*

◆ Slice 225 g (8 oz) mushrooms and set aside for the sauce. Finely chop the rest and place in a medium bowl.
◆ Add half the onion to the bowl along with the celery, garlic and 15 ml (1 tbsp) oil. Microwave on HIGH for 10 minutes or until the onion and celery are soft, stirring once. Stir in the walnuts, breadcrumbs, lemon rind, herbs and enough lemon juice to bind the mixture. Season to taste.
◆ Using a meat mallet or rolling pin, flatten the chicken breasts between 2 sheets of dampened greaseproof paper or cling film to a thickness of 0.5 cm (¼ inch). Spread the stuffing over the chicken, roll up and secure with wooden cocktail sticks.
◆ Place the chicken seam side up on a microwave roasting rack. Brush with half the remaining oil and microwave on HIGH for 16 minutes or until tender. Turn the chicken over halfway through cooking time and brush with the remaining oil. Leave to stand covered.
◆ In a large bowl, microwave the butter on HIGH for 45 seconds or until the butter melts. Stir in the remaining onion and microwave on HIGH for 5-7 minutes or until soft. Add the reserved mushrooms and continue to microwave for a further 7 minutes, stirring once.
◆ Stir in the flour and microwave on HIGH for 30 seconds. Gradually stir in the cream and wine and microwave on HIGH for 8 minutes or until the sauce is thick and smooth, stirring occasionally. Season to taste.
◆ Place the chicken in a shallow dish. Spoon over the sauce and microwave on HIGH for 2 minutes or until the roulades are heated through.

# CORONATION CHICKEN

## SERVES 2

| |
|---|
| 1 shallot or ½ small onion, skinned and finely chopped |
| 30 ml (2 tbsp) vegetable oil |
| 5 ml (1 tsp) hot curry paste |
| 5 ml (1 tsp) tomato purée |
| 30 ml (2 tbsp) red wine |
| 10 ml (2 tsp) lemon juice |
| 1 chicken quarter, about 225 g (8 oz), skinned |
| 60 ml (4 tbsp) mayonnaise |
| 15 ml (1 tbsp) apricot jam |
| salt and pepper |
| 50 g (2 oz) white rice |
| 15 ml (1 level tbsp) sultanas |
| 25 g (1 oz) dried apricots, chopped |
| watercress, to garnish |

◆ Put the shallot and 15 ml (1 tbsp) of the oil into a medium bowl and cover with cling film, pulling back one corner to allow the steam to escape. Microwave on HIGH for 3-4 minutes or until the shallot is softened.

◆ Stir in the curry paste, tomato purée, the red wine and half of the lemon juice. Microwave on HIGH for 5 minutes, uncovered, or until the liquid is reduced by about half. Strain and leave to cool.

◆ Meanwhile, put the chicken into a roasting bag, tie loosely and microwave on HIGH for 4-5 minutes or until it is cooked. Leave to cool, then remove the meat from the bones and cut into bite-sized pieces.

◆ Beat the mayonnaise and the apricot jam into the cooled curry sauce. Season with salt and pepper. Toss the chicken pieces in the sauce.

◆ Put the rice and salt to taste into a medium bowl and pour over 600 ml (1 pint) boiling water. Microwave on HIGH for 7-8 minutes or until the rice is tender.

◆ Meanwhile, make a dressing for the rice. Mix the remaining vegetable oil and lemon juice together and season with salt and pepper.

◆ Drain and rinse the rice, then stir in the dressing, sultanas and apricots while it is still hot. Leave to cool.

◆ Serve the chicken and the rice salad cold, garnished with the watercress.

# STUFFED ROAST CHICKEN

## SERVES 4

| |
|---|
| 30 ml (2 tbsp) vegetable oil |
| 1 small onion, skinned and chopped |
| 25 g (1 oz) dried apricots |
| 50 g (2 oz) fresh brown breadcrumbs |
| 25 g (1 oz) salted cashew nuts, chopped |
| 5 ml (1 tsp) chopped fresh rosemary or 2.5 ml (½ level tsp) dried |
| 2.5 ml (½ level tsp) lemon rind |
| salt and pepper |
| a little beaten egg |
| 1 oven-ready roasting chicken, weighing about 1.4 kg (3 lb) |
| 25 g (1 oz) butter or margarine |
| paprika to taste |
| 10 ml (2 level tsp) plain flour |

◆ To prepare the stuffing, put the oil in an ovenproof glass bowl and microwave on HIGH for 1 minute. Add the onion and microwave on HIGH for 4-5 minutes or until the onion is soft.

◆ Snip the apricots into small pieces and stir them into the bowl with the breadcrumbs, chopped nuts, rosemary, lemon rind and the seasonings. Add sufficient beaten egg to form a soft stuffing.

◆ Fill the neck end of the bird with the stuffing. Tie the chicken legs together with string. Spread the butter over the bird and sprinkle it lightly with paprika. Sprinkle the flour inside a roasting bag and then place the chicken inside. Tie the bag loosely with string, making sure there is room for the steam to escape.

◆ Weigh the bird and then place it in a shallow microwave dish. Microwave on MEDIUM for 9 minutes per 450 g (1 lb).

◆ Leave the chicken to stand for about 15 minutes before upwrapping it. Carve the bird and serve it accompanied by the cooking juices.

# CHICKEN WITH TOMATO AND PAPRIKA

### SERVES 4

| |
|---|
| 30 ml (2 tbsp) vegetable oil |
| 1 medium onion, skinned and finely chopped |
| 450 g (1 lb) chicken breast fillet, skinned and cut into 2.5 cm (1 inch) strips |
| 30 ml (2 level tbsp) paprika |
| 1.25 ml (¼ level tsp) chilli seasoning |
| 225 ml (8 fl oz) tomato juice |
| salt and pepper |
| 30 ml (2 level tbsp) cornflour |
| 100 ml (4 fl oz) soured cream |
| chopped fresh parsley, to garnish |

◆ Put the oil and onion in a large bowl and three-quarters cover with cling film or a lid. Microwave on HIGH for 5-7 minutes until softened, stirring occasionally.

◆ Add the chicken, paprika and chilli seasoning and mix well together. Gradually stir in the tomato juice and season with salt and pepper.

◆ Blend the cornflour to a smooth paste with about 45 ml (3 tbsp) water, then stir into the bowl.

◆ Microwave on HIGH for 6-7 minutes or until the chicken is tender and the sauce is bubbling and thickened, stirring frequently.

◆ Gradually stir in the soured cream and microwave on MEDIUM for 1 minute or until the sauce is heated through but not boiling. Garnish with chopped parsley. Serve with cooked rice, if liked.

# CHICKEN WITH APPLE AND MUSTARD SAUCE

### SERVES 4

| |
|---|
| 8 chicken thighs, skinned |
| 60-75 ml (4-5 tbsp) prepared English mustard |
| 25 g (1 oz) butter or margarine |
| 2 medium onions, skinned and thinly sliced |
| 1 medium cooking apple, peeled, cored and sliced |
| salt and pepper |
| 15 ml (1 level tbsp) plain flour |
| 150 ml (¼ pint) chicken stock |

◆ Prick the chicken with a fork and spread generously with the mustard. Place in a non-metal dish, cover and refrigerate for several hours or overnight.

◆ Place the butter in a large shallow casserole and microwave on HIGH for 45 seconds or until melted. Add the onion and apple and stir well. Microwave on HIGH for 5-7 minutes or until the onion is soft. Season to taste with salt and pepper.

◆ Arrange the chicken on top of the onion and apple, bone side up. Cover and microwave on HIGH for 10 minutes. Turn the chicken over, leave uncovered and microwave on HIGH for a further 10 minutes or until tender. Transfer the chicken to a heated serving dish and keep hot.

◆ Sprinkle the flour over the onions and apple and mix well. Microwave on HIGH for 1 minute, then gradually stir in the chicken stock. Season to taste and microwave on HIGH for 2 minutes or until thickened and smooth.

◆ Pour the sauce over the chicken and serve at once.

# CHICKEN FRICASSEE

### SERVES 4

| |
|---|
| 1 oven-ready roasting chicken, weighing about 1.4 kg (3 lb) |
| 25 g (1 oz) butter or margarine |
| salt and pepper |
| 225 g (8 oz) carrots, peeled and thinly sliced |
| 45 ml (3 tbsp) vegetable oil |
| 45 ml (3 level tbsp) plain flour |
| 300 ml (½ pint) chicken stock |
| 45 ml (3 tbsp) chopped fresh coriander |
| 425 g (15 oz) can chick-peas |
| chopped fresh coriander, to garnish |

◆ Place the chicken breast side down in a 2.3 litre (4 pint) microwave dish and spread it with the butter. Next, sprinkle it with pepper.

◆ Cover the chicken loosely with greaseproof paper and microwave on HIGH for 6 minutes per 450 g (1 lb); leave it to stand for 15 minutes.

◆ Cut all the flesh off the bone and divide it into pieces. Reserve the skin and bones for stock, if wished.

◆ Place the carrots in a casserole dish with the oil. Cover the microwave on HIGH for 4 minutes.

◆ Stir in the flour, followed by the stock, the seasonings and the coriander leaves. Add the chicken and the drained chick-peas, stirring well to mix.

◆ Cover the microwave on HIGH for 4 minutes, then stir well. Re-cover and microwave on HIGH for a further 4 minutes.

◆ Leave the chicken to stand for 5 minutes. Adjust the seasoning, garnish with fresh coriander and serve.

### CHICKEN FRICASSEE

*A substantial recipe combining chicken, carrots and chick-peas, served
here with Okra and coconut (page 136)*

SEE OPPOSITE

## SPICED TURKEY

### SERVES 4

| |
|---|
| 450 g (1 lb) turkey fillet, cut into 2.5 cm (1 inch) strips |
| 5 ml (1 level tsp) paprika |
| 5 ml (1 level tsp) ground cumin |
| 5 ml (1 level tsp) ground coriander |
| pinch of ground ginger |
| pinch of ground cloves |
| 5 ml (1 level tsp) ground cinnamon |
| 150 ml (¼ pint) natural yogurt |
| 15 ml (1 tbsp) vegetable oil |
| 15 ml (1 level tbsp) plain flour |
| 25 g (1 oz) ground almonds |
| 1 garlic clove, skinned and crushed |
| salt and pepper |

◆ Place the turkey in a large bowl. Add the paprika, cumin, coriander, ginger, cloves, cinnamon and yogurt. Mix thoroughly. Cover and leave to marinate for at least 1 hour.
◆ Preheat a browning dish to maximum according to the manufacturer's instructions, adding the oil for the last 30 seconds.
◆ Add the flour and almonds and microwave on HIGH for 30 seconds. Stir in the turkey and marinade, garlic and seasoning, and mix together well.
◆ Microwave on HIGH for 2 minutes, stirring occasionally, then cover and microwave on LOW for 20-25 minutes, or until the turkey is tender, stirring occasionally.

## TURKEY WITH HAZELNUT SAUCE

### SERVES 4

| |
|---|
| 25 g (1 oz) butter or margarine |
| 450 lb (1 lb) turkey breast fillets, cut into 0.5 cm (¼ inch) slices |
| 60 ml (4 tbsp) sweet sherry |
| 60 ml (4 tbsp) double cream |
| 25 g (1 oz) hazelnuts, finely chopped |
| salt and pepper |
| paprika, to garnish |

◆ Place the butter in a shallow casserole and microwave on HIGH for 45 seconds or until the butter melts. Stir in the turkey slices and microwave on HIGH for 5-6 minutes or until the turkey is just cooked, stirring once or twice.

◆ Add the sherry, cream and hazelnuts. Stir well and microwave on HIGH for 7 minutes or until the sauce is boiling, stirring occasionally. Sprinkle with paprika and serve.

## SHREDDED TURKEY WITH COURGETTES

### SERVES 4

| |
|---|
| 450 g (1 lb) turkey or chicken breast fillet |
| 450 g (1 lb) courgettes, trimmed |
| 1 red pepper, cored, seeded and thinly sliced |
| 45 ml (3 tbsp) vegetable oil |
| 45 ml (3 tbsp) dry sherry |
| 15 ml (1 tbsp) soy sauce |
| salt and pepper |
| 60 ml (4 tbsp) natural yogurt or soured cream |

◆ Cut all the dry ingredients into fine strips to ensure even cooking.
◆ Place all the ingredients except the yogurt in a 2.3 litre (4 pint) microwave dish, season and stir well to mix.
◆ Cover with a lid or cling film and microwave on HIGH for 4 minutes.
◆ Leave to stand for 5 minutes, then add the yogurt, adjust the seasoning and serve.

## — SHREDDED TURKEY WITH COURGETTES —

*An Oriental-tasting dish, with turkey, red peppers and courgettes,*
*seasoned with soy-sauce, sherry and yogurt*

SEE OPPOSITE

## CHICKEN, MANGO AND PISTACHIO NUT SALAD

### SERVES 2

2 chicken breast fillets, skinned and cut into bite-sized pieces

15 ml (1 tbsp) olive or vegetable oil

1 small lime

salt and pepper

paprika

1 large ripe mango

1 garlic clove, skinned and crushed

30 ml (2 tbsp) mayonnaise

a few salad leave such as endive, radicchio or oak leaf lettuce

15 g (½ oz) blanched pistachio nuts, coarsely chopped

◆ Put the chicken into a shallow dish with the oil.
◆ Cut half the lime into thin slices and lay on top of the chicken.
◆ Cover with cling film, pulling back one corner to allow the steam to escape, and microwave on HIGH for 2 minutes.
◆ Uncover the chicken and stir, pressing the lime slices to extract the juice. Microwave on HIGH for 2-3 minutes or until the chicken is tender, stirring occasionally.
◆ Season the chicken with salt, pepper and paprika and leave until cold.
◆ When ready to serve, slice the mango twice lengthways either side of the stone. Scrape the flesh away from the stone and put into a blender or food processor.
◆ Using a teaspoon, scoop out the flesh from one of the mango halves and put in the blender with the garlic, 30 ml (2 tbsp) cooking liquid from the chicken and the mayonnaise.
◆ Liquidise until smooth, then season with salt, pepper and paprika. Cut the remaining mango into neat cubes and put into a serving bowl.
◆ Remove the chicken from the liquid with a slotted spoon and add to the bowl with the chopped mango. Pour over the dressing and mix together carefully to coat the chicken.
◆ Tear the salad leaves into small pieces and add to the bowl. Toss together to coat lightly in dressing.
◆ Spoon the salad on to 2 individual serving plates and sprinkle with the pistachio nuts. Serve immediately.

## SWEET AND SOUR CHICKEN

### SERVES 4

75 g (3 oz) soft brown sugar

75 ml (5 tbsp) wine vinegar

45 ml (3 tbsp) soy sauce

45 ml (3 level tbsp) cornflour

1 green pepper, cored, seeded and thinly sliced

225 g (8 oz) carrots, peeled and cut into thin strips

397 g (14 oz) can tomatoes

450 g (1 lb) chicken breast, skinned and the flesh cut into 2.5 cm (1 inch) strips

50 g (2 oz) beansprouts

◆ In a large casserole, blend together the sugar, vinegar, soy sauce and cornflour. Microwave on HIGH for 3 minutes or until the liquid is just boiling, stirring occasionally.
◆ Stir in the green pepper, carrots, tomatoes and juice, and add the chicken. Cover and microwave on HIGH for 5 minutes or until the liquid boils, then continue microwaving on HIGH for 12-15 minutes or until the chicken is tender, stirring occasionally.
◆ Add the beansprouts and microwave, uncovered, on HIGH for 2 minutes. Serve immediately with rice, if liked.

## CHICKEN LIVER BOLOGNESE

### SERVES 4

50 g (2 oz) butter or margarine

2 medium onions, skinned and chopped

125 g (4 oz) carrot, peeled and finely chopped

125 g (4 oz) celery, trimmed and finely chopped

100 g (4 oz) streaky bacon rashers, rinded and chopped

450 g (1 lb) chicken livers, trimmed and chopped

150 ml (¼ pint) red wine

15 ml (1 tbsp) tomato purée

150 ml (¼ pint) beef stock

2.5 ml (½ level tsp) dried oregano

1 bay leaf

salt and pepper

spaghetti, to serve

◆ Put the butter into a shallow ovenproof casserole and microwave on HIGH for 1 minute until the butter melts. Stir in the vegetables, and cover them with a lid, or with cling film, pulling back one corner to allow the steam to escape. Microwave on HIGH for 5-6 minutes or until the vegetables are softened.

◆ Uncover the dish, stir in the bacon and livers and microwave on HIGH for 3-4 minutes, stirring twice.

◆ Add the wine, tomato purée, stock, oregano and bay leaf to the chicken livers, season well with salt and pepper and stir well. Microwave on HIGH for 1 minute or until the sauce is boiling. Boil for 1 minute, stirring twice. Cover the dish with a lid, or with cling film, pulling back one corner to allow the steam to escape. Microwave on HIGH for 8 minutes, stirring twice. Serve the Bolognese poured over hot, buttered spaghetti.

# CHICKEN CURRY

### SERVES 4

| |
|---|
| 15 g (½ oz) butter or margarine |
| 1 medium onion, skinned and finely chopped |
| 4 chicken quarters, skinned and halved |
| 30 ml (2 level tbsp) medium curry powder |
| 15 ml (1 level tbsp) plain flour |
| 600 ml (1 pint) chicken stock |
| 5 ml (1 tsp) Worcestershire sauce |
| 15 ml (1 tbsp) tomato purée |
| 15 ml (1 tbsp) lemon juice |
| 30 ml (2 level tbsp) mango chutney |
| 50 g (2 oz) sultanas |
| 1 eating apple, peeled, cored and chopped |
| salt and pepper |

◆ Put the butter and onion in a large round casserole. Add the chicken, placing the thinnest parts towards the centre. Microwave on HIGH for 10-12 minutes or until the chicken is tender, turning the quarters over once. Remove the chicken from the dish and set aside.

◆ Stir the curry powder and flour into the casserole and microwave on HIGH for 30 seconds.

◆ Gradually blend in the stock. Microwave on HIGH for 4 minutes, stirring occasionally, until the sauce has thickened.

◆ Stir in the Worcestershire sauce, tomato purée, lemon juice, chutney, sultanas, apple and season with salt and pepper. Return the chicken to the casserole.

◆ Cover and microwave on HIGH for 8 minutes until heated through.

◆ Leave to stand, covered, for 5 minutes. Serve with cooked rice, if liked.

# CHICKEN MEAT LOAF

### SERVES 6

| |
|---|
| 225 g (8 oz) streaky bacon rashers, rinded |
| 25 g (1 oz) butter or margarine |
| 1 small onion, skinned and finely chopped |
| 2 garlic cloves, skinned and crushed |
| 225 g (8 oz) chicken breast fillet, skinned and finely chopped |
| 225 g (8 oz) lean pork, finely chopped |
| 175 g (6 oz) chicken livers, finely chopped |
| 15 ml (1 tbsp) brandy |
| 1 egg, beaten |
| salt and pepper |
| 10 ml (2 tsp) chopped fresh thyme or 5 ml (1 level tsp) dried |
| 60 ml (4 tbsp) double cream |

◆ Stretch the bacon with the back of a knife and use it to line a 700 g (1½ lb) loaf dish, reserving a few slices.

◆ Put the butter in a large bowl and microwave on HIGH for 30 seconds or until the butter melts.

◆ Add the onion and garlic and three-quarters cover with cling film or a lid. Microwave on HIGH for 5-7 minutes until soft, stirring occasionally.

◆ Add the chicken, pork and chicken livers to the onion mixture with the remaining ingredients. Mix together well.

◆ Spread the mixture into the loaf dish taking care not to disturb the bacon. Fold the ends of the bacon over the mixture. Cover with the reserved bacon and then loosely cover with greaseproof paper.

◆ Microwave on HIGH for 25 minutes until the juices run clear when a wooden cocktail stick is inserted in the centre. Remove the greaseproof paper after 15 minutes and, if the oven does not have a turntable, give the dish a quarter turn three times during cooking.

◆ When cooked, place a plate on top of the meat loaf and weight it down. Allow it to cool, then chill it overnight. Serve cut into slices with French bread and a salad, if liked.

## SPANISH CHICKEN IN RED WINE

*The olives in this recipe provide a pleasing sharp taste contrasting
perfectly with that of the chicken*

SEE PAGE 102

### —— PEKING-STYLE DUCK ——
*A classic Chinese dish, perfectly adapted for microwave cooking*

SEE PAGE 102

## SPANISH CHICKEN IN RED WINE

### SERVES 4

| |
|---|
| 15 ml (1 tbsp) vegetable oil |
| 4 chicken pieces |
| 100 g (4 oz) bacon rashers, rinded and chopped |
| 225 g (8 oz) button mushrooms |
| 45 ml (3 level tbsp) plain flour |
| 150 ml (¼ pint) red wine |
| salt and pepper |
| 50 g (2 oz) black or green olives, stoned |

◆ Preheat a browning dish to maximum according to the manufacturer's instructions, adding the oil for the last 30 seconds. Add the chicken and quickly brown.
◆ Add the bacon and mushrooms and microwave on HIGH for 2 minutes. Stir in the flour and microwave on HIGH for 30 seconds.
◆ Gradually stir in the red wine and microwave on HIGH for 5 minutes or until boiling, stirring occasionally. Season to taste.
◆ Pour the sauce over the chicken and add the olives. Cover and microwave on HIGH for 10 minutes. Turn chicken over and microwave, uncovered, on HIGH for 8 minutes or until chicken is tender.

## CHINESE-STYLE CHICKEN WITH VEGETABLES

### SERVES 4

| |
|---|
| 450 g (1 lb) boned chicken breasts, skinned and the flesh cut into 1 cm (½ inch) wide strips |
| 30 ml (2 tbsp) dry sherry |
| 15 ml (1 tbsp) soy sauce |
| 100 g (4 oz) carrots, peeled |
| 1 large green pepper, cored, seeded and thinly sliced |
| 1 large red pepper, cored, seeded and thinly sliced |
| 100 g (4 oz) mange-tout, trimmed |
| 50 g (2 oz) baby corn on the cobs |
| 2 large courgettes, trimmed and sliced |
| pepper to taste |

◆ Place the chicken strips in a medium casserole. Mix the sherry and soy sauce together, add to the chicken and leave to marinate for 30 minutes.
◆ Cut the carrots into strips about 5 cm (2 inches) long and 1 cm (½ inch) wide. Put into a polythene bag together with the green and red peppers, mange-tout and courgettes.

Loosely fold over the top of the bag and microwave on HIGH for 2 minutes.
◆ Mix the corn with the chicken. Three-quarters cover and microwave on HIGH for 6 minutes or until tender, stirring twice.
◆ Stir in the vegetables. Season to taste with pepper and microwave on HIGH for 3 minutes or until the vegetables are tender but still firm.

## PEKING-STYLE DUCK

### SERVES 4

| |
|---|
| 1 bunch spring onions, trimmed |
| ½ cucumber |
| 2 kg (4-4½ lb) oven-ready duckling |
| soy sauce to taste |
| 100 ml (4 fl oz) hoi sin sauce |
| For the pancakes: |
| 450 g (1 lb) plain flour |
| pinch of salt |
| 15 ml (1 tbsp) vegetable oil, plus extra for brushing |

◆ Trim off the root end of the spring onions, and trim the green leaves down to about 5 cm (2 inches). Skin, then cut twice lengthways to within 2.5 cm (1 inch) off the end. Place in a bowl of iced water and refrigerate for 1-2 hours or until the onion curls. Cut the cucumber into 5 cm (2 inch) fingers.
◆ To make the pancakes, place the flour and salt in a large bowl. Gradually mix in 15 ml (1 tbsp) oil and 375 ml (13 fl oz) boiling water, stirring vigorously with a wooden spoon. When the dough is slightly cool, shape into a ball and turn on to a lightly floured surface. Knead for about 5 minutes to make a soft smooth dough. Leave to stand in a bowl for 30 minutes covered with a damp cloth or cling film.
◆ Cut the dough in half and shape each half into a roll 40 cm (16 inches) long. Cut each roll into 16 even slices. On a lightly floured surface, roll out 2 slices of dough into circles about 7.5 cm (3 inches) across. Brush the tops with oil. Put the oiled surfaces together and roll out to a thin 15 cm (6 inch) circle. Repeat with the remaining dough to make a total of 16 pairs of pancakes.
◆ Heat an ungreased frying pan or griddle and cook each pair of pancakes for about 1-2 minutes on each side, turning when air bubbles start to form. Remove from the frying pan and while they are still hot separate the pancakes. Stack in a clean damp tea towel.
◆ Pat the duck dry with absorbent kitchen paper. Calculate the cooking time at 10 minutes per 450 g (1 lb). Place the duck breast side down on a microwave roasting rack and brush with soy sauce.

◆ Cover and microwave on HIGH for the calculated cooking time. Turn the duck over halfway through cooking, brush with soy sauce and continue to microwave on HIGH, uncovered, until the duck is tender. Leave the duck to stand, loosely covered with foil.

◆ Grill the duck under a hot grill for about 2 minutes or until the duck is golden brown and the skin is crisp on all sides.

◆ Microwave the hoi sin sauce on HIGH for about 2 minutes or until the sauce is just bubbling.

◆ Cut the duck into small pieces. Meanwhile, microwave the pancakes wrapped in the damp tea towel on HIGH for 2 minutes or until just warm.

◆ Serve each person with 8 pancakes and some of the duck, including the skin. Hand the vegetables and sauce separately. To eat, spread a little sauce on a pancake and top with vegetables and duck. Roll up and eat with your fingers.

# DUCK WITH PEACH SAUCE

## SERVES 4

| |
|---|
| 4 duckling portions, each weighing about 300 g (11 oz) |
| 30 ml (2 tbsp) soy sauce |
| 411 g (14½ oz) can peach slices in natural juice |
| 15 ml (1 level tbsp) plain flour |
| 15 ml (1 tbsp) wholegrain mustard |
| salt and pepper |
| 60 ml (4 tbsp) peach chutney |

◆ Pat the duckling portions dry with absorbent kitchen paper. Place them skin side down on a microwave roasting rack and brush with half the soy sauce.

◆ Cover and microwave on HIGH for 10 minutes. Switch to MEDIUM and microwave for 30 minutes, repositioning the portions once or twice. Turn the duckling skin side up and brush with the remaining soy sauce. Microwave on HIGH for 5 minutes or until the duck is tender.

◆ Transfer the duckling to a hot grill and grill until the skins are crisp.

◆ To make the sauce, drain the peaches, reserving the juice. Blend the juice with the flour and mustard in a serving jug or bowl and season to taste. Microwave on HIGH for 3 minutes or until the sauce is thickened and smooth, stirring once or twice.

◆ Put the peach slices in a blender or food processor and add the sauce. Liquidise until smooth and add to the flour and juice mixture. Stir in the chutney and microwave on HIGH for 2 minutes or until hot. Serve the duck with the sauce handed separately.

# DUCK BREASTS WITH PORT AND ORANGE

## SERVES 2

| |
|---|
| 2 duck breast fillets, weighing about 200 g (7 oz) each, skinned |
| salt and pepper |
| thinly pared rind and juice of ½ large orange |
| 15 ml (1 tbsp) olive or vegetable oil |
| 15 ml (1 level tbsp) redcurrant jelly |
| 75 ml (3 fl oz) port |
| juice of ½ lemon |
| pinch of mustard powder |
| pinch of cayenne pepper |
| orange twists, to garnish |

◆ Preheat a browning dish to maximum according to the manufacturer's instructions.

◆ Meanwhile, season the meat with salt and pepper. Cut the pared orange rind into very thin strips.

◆ Add the oil to the browning dish, then quickly put the meat into the dish. Microwave on HIGH for 2 minutes, turn over, stir in the orange strips and juice, redcurrant jelly and the port and microwave on HIGH for 4-5 minutes, or until the meat is tender, turning the duck once.

◆ Remove the duck from the dish. Slice thinly, and arrange on 2 warmed serving plates.

◆ Stir the lemon juice, mustard and cayenne into the dish and microwave on HIGH for 2-3 minutes or until reduced and thickened. Pour over the duck, garnish with orange twists and serve immediately.

## BRAISED PHEASANT WITH FORCEMEAT BALLS

### SERVES 4

| |
|---|
| 2 oven-ready pheasants, total weight about 2 kg (4 lb) |
| 300 ml (½ pint) chicken stock |
| 1 medium onion, skinned and chopped |
| 15 ml (1 tbsp) brandy |
| 15 ml (1 level tbsp) cornflour |
| 60 ml (4 tbsp) redcurrant jelly |
| 15 ml (1 tbsp) lemon juice |
| For the forcemeat balls: |
| 225 g (8 oz) pork sausagemeat |
| 30 ml (2 tbsp) chopped fresh parsley |
| salt and pepper |
| 30 ml (2 level tbsp) toasted wheatgerm |

◆ Pat the pheasants dry with absorbent kitchen paper. Using poultry shears, cut each pheasant along the breastbone and backbone, so it is cut in half.

◆ Place the pheasants breast side down in a shallow casserole. Pour in the stock and add the onion. Cover and microwave on HIGH for 15 minutes.

◆ Meanwhile, mix the sausagemeat and parsley together. Season to taste and shape into 8 balls. Roll each ball in the wheatgerm to coat all over.

◆ Add the forcemeat balls to the casserole. Turn the pheasants over and microwave on HIGH, uncovered, for 15 minutes or until the pheasants are tender.

◆ Using a slotted spoon, transfer the pheasant and forcemeat balls to a heated serving dish. Loosely cover and keep hot.

◆ Blend the brandy, cornflour, redcurrant jelly and lemon juice together and add to the pan juices. Season to taste. Microwave on HIGH for 5 minutes or until thickened and smooth, stirring occasionally.

◆ Pour a little sauce over the pheasant and hand the remaining sauce separately.

## QUAIL WITH MUSHROOMS AND JUNIPER

### SERVES 2

| |
|---|
| 4 quail, cleaned |
| 15 ml (1 tbsp) olive or vegetable oil |
| 150 ml (¼ pint) chicken stock |
| 4 juniper berries |
| 5 ml (1 tsp) chopped fresh thyme or 2.5 ml (½ level tsp) dried |
| 15 ml (1 tbsp) gin |
| 100 g (4 oz) button mushrooms, sliced |
| salt and pepper |
| watercress, to garnish |

◆ Preheat a browning dish to maximum according to the manufacturer's instructions. Meanwhile, using a rolling pin, beat each quail three or four times to flatten slightly.

◆ Add the oil to the dish. Quickly add the quail, breast side down, and microwave on HIGH for 2 minutes. Turn over and microwave on HIGH for 1 minute.

◆ Stir in the stock, juniper berries, thyme, gin, mushrooms, salt and pepper. Microwave on HIGH for 6 minutes or until tender, turning the quail once during cooking.

◆ Transfer the quail to a warmed serving dish then microwave the cooking liquid on HIGH for 3 minutes or until it is slightly reduced. Season, if necessary, with salt and pepper then pour over the quail. Garnish with watercress and serve immediately.

## QUAIL WITH
—— MUSHROOMS AND JUNIPER ——

*A marvellous celebration meal, these elegant quail are stuffed with a
tangy juniper, mushroom and thyme mixture*

SEE OPPOSITE

# TURKEY WITH MUSHROOMS AND YOGURT

SERVES 4

| |
|---|
| 450 g (1 lb) turkey breast, skinned and the flesh cut into 2.5 cm (1 inch) cubes |
| 25 g (1 oz) butter or margarine |
| 1 medium onion, skinned and chopped |
| 25 g (1 oz) plain flour |
| 300 ml (½ pint) milk |
| 100 g (4 oz) mushrooms, sliced |
| salt and pepper |
| grated nutmeg to taste |
| 1.25 ml (¼ level tsp) ground ginger |
| 150 ml (¼ pint) natural yogurt |
| 2 egg yolks |
| lemon slices and chopped fresh parsley, to garnish |

◆ Put the turkey cubes in a small roasting bag. Loosely tie the end of the bag with a plastic tie or a rubber band. Microwave on HIGH for 6 minutes or until the turkey is cooked.
◆ Put the butter in an ovenproof casserole and microwave on HIGH for 45 seconds or until the butter melts, then stir in the onion. Cover with a lid or with cling film, pulling back one corner to allow the steam to escape. Microwave on HIGH for 5-7 minutes or until the onion softens.
◆ Stir the flour into the onion and microwave on HIGH for 1 minute. Gradually stir in the milk. Microwave on HIGH for 45 seconds, then whisk. Continue to microwave on HIGH for 1¾-2 minutes, whisking every 30 seconds, until the sauce is boiling.
◆ Add the turkey and any juices in the roasting bag and the mushrooms to the sauce. Season well with the salt, pepper, nutmeg and ginger. Microwave on HIGH for 2-3 minutes, stirring once.
◆ Blend the yogurt and egg yolks together until smooth and stir this into the turkey mixture. Microwave on HIGH for 1½-2 minutes or until the sauce is very hot but not boiling, stirring two or three times during the cooking time.
◆ Serve the turkey garnished with the lemon slices and parsley.

# STIR-FRIED TURKEY AND MANGE-TOUT

SERVES 4

| |
|---|
| 450 g (1 lb) turkey fillet, cut into 2.5 cm (1 inch) strips |
| 2.5 cm (1 inch) piece of fresh root ginger, grated |
| 60 ml (4 tbsp) soy sauce |
| 60 ml (4 tbsp) dry sherry |
| 5 ml (1 level tsp) five-spice powder |
| 1 garlic clove, skinned and crushed |
| 30 ml (2 tbsp) vegetable oil |
| 30 ml (2 level tbsp) cornflour |
| 150 ml (¼ pint) chicken stock |
| salt and pepper |
| 175 g (6 oz) mange-tout, trimmed |
| 25 g (1 oz) cashew nuts (optional) |
| spring onion tassels, to garnish |

◆ Put the turkey strips into a large bowl with the ginger, soy sauce, sherry, five-spice powder and garlic. Stir well, then cover and leave to marinate for at least 1 hour.
◆ Preheat a browning dish to maximum according to the manufacturer's instructions, adding the oil for the last 30 seconds.
◆ Remove the turkey from the marinade with a slotted spoon and add it to the browning dish. Reserve the marinade. Quickly stir the turkey in the oil and microwave on HIGH for 2 minutes.
◆ Meanwhile, blend the cornflour with the reserved marinade, then stir in the stock.
◆ Add the marinade mixture to the turkey and mix thoroughly. Season and then stir in the mange-tout.
◆ Microwave on HIGH for 4-5 minutes or until the turkey is tender, stirring occasionally.
◆ Stir in the cashew nuts, if using, and microwave on HIGH for 1 minute. Serve hot garnished with spring onion tassels.

# INDONESIAN SPICED TURKEY

### SERVES 6

| |
|---|
| 900 g (2 lb) boneless turkey breast |
| 7.5 ml (1½ level tsp) ground cumin |
| 7.5 ml (1½ level tsp) ground coriander |
| 2.5 ml (½ level tsp) ground turmeric |
| 2.5 ml (½ level tsp) ground ginger |
| 30 ml (2 tbsp) lemon juice |
| 300 ml (½ pint) natural yogurt |
| salt and pepper |
| 1 large onion, skinned and chopped |
| 15 ml (1 tbsp) vegetable oil |
| 30 ml (2 level tbsp) plain flour |
| 45 ml (3 level tbsp) desiccated coconut |
| chopped fresh coriander, to garnish |

◆ Cut the turkey breast into bite-sized pieces, making sure they are all the same size.
◆ In a large bowl, mix the spices, lemon juice and yogurt together and season to taste. Add the turkey and coat thoroughly with the sauce. Cover and refrigerate for at least 3 hours or overnight. Stir once or twice during marinating.
◆ Place the onion and oil in a large casserole, mix together and microwave on HIGH for 5-7 minutes or until the onion is softened. Stir in the flour and coconut and microwave on HIGH for 1 minute.
◆ Add the turkey and yogurt mixture, cover and microwave on HIGH for 15 minutes, or until the turkey is tender, stirring occasionally. Sprinkle with coriander and serve with rice, if liked.

# SPICY SPATCHCOCKED POUSSIN WITH GARLIC BUTTER

### SERVES 2

| |
|---|
| 25 g (1 oz) butter or margarine |
| ½ small garlic clove, skinned and crushed |
| salt and pepper |
| 700 g (1½ lb) poussin |
| 15 ml (1 level tbsp) paprika |
| 5 ml (1 level tsp) ground cumin |
| 5 ml (1 level tsp) ground turmeric |
| 15 ml (1 tbsp) tomato purée |
| 10 ml (2 tsp) lemon juice |
| 2.5-5 ml (½-1 tsp) chilli sauce |
| 15 ml (1 tbsp) vegetable oil |

◆ To make the garlic butter, put the butter into a small bowl and microwave on HIGH for 10-15 seconds or until the butter is just soft enough to beat.
◆ Beat in the garlic, salt and pepper. Push to the side of the bowl to form a small pat and chill while cooking the poussin.
◆ Place the poussin on a chopping board, breast side down. Using poultry scissors or a small sharp knife, cut through the backbone to open the poussin up.
◆ Turn the poussin breast side upwards and flatten with a rolling pin. Insert 2 wooden skewers through the poussin, one through the wings and the breast and one through the drumsticks. These will fold it flat during cooking.
◆ Preheat a browning dish to maximum according to the manufacturer's instructions. Mix together the paprika, cumin, turmeric, tomato purée, lemon juice, chilli sauce and 10 ml (2 tsp) water. Season with salt and pepper, then spread all over the poussin.
◆ Put the oil in the browning dish then quickly add the poussin, breast side down. Microwave on HIGH for 3 minutes.
◆ Turn over and microwave on HIGH for 8-10 minutes or until the poussin is tender. Leave to stand for 2-3 minutes.
◆ To serve, remove the skewers, then cut the poussin in half lengthways along the breast. Arrange on 2 warmed serving plates, spoon over some of the cooking juices, and top with the garlic butter. Serve immediately.

# MEAT

## SPICY MINI MEATBALLS WITH
### —— TOMATO AND CORIANDER SAUCE ——

*Spiced with cumin and coriander, these meatballs are perfectly set off by the tomato sauce*

SEE PAGE 111

# Cooking Tips

◆

*Do not add salt directly on to meat before cooking as this draws out moisture and toughens the outside.*

◆

*Start meat cooking with the fat side down and turn it halfway through cooking if more than 5 cm (2 inches) thick.*

◆

*Improve browning of meat by microwaving in a roasting bag.*

◆

*Joints of meat cook more evenly if symmetrically shaped, such as boned and rolled.*

◆

*Position joints of meat so that the thickest parts are pointing towards the edge of the dish.*

◆

*Turn large joints or cuts over at least once during cooking for even cooking.*

◆

*Arrange meatballs in a circle on a dish to ensure even cooking and try to leave a space in the middle so that microwaves can penetrate from the inner as well as the outer edges.*

◆

*Cover bacon with absorbent kitchen paper to absorb the fat as it is likely to spatter during cooking.*

◆

*Pierce liver, since the thin membrane surrounding it can cause it to explode and spatter the oven.*

◆

*As large joints need 15–20 minutes standing time, cover them with aluminium foil to kept the heat in and leave in a warm place.*

◆

# SPICY MINI MEATBALLS WITH TOMATO AND CORIANDER SAUCE

### SERVES 2

| |
|---|
| 1 small onion, skinned and quartered |
| 1 garlic clove, skinned and crushed |
| 2.5 cm (1 inch) piece of fresh root ginger, peeled and crushed |
| 350 g (12 oz) lean minced beef |
| 15 ml (1 level tbsp) mango chutney |
| 2.5 ml (½ level tsp) ground cumin |
| 2.5 ml (½ level tsp) ground coriander |
| 30 ml (2 tbsp) chopped fresh coriander |
| salt and pepper |
| 1 egg, size 6, beaten |
| 200 g (7 oz) can tomatoes |
| 15 ml (1 tbsp) chicken stock |
| 10 ml (2 tsp) tomato purée |
| 5 ml (1 level tsp) sugar |
| fresh coriander, to garnish |

◆ Put the onion, garlic and ginger in a blender or food processor and liquidise until very finely chopped.
◆ Add the beef, chutney, cumin, ground coriander and half the fresh chopped coriander and season with salt and pepper. Pour in the egg and blend until well mixed. Shape into 16 small balls.
◆ Arrange in a single layer in a shallow dish. Microwave on HIGH for 5-6 minutes or until the meat is cooked, rearranging once during cooking. Leave to stand, covered, while making the sauce.
◆ To make the sauce, put the tomatoes and their juice into a large bowl. Stir in the chicken stock, tomato purée, sugar, salt and pepper.
◆ Microwave on HIGH for 5 minutes, stirring occasionally, then stir in the remaining fresh coriander and microwave on HIGH for 2-3 minutes or until the sauce is reduced and thickened.
◆ Microwave the meatballs on HIGH for 1-2 minutes or until reheated. Serve the meatballs with the sauce, garnished with coriander.

# COTTAGE PIE WITH ALE

### SERVES 4

| |
|---|
| 15 ml (1 tbsp) vegetable oil |
| 2 medium onions, skinned and thinly sliced |
| 10 ml (2 level tsp) demerara sugar |
| 1 small garlic clove, skinned and crushed |
| 450 g (1 lb) lean minced beef |
| 30 ml (2 level tbsp) plain flour |
| 300 ml (½ pint) beef stock |
| 150 ml (¼ pint) brown ale |
| 2 bay leaves |
| salt and pepper |
| 900 g (2 lb) potatoes, peeled and diced evenly |
| 10 ml (2 tbsp) French mustard |
| 60 ml (4 tbsp) milk |
| 1 egg, size 2, beaten |
| 25 g (1 oz) butter or margarine |
| chopped fresh parsley, to garnish |

◆ Put the oil into a 1.7 litre (3 pint) ovenproof glass bowl and microwave on HIGH for 1 minute until hot. Stir in the onions, sugar and garlic and cover the bowl with cling film, pulling back one corner to allow the steam to escape. Microwave on HIGH for 5 minutes or until the onions are softened.
◆ Uncover the bowl and add the mince, then stir well and microwave on HIGH for 2 minutes, stirring to break up the mince. Stir the flour into the mince, then add the stock, ale and bay leaves. Three-quarters cover with cling film, then microwave on HIGH for 20-25 minutes until cooked.
◆ Remove the cooked minced beef from the oven and skim any excess fat from the surface. Season it very well with salt and pepper, cover the meat and put it aside.
◆ Put the potatoes into a 2.8 litre (5 pint) ovenproof glass bowl and add 60 ml (4 tbsp) cold water. Three-quarters cover with cling film and microwave on HIGH for 8-10 minutes until the potatoes are cooked, stirring once or twice. Remove them from the oven and allow them to stand for 2-3 minutes.
◆ Drain any excess water from the potatoes, then mash them well and beat in the mustard, milk, egg and butter, beating the potatoes until they are smooth and creamy. Season well.
◆ Spoon the cooked minced beef into a shallow, ovenproof serving dish, then spoon or pipe the mashed potato over the top of the mince.
◆ Microwave, uncovered, on HIGH for 4-5 minutes until the cottage pie is piping hot. Garnish with parsley. (If liked, the pie may be browned under a grill before serving).

# BOEUF BOURGUIGNONNE

## SERVES 4

| |
|---|
| *100 g (4 oz) streaky bacon, rinded and chopped* |
| *700 g (1½ lb) sirloin steak, trimmed and cut into 2.5 cm (1 inch) cubes* |
| *1 garlic clove, skinned and chopped* |
| *175 g (6 oz) silverskin or baby onions, skinned and left whole* |
| *100 g (4 oz) button mushrooms* |
| *10 ml (2 tsp) chopped fresh mixed herbs or 5 ml (1 level tsp) dried* |
| *salt and pepper* |
| *15 ml (1 tbsp) plain flour* |
| *225 ml (8 fl oz) red wine* |
| *chopped fresh parsley, to garnish* |

◆ Put the chopped bacon in a large casserole and microwave on HIGH for 3 minutes.

◆ Add the steak, garlic, onions, mushrooms, herbs and seasoning and mix together. Sprinkle over the flour and stir in. Microwave on HIGH for 1 minute, then gradually stir in the red wine.

◆ Three-quarters cover with cling film or a lid and microwave on HIGH for 5 minutes until boiling. Reduce to LOW and cook for 40-50 minutes or until the meat is tender, stirring occasionally. Serve garnished with chopped parsley.

# CHILLI CON CARNE

## SERVES 8

| |
|---|
| *1 large onion, skinned and chopped* |
| *1 green pepper, cored, seeded and cut into strips* |
| *15 ml (1 tbsp) vegetable oil* |
| *700 g (1½ lb) minced fresh beef* |
| *397 g (14 oz) can chopped tomatoes* |
| *30 ml (2 tbsp) tomato purée* |
| *15 ml (1 tbsp) red wine vinegar* |
| *5 ml (1 level tsp) soft dark brown sugar* |
| *5-10 ml (1-2 level tsp) chilli powder* |
| *30 ml (2 level tbsp) ground cumin* |
| *salt and pepper* |
| *439 g (15½ oz) can red kidney beans, drained* |

◆ In a large bowl, stir together the onion, pepper and oil. Microwave on HIGH for 5 minutes or until the vegetables are softened, stirring once. Add the beef, breaking up any large pieces. Microwave on HIGH for 6-8 minutes or until the meat starts to change colour, stirring once.

◆ Mix together the tomatoes, tomato purée, vinegar, sugar and spices. Season to taste and stir into the meat. Cover and microwave on HIGH for 30 minutes, stirring once.

◆ Add the beans, re-cover and microwave on HIGH for 5 minutes. Serve hot.

# LAMB AND CABBAGE PARCELS

## SERVES 4

| |
|---|
| *8 medium cabbage leaves* |
| *450 g (1 lb) lean minced lamb* |
| *1 small onion, skinned and finely chopped* |
| *1 garlic clove, skinned and crushed* |
| *30 ml (2 tbsp) chopped fresh mint* |
| *1.25 ml (¼ level tsp) ground cinnamon* |
| *100 g (4 oz) fresh breadcrumbs* |
| *salt and pepper* |
| *about 15 ml (1 tbsp) lemon juice* |
| *10 ml (2 level tsp) cornflour* |
| *397 g (14 oz) can chopped tomatoes, sieved* |
| *15 ml (1 level tbsp) soft light brown sugar* |
| *30 ml (2 tbsp) chopped fresh parsley* |

◆ Cut out the centre stem of each cabbage leaf and place the leaves in a large shallow casserole. Cover and microwave on HIGH for 2-3 minutes or until the leaves are soft.

◆ Mix the lamb, onion, garlic, mint, cinnamon, breadcrumbs and seasoning together with enough lemon juice to bind. Shape into 8 even-sized cigar-shaped rolls.

◆ Wrap each roll in a cabbage leaf and place in the casserole, seam side down.

◆ Mix the cornflour to a smooth paste with a little of the tomato liquid, add the remaining tomatoes, the sugar and parsley. Spoon the tomato mixture over the cabbage rolls, cover and microwave on HIGH for 20 minutes.

## LAMB AND CABBAGE PARCELS

*An elegant and healthy way of serving lean lamb*

SEE OPPOSITE

# BEEF AND MUSHROOM LASAGNE

### SERVES 4

| |
|---|
| 175 g (6 oz) lasagne |
| 45 ml (3 tbsp) vegetable oil |
| 1 medium onion, skinned and finely chopped |
| 450 g (1 lb) minced fresh beef |
| 30 ml (2 level tbsp) plain flour |
| 30 ml (2 tbsp) chopped fresh basil or 15 ml (1 level tbsp) dried |
| 397 g (14 oz) can chopped tomatoes |
| 150 ml (¼ pint) hot beef stock |
| 175 g (6 oz) mushrooms, sliced |
| salt and pepper |
| 300 ml (½ pint) white sauce (see p. 211) |
| 100 g (4 oz) Cheddar cheese, grated |

◆ Place the lasagne in a 5 cm (2 inch) deep rectangular casserole. Spoon over 5 ml (1 tsp) oil and add 900 ml (1½ pint) boiling water and a pinch of salt. Cover and microwave on HIGH for 9 minutes. Leave to stand for 15 minutes, then drain and rinse.

◆ To make the sauce, mix the remaining oil and the onion in a medium bowl. Microwave on HIGH for 3 minutes, stirring once. Add the meat, breaking up any large pieces, and microwave on HIGH for 5 minutes, stirring once.

◆ Stir in the flour, basil, tomatoes, stock and mushrooms. Season. Microwave on HIGH for 20 minutes, stirring once.

◆ Layer the lasagne and meat sauce in the casserole dish, finishing with a layer of sauce. Pour over the white sauce and microwave on HIGH for 2 minutes or until heated through. Sprinkle with the cheese, and melt under a hot grill.

# STEAK AU POIVRE

### SERVES 2

| |
|---|
| 15 ml (1 level tbsp) black peppercorns |
| 2 fillet steaks, weighing about 175 g (6 oz) each |
| 15 g (½ oz) butter or margarine, cut into pieces |
| 15 ml (1 tbsp) vegetable oil |
| 15 ml (1 tbsp) brandy |
| 75 ml (3 fl oz) double cream |
| salt |

◆ Preheat a browning dish to maximum according to the manufacturer's instructions.

◆ Using a pestle and mortar, coarsely crush the peppercorns. Spread on a board, then place the steaks on top and press down firmly with the flat of your hand to coat the surface of the meat. Repeat with the other side.

◆ Put the butter and the oil in the browning dish then quickly add the steaks. Microwave on HIGH for 1 minute, then turn over and microwave on HIGH for 2-3 minutes or until the meat is cooked to taste. Transfer the meat to a warmed serving dish.

◆ Stir the brandy and cream into the cooking juices and microwave on HIGH for 2-3 minutes or until the sauce has reduced and thickened, stirring occasionally. Season with salt, pour over the steaks and serve immediately.

# ONION-TOPPED MEATLOAF

### SERVES 6

| |
|---|
| 15 ml (1 tbsp) vegetable oil |
| 1 garlic clove, skinned and crushed |
| 2 large onions, skinned and thinly sliced |
| 2 celery sticks, finely chopped |
| 2 eggs |
| 60 ml (4 tbsp) tomato purée |
| 700 g (1½ lb) minced fresh beef |
| 100 g (4 oz) fresh breadcrumbs |
| 45 ml (3 tbsp) chopped fresh parsley |
| 15 ml (1 tbsp) chopped fresh basil or 5 ml (1 level tsp) dried |
| salt and pepper |

◆ Place the oil, garlic and onions in a medium bowl and microwave on HIGH for 5-7 minutes or until the onion is soft, stirring twice.

◆ Using a fork, transfer half the onions to the base of a 1.5 litre (2½ pint) microwave ring mould.

◆ Stir the celery into the remaining onions and microwave on HIGH for 3 minutes or until the vegetables are softened.

◆ Beat the eggs and tomato purée together in a large mixing bowl. Mix in the meat, breadcrumbs, parsley, basil and onion and celery mixture. Season to taste with salt and pepper.

◆ Spoon into the ring mould, pressing the mixture down lightly. Microwave on HIGH for 20 minutes. Leave to stand for 5 minutes. Unmould on to a heated serving dish.

# SPICED BEEF CASSEROLE

## SERVES 4

15 ml (1 tbsp) vegetable oil

1 medium onion, skinned and sliced

3 celery sticks, trimmed and chopped

1 garlic clove, skinned and crushed

50 g (2 oz) lean streaky bacon, rinded and diced

15 ml (1 level tbsp) plain flour

15 ml (1 level tbsp) mild curry powder

2.5 ml (½ level tsp) ground allspice

450 g (1 lb) lean minced beef

5 ml (1 level tsp) tomato purée

225 g (8 oz) can tomatoes

salt and pepper

½ a cucumber, chopped

25 g (1 oz) cashew nuts (optional)

150 ml (¼ pint) natural yogurt

◆ Put the oil into a large ovenproof casserole with the onion, celery, garlic and bacon. Cover with cling film, pulling back one corner to allow the steam to escape, and microwave on HIGH for 5-7 minutes or until the onions and celery are soft. Stir in the flour, curry powder and allspice and microwave on HIGH for 2 minutes, stirring occasionally.

◆ Stir in the minced beef, tomato purée, tomatoes, cucumber and nuts, if using.

◆ Three-quarters cover with cling film or a casserole lid. Microwave on HIGH for 20-25 minutes, stirring frequently. Gradually stir in the yogurt, re-cover and microwave on HIGH for 2 minutes. Remove from the oven and allow to stand for 5 minutes. Season well with salt and pepper.

# STEAK AND KIDNEY PUDDING

## SERVES 2

100 g (4 oz) wholemeal self raising flour

large pinch of ground mace

15 ml (1 tbsp) chopped fresh parsley

50 g (2 oz) shredded suet

salt and pepper

1 egg, beaten

15 ml (1 tbsp) vegetable oil

1 medium onion, skinned and chopped

225 g (8 oz) rump steak, cut into thin strips

1-2 lamb's kidneys, skinned, halved, cored and chopped

30 ml (2 level tbsp) plain flour

150 ml (¼ pint) red wine

1 bay leaf

◆ To make the pastry, put the flour, mace, parsley, suet, salt and pepper into a bowl and mix together. Make a well in the centre, then stir in the egg and 30-45 ml (2-3 tbsp) cold water to make a soft, light elastic dough. Knead until smooth.

◆ Roll out two thirds of the pastry on a floured surface, and use to line a 600 ml (1 pint) pudding basin.

◆ Put the oil and onion in a medium bowl, cover with cling film and pull back one corner to allow the steam to escape. Microwave on HIGH for 5-7 minutes or until the onion is softened.

◆ Toss the steak and the halved kidneys in the flour and stir into the softened onion. Microwave on HIGH for 3 minutes, then stir in the wine, bay leaf, salt and pepper. Re-cover and microwave on HIGH for 5 minutes, stirring occasionally.

◆ Spoon the mixture into the lined pudding basin. Roll out the remaining pastry to a circle to fit the top of the pudding. Dampen the edges and press firmly together to seal.

◆ Cover loosely with cling film and microwave on HIGH for 5 minutes, or until the pastry looks 'set'.

◆ Leave to stand for 5 minutes, then turn out on to a warmed serving dish or wrap a clean table napkin round the bowl and serve from the bowl. Serve immediately.

## MINTED LAMB MEAT BALLS

### SERVES 4

| |
|---|
| 225 g (8 oz) crisp green cabbage, roughly chopped |
| 1 medium onion, skinned and quartered |
| 450 g (1 lb) lean minced lamb |
| 2.5 ml (½ level tsp) ground allspice |
| salt and pepper |
| 397 g (14 oz) can tomato juice |
| 1 bay leaf |
| 10 ml (2 tsp) chopped fresh mint or 5 ml (1 level tsp) dried |
| 15 ml (1 tbsp) chopped fresh parsley |

◆ Put the cabbage and onions in a food processor or blender and liquidise until finely chopped. Transfer to an ovenproof glass bowl, cover the top with cling film, pulling back one corner to allow the steam to escape, and microwave on HIGH for 2-3 minutes or until the vegetables are softened. Leave for 5 minutes to cool.
◆ Add the lamb and allspice and season with salt and pepper. Beat together well.
◆ Using wet hands, shape the lamb mixture into 16 small balls and place them in a single layer in a shallow ovenproof dish. Microwave them uncovered for 5 minutes, carefully turning and repositioning the meat balls after 3 minutes.
◆ Mix the tomato juice with the bay leaf, mint and parsley and pour this over the meat balls. Three-quarters cover the dish with cling film and microwave on HIGH for 5-6 minutes or until the sauce is boiling and the meat balls are cooked. Allow them to stand for 5 minutes. Skim off any fat and serve with rice or noodles, if liked.

## SPINACH-STUFFED SADDLE OF LAMB

### SERVES 6

| |
|---|
| 25 g (1 oz) butter or margarine |
| 1 medium onion, skinned and chopped |
| 300 g (10.6 oz) packet frozen spinach, thawed |
| 25 g (1 oz) fresh breadcrumbs |
| finely grated rind and juice of ½ a lemon |
| salt and pepper |
| about 1.5 kg (3 lb) saddle of lamb, boned |
| 30 ml (2 tbsp) redcurrant jelly |

◆ Place the butter in a small ovenproof bowl and microwave on HIGH for 45 seconds or until the butter melts. Add the onion and cover with cling film, pulling back one corner to allow the steam to escape, and microwave on HIGH for 5-7 minutes until softened.
◆ Drain and discard all the excess liquid from the spinach, then add it to the onion with the breadcrumbs, lemon rind and juice; season to taste and mix together well.
◆ Place the meat fat side uppermost on a flat surface and score the fat with a sharp knife. Turn the meat over and spread it with the stuffing. Fold over to enclose the stuffing and sew the edges together with fine string to form a neat and even shape.
◆ Weigh the joint and calculate the cooking time at 8 minutes per 450 g (1 lb). Place the joint in a roasting bag, securing the end with string or an elastic band, and place it on a roasting rack. Microwave on HIGH for half the cooking time. Remove from the oven and remove the meat from the roasting bag.
◆ Place the redcurrant jelly in a small ovenproof bowl and heat for 30 seconds or until melted, then brush it over the lamb. Return the meat to the oven, uncovered, and cook for the remaining time. Leave to stand for 10-15 minutes. To serve, remove the string and carve into thick slices.

## LAMB BURGERS

### MAKES 4

| |
|---|
| 450 g (1 lb) lean minced lamb |
| 1 large onion, skinned and finely grated |
| 5 ml (1 level tsp) salt |
| 1.25 (¼ level tsp) cayenne pepper |
| 30 ml (2 tbsp) vegetable oil |
| plain or toasted hamburger buns, to serve |

◆ Mix the lamb and onion together and season with salt and cayenne pepper.
◆ Divide the lamb mixture into four and shape each piece into a neat pattie about 2.5 cm (1 inch) thick.
◆ Preheat a large browning dish to maximum according to the manufacturer's instructions, adding the oil for the last 30 seconds. (Or put the oil into a large shallow ovenproof dish and microwave on HIGH for 1-2 minutes until the oil is hot.)
◆ Without removing the dish from the oven, press 2 lamb burgers flat on to the hot surface and microwave on HIGH for 2-3 minutes. Turn the burgers over and reposition them and microwave on HIGH for 2-3 minutes until cooked. Repeat with the remaining burgers.
◆ Serve the lamb burgers in plain or toasted hamburger buns.

## LAMB BURGERS

*A variation on the hamburger theme, and a guaranteed favourite with children*

SEE OPPOSITE

# LAMB AND APRICOT KEBABS

### SERVES 4

| |
|---|
| 700 g (1½ lb) lamb fillet or boned leg of lamb |
| 60 ml (4 tbsp) olive oil |
| juice of 1 lemon |
| 1 garlic clove, skinned and crushed |
| pinch of salt |
| 5 ml (1 level tsp) ground cumin |
| 5 ml (1 level tsp) ground coriander |
| 5 ml (1 level tsp) ground cinnamon |
| 2 large onions, skinned and quartered |
| 75 g (3 oz) apricots, diced |
| 8 bay leaves |

◆ Cut the lamb into 2.5 cm (1 inch) thick slices if using fillet, or cubes, if using leg.
◆ Put the olive oil, lemon juice, garlic, salt, cumin, coriander and cinnamon into a large glass bowl and whisk the ingredients together well. Stir in the lamb, cover and leave it to marinate at room temperature for at least 4 hours.
◆ Put the onion quarters and the apricots into an oven-proof glass bowl, add 150 ml (¼ pint) water, cover and microwave on HIGH for 3 minutes. Drain them well, cover and set them aside until lamb is ready for cooking.
◆ Put alternate pieces of lamb, apricot, onion quarters and bay leaves on to 8 wooden kebab skewers.
◆ Arrange the kebabs in a double layer on a roasting rack in a shallow ovenproof dish and spoon over any remaining marinade. Microwave on HIGH for 8 minutes, then re-position them so that the inside skewers are moved to the outside of the dish. Microwave on HIGH for 10 minutes, repositioning the kebabs twice during this cooking period. Allow them to stand for 5 minutes.
◆ Serve with rice, if liked. The juices left in the cooking dish may be reheated and served with the kebabs.

# BARBECUED LAMB

### SERVES 6

| |
|---|
| 1.25 kg-1.5 kg (2½-3 lb) leg of lamb, boned |
| 150 ml (¼ pint) tomato ketchup |
| 15 ml (1 level tbsp) soft light brown sugar |
| 1 small onion, skinned and finely chopped |
| 15 ml (1 tbsp) chopped fresh rosemary or 5 ml (1 level tsp) dried |
| 30 ml (2 tbsp) red wine vinegar |
| salt and pepper |

◆ With a sharp knife, score the meat on both sides in a diamond pattern. This ensures good penetration of the marinade when added. Tie the meat into a neat compact shape and place in a large shallow dish.
◆ Combine all the remaining ingredients and season to taste. Pour the marinade over the meat. Cover and refrigerate overnight, turning the meat over at least once.
◆ Place the meat on a roasting rack and microwave on HIGH for 7-8 minutes per 450 g (1 lb) or until the meat is cooked, turning at least once. The meat should still be pink in the centre. Serve cut into thick slices.

# LAMB WITH MINT AND YOGURT

### SERVES 4

| |
|---|
| 15 ml (1 tbsp) vegetable oil |
| 1 medium onion, skinned and sliced |
| 3 bay leaves |
| 75 ml (5 tbsp) white wine vinegar |
| salt and pepper |
| 1.25 kg (2¾ lb) leg of lamb, boned and cut into 2.5 cm (1 inch) cubes |
| 15 ml (1 level tbsp) cornflour |
| 5 ml (1 level tsp) granulated sugar |
| 150 ml (¼ pint) natural yogurt |
| 45 ml (3 tbsp) chopped fresh mint |
| 30 ml (2 tbsp) chopped fresh parsley |

◆ Place the oil, onion, bay leaves, vinegar and seasoning in a large casserole. Microwave on HIGH for about 5 minutes or until the liquid is boiling. Add the lamb to the casserole, cover and microwave on MEDIUM for 30 minutes or until the meat is tender. Leave to stand for 5 minutes.
◆ Meanwhile, mix the cornflour and sugar to a smooth paste with 15 ml (1 tbsp) water. Add to the pan, stirring well, and microwave on HIGH for about 3 minutes, stirring after each minute, until thickened. Stir in the yogurt, mint and parsley and season to taste. Serve with noodles or rice, if liked.

## SWEET AND SOUR PORK

### SERVES 6

*30 ml (2 level tbsp) soft dark brown sugar*

*30 ml (2 level tbsp) cornflour*

*450 g (1 lb) pork tenderloin, cut into matchsticks*

*1 large onion, skinned and thinly sliced*

*2 garlic cloves, skinned and crushed*

*15 ml (1 tbsp) vegetable oil*

*30 ml (2 tbsp) soy sauce*

*50 ml (2 fl oz) cider vinegar*

*225 g (8 oz) carrots, peeled and cut into matchsticks*

*439 g (15½ oz) can pineapple chunks in natural juice, drained with juice reserved*

*1 large green pepper, cored, seeded and cut into matchsticks*

*230 g (8 oz) can water chestnuts, drained and sliced (optional)*

◆ Place the sugar and cornflour in a large polythene bag and add the pork. Toss together to coat the pork all over.
◆ Mix the onion, garlic and oil in a large bowl. Microwave on HIGH for 5-7 minutes or until soft, stirring once.
◆ Stir in the pork along with any cornflour mixture left in the bag. Add the soy sauce, vinegar, carrots and pineapple juice. Three-quarters cover and microwave on HIGH for 12-15 minutes or until the pork is tender, stirring once.
◆ Stir in the pineapple chunks, green pepper and water chestnuts, if using. Microwave on HIGH, uncovered, for 5 minutes. Serve immediately, with rice, if liked.

## PORK FILLET WITH CIDER AND CORIANDER

### SERVES 4

*450 g (1 lb) pork fillet (tenderloin)*

*15 ml (1 tbsp) vegetable oil*

*1 small green pepper, cored, seeded and sliced into rings*

*1 medium onion, skinned and chopped*

*15 ml (1 level tbsp) ground coriander*

*15 ml (1 level tbsp) plain flour*

*150 ml (¼ pint) dry cider*

*150 ml (¼ pint) chicken stock*

*salt and pepper*

◆ Trim the pork fillet of all fat and membrane. Cut it into 0.5 cm (¼ inch) thick pieces, place between 2 sheets of greaseproof paper and flatten with a mallet until thin.

◆ Put the oil in a shallow ovenproof dish or casserole and microwave on HIGH for about 1 minute. Stir in the pepper and onion, cover with cling film, pulling back one corner to allow the steam to escape, and microwave on HIGH for 5-7 minutes or until the vegetables soften.
◆ Stir in the flour and coriander and microwave on HIGH for 2 minutes. Gradually stir in the cider and stock and microwave on HIGH for 3-4 minutes, stirring frequently until boiling and thickened. Add the pork, cover with cling film, pulling back one corner to allow the steam to escape, and microwave on HIGH for 5-6 minutes until boiling. Stir. Reduce the setting, microwave on LOW for 7-8 minutes or until the pork is tender. Allow it to stand for 5 minutes before serving.

## SPICY PORK CHOPS

### SERVES 4

*4 pork spare rib back chops*

*1 garlic clove, skinned and crushed*

*1 small onion, skinned and finely chopped*

*15 ml (1 level tbsp) cornflour*

*150 ml (¼ pint) natural yogurt*

*15 ml (1 tbsp) tomato purée*

*5 ml (1 level tsp) ground turmeric*

*5 ml (1 level tsp) paprika*

*2.5 ml (½ level tsp) chilli powder*

*salt and pepper*

◆ Trim off any excess fat from the chops and arrange them in a single layer in a round shallow dish. Prick all over with a fork.
◆ Mix all the remaining ingredients together and spread over both sides of the chops. Cover and leave to marinate for at least 4 hours, preferably overnight.
◆ Cover with cling film, pulling back one corner to allow the steam to escape. Microwave on HIGH for 5 minutes. Turn the chops over, reposition, re-cover and microwave on HIGH for 10-12 minutes until tender. Leave to stand, covered, for 5 minutes.

## PORK AND VEGETABLES

*An Oriental, stir-fried dish, simply made in seconds*

SEE OPPOSITE

## PORK AND VEGETABLES

### SERVES 4

| |
|---|
| 30 ml (2 tbsp) vegetable oil |
| 60 ml (4 tbsp) soy sauce |
| 15 ml (1 tbsp) dry sherry |
| 12.5 ml (2½ level tsp) cornflour |
| 6.25 ml (1¼ level tsp) sugar |
| 2.5 ml (½ tsp) finely chopped fresh ginger or 1.25 ml (¼ level tsp) ground ginger |
| 1 garlic clove, skinned and crushed |
| 450 g (1 lb) pork fillet, cut into matchstick strips |
| 2 large carrots, peeled and cut into matchstick strips |
| 1 green pepper, cut into thin strips |
| 3 spring onions, cut into 2.5 cm (1 inch) lengths |
| 225 g (8 oz) mushrooms, sliced |
| cooked rice, to serve |

◆ Stir the oil, soy sauce, sherry, cornflour, sugar, ginger and garlic together in a medium casserole. Add the pork, mix well and leave to marinate for at least 30 minutes.
◆ Stir in the remaining ingredients and microwave on HIGH for 7-8 minutes until the pork is tender and the juices run clear and the vegetables are tender but still firm, stirring occasionally. Serve with cooked rice.

## PORK AND LEEKS IN CREAM

### SERVES 4

| |
|---|
| 50 g (2 oz) butter or margarine |
| 225 g (8 oz) leeks, trimmed and thickly sliced |
| 1 garlic clove, skinned and crushed |
| 350 g (12 oz) pork tenderloin |
| 60 ml (4 tbsp) dry white wine or vermouth |
| 150 ml (5 fl oz) double cream |
| 15 ml (1 tbsp) wholegrain mustard |
| salt and pepper |

◆ Place half the butter in a medium shallow casserole and microwave on HIGH for 45 seconds or until the butter melts. Toss in the leeks and garlic and microwave on HIGH for 5-7 minutes or until soft, stirring once.
◆ Cut the pork diagonally into very thin slices. Fry the slices conventionally in the remaining butter until golden brown on both sides.

◆ Arrange the meat on top of the leeks. Deglaze the frying pan with the wine or vermouth and pour the liquid over the meat.
◆ Blend the cream and mustard together and pour it over the meat and season to taste. Cover and microwave on HIGH for 15 minutes. Leave to stand for 5 minutes. Serve with rice or noodles, if liked.

## SPARE RIBS WITH REDCURRANT AND HONEY GLAZE

### SERVES 1

| |
|---|
| 1 small onion, skinned and very finely chopped |
| 1 garlic clove, skinned and crushed |
| 45 ml (3 tbsp) redcurrant jelly |
| 15 ml (1 tbsp) clear honey |
| 15 ml (1 tbsp) soy sauce |
| 15 ml (1 tbsp) red wine vinegar |
| dash of hot chilli sauce |
| salt and pepper |
| 450 g (1 lb) Chinese style pork spare ribs |
| 15 ml (1 level tbsp) cornflour |

◆ Blend the onion, garlic, redcurrant jelly, honey, soy sauce and vinegar together in a large bowl. Season to taste with chilli sauce, salt and pepper.
◆ Stir in the ribs and coat in the marinade. Cover and leave in the refrigerator for at least 30 minutes for the ribs to absorb the flavour.
◆ Remove the ribs from the marinade, reserving the marinade for the sauce. Arrange the ribs in a single layer in a shallow dish. Cover with absorbent kitchen paper and microwave on HIGH for 5 minutes.
◆ Rearrange the ribs, then microwave on MEDIUM for 15-20 minutes or until the meat is tender, rearranging and turning once during cooking.
◆ Blend the cornflour with a little cold water to make a smooth paste then stir into the reserved marinade.
◆ Pour over the ribs making sure that they are all covered, and microwave on HIGH for 5 minutes, or until the ribs are thoroughly glazed and the sauce thickened, basting occasionally during cooking.

*To serve 2:* increase the cornflour to 45 ml (3 level tbsp) and double the remaining ingredients, then follow the recipe as above, but in point 4 microwave on MEDIUM for 20-25 minutes; in point 6 microwave on HIGH for 8-10 minutes.

## PORK CHOPS WITH PEPPERS

### SERVES 4

1 large onion, skinned and sliced

1 large red pepper, cored, seeded and sliced

15 ml (1 tbsp) vegetable oil

4 boneless pork chops

30 ml (2 level tbsp) paprika

150 ml (¼ pint) double cream

salt and pepper

◆ Mix the onion, red pepper and oil in a shallow casserole. Microwave on HIGH for 5-7 minutes or until the vegetables are softened, stirring once.
◆ Arrange the pork chops in a single layer on top of the vegetables. Blend the paprika and cream together. Season to taste and pour it over the meat.
◆ Cover and microwave on HIGH for 20 minutes or until the pork is tender.

## GLAZED BACON WITH ORANGE SAUCE

### SERVES 4

700 g (1½ lb) boneless lean bacon joint

60 ml (4 level tbsp) orange marmalade

45 ml (3 level tbsp) soft dark brown sugar

2.5 ml (½ level tsp) ground cinnamon

4-5 drops Tabasco sauce

60 ml (4 tbsp) orange juice

◆ Place the bacon in a roasting bag and fasten with string or an elastic band. Prick the bag with a fork and microwave on HIGH for 5 minutes. Turn the joint over and microwave on MEDIUM for 10 minutes.
◆ 2 Mix the marmalade, sugar, cinnamon and Tabasco together in a small bowl.
◆ Remove the meat from the bag and place in a shallow dish. Remove the rind, if necessary. Score the fat in a diamond pattern and spoon over half the marmalade mixture.
◆ Brown the meat under a preheated grill until golden, turning if necessary.
◆ Add the orange juice to the remaining marmalade mixture and microwave on HIGH for about 1½ minutes until bubbling. Serve the sauce with the meat.

## VEAL STROGANOFF

### SERVES 4

50 g (2 oz) butter or margarine

1 large onion, skinned and sliced

450 g (1 lb) veal escalopes, cut into thin strips

225 g (8 oz) mushrooms, sliced

150 ml (¼ pint) white wine or chicken stock

150 ml (¼ pint) soured cream

30 ml (2 tbsp) tomato purée

15 ml (1 tbsp) wholegrain mustard

10 ml (2 level tsp) paprika

salt and pepper

1 egg yolk

◆ Place the butter in a medium casserole and microwave on HIGH for 45 seconds or until the butter melts. Stir in the onion and microwave on HIGH for 5-7 minutes, or until the onion is soft, stirring once.
◆ Stir in the veal, mushrooms and wine or stock. Cover and microwave on HIGH for 15 minutes or until the veal is tender, stirring once.
◆ Mix the remaining ingredients together. Season to taste and add to the meat. Microwave on MEDIUM for 5 minutes, stirring after each minute until thickened. Do not allow to boil. Leave to stand for 3 minutes. Serve with noodles and a green salad, if liked.

## WIENER SCHNITZEL

### SERVES 6

6 veal or pork escalopes, cut about 0.5 cm (¼ inch) thick

2 eggs

salt and pepper

75 ml (5 level tbsp) plain flour

175 g (6 oz) dried breadcrumbs

30-60 ml (2-4 tbsp) vegetable oil

lemon wedges and chopped fresh parsley, anchovy fillets and capers (optional), to garnish

◆ Using a mallet or rolling pin, beat the escalopes between 2 sheets of dampened greaseproof paper until they are about 0.3 cm (⅛ inch) thick. Trim off any excess fat.
◆ Beat the eggs with salt and pepper in a shallow dish. Spread the flour on a sheet of greaseproof paper and the breadcrumbs on another.
◆ Coat the escalopes in the flour, shaking off the excess,

then dip them in the egg and coat them with the breadcrumbs.

◆ Preheat a large browning dish to maximum according to the manufacturer's instructions, adding half of the oil for the last 30 seconds.

◆ Without removing the dish from the oven, place 2 escalopes in the hot oil and microwave on HIGH for 1 minute, then turn over the escalopes and microwave on HIGH for ½-1 minute, or until the escalopes are cooked through. Transfer the schnitzels to a hot serving dish, cover and keep them warm.

◆ Wipe the browning dish clean with absorbent kitchen paper. Reheat the dish and add the remaining oil for the last 30 seconds. Cook the remaining 2 escalopes as above and place them on the serving dish.

◆ Garnish the escalopes with lemon wedges and parsley, adding anchovy fillets and capers if you wish. Serve the schnitzels with a green salad, if liked.

## VEAL MARENGO

SERVES 4

| 4 veal escalopes |
| 4 thin slices ham |
| 15 ml (1 tbsp) vegetable oil |
| 2 carrots, peeled and finely chopped |
| 2 celery sticks, trimmed and chopped |
| 1 medium onion, skinned and finely chopped |
| 50 g (2 oz) streaky bacon, rinded and chopped |
| 54 ml (3 level tbsp) plain flour |
| 150 ml (¼ pint) hot chicken stock |
| 397 g (14 oz) can chopped tomatoes |
| 30 ml (2 tbsp) sherry |
| salt and pepper |
| 100 g (4 oz) mushrooms, sliced |
| chopped fresh parsley, to garnish |

◆ Using a mallet or rolling pin, beat the veal escalopes between 2 sheets of dampened greaseproof paper until they are thin. Trim off any excess fat.

◆ Place a slice of ham on each escalope and roll up. Secure with wooden cocktail sticks and arrange in a deep casserole.

◆ Place the oil, vegetables and bacon in a medium bowl. Microwave on HIGH for 5 minutes, stirring once. Stir in the flour and microwave on HIGH for 30 seconds. Gradually stir in the stock. Microwave on HIGH for 2 minutes, stirring once.

◆ Add the tomatoes, sherry, seasoning and mushrooms. Pour the sauce over the veal, cover and microwave on HIGH for 20 minutes. Remove sticks and sprinkle with parsley.

## LIVER WITH ONIONS AND MUSHROOMS

SERVES 4

| 450 g (1 lb) lamb's liver |
| 15 ml (1 level tbsp) plain flour |
| 50 g (2 oz) butter or margarine |
| 450 g (1 lb) onions, skinned and thinly sliced |
| 4 streaky bacon rashers, rinded and chopped |
| 100 g (4 oz) mushrooms, sliced |
| salt and pepper |
| 15 ml (1 tbsp) wine vinegar |

◆ Cut the liver, diagonally, into thick slices and toss them gently in the flour, ensuring that they are evenly coated.

◆ Preheat a large browning dish to maximum according to the manufacturer's instructions, adding 25 g (1 oz) butter for the last minute. (Or put the butter into a shallow ovenproof dish and microwave on HIGH for 1 minute until the butter is bubbling.)

◆ Without removing the dish from the oven, place the liver in the hot butter and microwave on HIGH for about 5 minutes, turning the slices over and repositioning them after 3 minutes. Remove the liver to a hot dish, cover and keep warm.

◆ Add the remaining butter to the cooking dish and microwave on HIGH for about 1 minute until bubbling.

◆ Stir the onions, bacon and mushrooms into the butter, three-quarters cover the dish with cling film and microwave on HIGH for 5-7 minutes until softened, stirring frequently.

◆ Season the onions very well with salt and pepper and stir in the vinegar and liver. Microwave on HIGH for 1 minute and serve hot.

—— SAGE- AND BACON-STUFFED PORK ——

*A beautifully succulent dish that is ideal for a Sunday lunch*

SEE PAGE 126

### CALF'S LIVER WITH APPLE, BACON
### AND SAGE

*The apple used in this dish goes perfectly with the more traditional
combination of liver and bacon*

SEE PAGE 126

## SAGE- AND BACON-STUFFED PORK

### SERVES 6-8

about 1.8 kg (4 lb) loin of pork, boned and rinded

8 streaky bacon rashers, rinded

12 fresh sage leaves

2 garlic cloves, skinned and cut into slivers

salt and pepper

fresh sage, to garnish

◆ Place the pork, fat side uppermost, on a flat surface and remove most of the fat. Score the remaining fat with a sharp knife.
◆ Turn over the meat and lay half of the bacon, the sage and the garlic over the flesh. Season well with salt and pepper. Roll up and secure with string. Lay the remaining bacon on top of the joint.
◆ Weigh the joint and calculate the cooking time at 8 minutes per 450 g (1 lb). Place the joint in a roasting bag, securing the end with string and place on a roasting rack, bacon side down. Microwave on HIGH for half of the calculated cooking time, then turn over and cook for the remaining time. Leave to stand for 10-15 minutes. Garnish with fresh sage and serve cut into slices.

## CALF'S LIVER WITH APPLE, BACON AND SAGE

### SERVES 2

225 g (8 oz) calf's liver, sliced into thin strips

15 ml (1 level tbsp) plain flour

salt and pepper

paprika to taste

15 ml (1 tbsp) vegetable oil

15 g (½ oz) butter or margarine

3 streaky bacon rashers, rinded

1 red eating apple

1 medium onion, skinned and thinly sliced

200 ml (7 fl oz) medium dry cider

30 ml (2 tbsp) soured cream

5 ml (1 tsp) chopped fresh sage or 2.5 ml (½ level tsp) dried

fresh sage, to garnish

◆ Coat the liver in the flour and season well with salt, pepper and paprika.

◆ Put the oil and the butter into a shallow dish and microwave on HIGH for 30 seconds or until the butter melts.
◆ Meanwhile, cut the bacon into thin strips. Core the apple, cut into rings, then cut each ring in half.
◆ Stir the onion and bacon into the fat and microwave on HIGH for 5-6 minutes or until the onion is softened, stirring frequently.
◆ Stir in the liver and microwave on HIGH for 1-2 minutes or until the liver just changes colour, stirring occasionally.
◆ Stir in the apple slices and 150 ml (5 fl oz) cider and microwave on HIGH for 2-3 minutes or until the liver is tender, stirring occasionally.
◆ Remove the liver, bacon, apple and onion with a slotted spoon and transfer to a warmed serving dish.
◆ Stir in the remaining cider, the cream and the sage and microwave on HIGH for 4-5 minutes or until thickened and reduced. Adjust the seasoning, if necessary.
◆ Microwave the liver and apple mixture on HIGH for 1 minute to reheat, if necessary, then pour over the sauce. Garnish with sage and serve immediately.

## LIVER AND BEAN CASSEROLE

### SERVES 4

350 g (12 oz) lamb's liver, cut into 1 cm (½ inch) strips

25 g (1 oz) plain flour

15 ml (1 tbsp) vegetable oil

1 medium onion, skinned and finely chopped

150 ml (¼ pint) beef stock

75 ml (3 fl oz) milk

30 ml (2 tbsp) tomato purée

10 ml (2 tsp) chopped fresh mixed herbs or
5 ml (1 level tsp) dried

100 g (4 oz) mushrooms, sliced

475 g (17 oz) can red kidney beans, drained

salt and pepper

◆ Toss the liver strips in the flour, ensuring that they are evenly coated.
◆ Preheat a browning dish to maximum according to the manufacturer's instructions, adding the oil for the last 30 seconds.
◆ Add the liver, any excess flour and the onion and mix well. Microwave on HIGH for 3 minutes, stirring.
◆ Add the stock, milk, purée and herbs and mix well together. Microwave on HIGH for 10 minutes or until boiling, stirring occasionally.
◆ Add the mushrooms, kidney beans and seasoning and microwave on HIGH for 5-7 minutes or until the liver is tender. Serve hot.

# EASTERN SPICED LIVER

### SERVES 4

| |
|---|
| 25 g (1 oz) desiccated coconut |
| 45 ml (3 tbsp) vegetable oil |
| 2 medium onions, skinned and thinly sliced |
| 5 ml (1 level tsp) chilli powder |
| 15 ml (1 level tbsp) ground coriander |
| 5 ml (1 level tsp) paprika |
| 2.5 ml (½ level tsp) ground turmeric |
| 450 g (1 lb) lamb's liver, cut into small thin strips |
| 30 ml (2 level tbsp) plain flour |
| 300 ml (½ pint) chicken stock |
| 30 ml (2 level tbsp) mango chutney |
| salt and pepper |

◆ Place the coconut and 150 ml (¼ pint) water in a large bowl. Cover and microwave on HIGH for 5 minutes or until the water is boiling. Leave to stand for 15 minutes, then strain, reserving the liquid.

◆ In a large shallow dish, mix the oil, onions and spices together and microwave on HIGH for 5 minutes, stirring frequently, until the onion is slightly softened. Add the liver.

◆ Stir in the flour and microwave on HIGH for 30 seconds. Blend in the stock, coconut liquid, chutney and seasoning. Microwave on HIGH for 5-7 minutes or until liver is tender.

# KIDNEYS IN RED WINE

### SERVES 4

| |
|---|
| 8 lamb's kidneys |
| 50 g (2 oz) butter or margarine |
| 1 large onion, skinned and chopped |
| 25 g (1 oz) plain flour |
| 150 ml (¼ pint) red wine |
| 150 ml (¼ pint) beef stock |
| 15 ml (1 tbsp) tomato purée |
| 1 bouquet garni |
| 100 g (4 oz) mushrooms, sliced |
| salt and pepper |
| chopped fresh parsley, to garnish |

◆ Skin the kidneys, cut them in half and remove the cores.

◆ Put the butter into a shallow ovenproof dish and microwave on HIGH for 45 seconds until the butter melts. Stir in the onion, cover with cling film and pull back one corner to allow the steam to escape. Microwave on HIGH for 5-7 minutes or until the onion softens.

◆ Uncover the dish, stir in the flour and microwave on HIGH for 1 minute. Add the kidneys and microwave on HIGH for 3-4 minutes, stirring occasionally. Stir in the wine, stock, tomato purée, bouquet garni and mushrooms, three-quarters cover with cling film and microwave on HIGH for 5 minutes, or until the kidneys are cooked, stirring twice during the cooking time. Uncover and microwave on HIGH for 1 minute.

◆ Remove the bouquet garni from the dish and season the kidneys well with salt and pepper. Sprinkle them with chopped parsley and serve with rice, if liked.

# KIDNEY AND CELERY SAUTE

### SERVES 4

| |
|---|
| 450 g (1 lb) lamb's kidneys |
| 2 celery sticks, trimmed |
| 15 ml (1 tbsp) vegetable oil |
| 25 g (1 oz) butter or margarine |
| 30 ml (2 tbsp) brandy (optional) |
| 150 ml (¼ pint) beef stock |
| 1 garlic clove, skinned and crushed |
| salt and pepper |
| chopped fresh parsley, to garnish |

◆ Remove the skin from each kidney, cut them in half and snip out the cores, then halve the kidneys again. Slice the celery into 2.5 cm (1 inch) diagonal pieces.

◆ Preheat a large browning dish to maximum according to the manufacturer's instructions, adding the oil and butter for the last 30 seconds. (Or put the oil and butter into a shallow ovenproof dish and microwave on HIGH for 1 minute until the butter is bubbling.)

◆ Without removing the dish from the oven, place the kidney pieces in the hot oil, turning them quickly so that they are well coated. Microwave on HIGH for 2-4 minutes or until the kidneys are cooked. Remove the kidney pieces from the dish and keep them warm.

◆ Add the sliced celery to the cooking dish, cover the top with cling film, pulling back one corner to allow the steam to escape, and microwave on HIGH for 3-4 minutes, stirring occasionally, until the celery has softened.

◆ Add the kidneys to the celery and stir in the brandy, if using, then microwave on HIGH for 1 minute. Remove the dish from the oven and set the brandy alight, then, when the flame subsides, stir in the stock, garlic, salt and pepper. Microwave on HIGH for 4-5 minutes until the liquid is boiling, stirring once during cooking. Garnish with parsley.

# VEGETABLES & PULSES

## POTATO AND LEEK RAMEKINS

*A lightly spiced potato dish served with a delightful salad of cherry tomatoes (page 131)*

SEE PAGE 131

# Cooking Tips

◆

*Cut vegetables into uniformly sized pieces so that they cook evenly.*

◆

*Frozen vegetables need no added liquid. Fresh vegetables require only a very small amount of water, butter or margarine to create steam for cooking.*

◆

*Small frozen vegetables such as peas, sweetcorn kernels and mixed vegetables can be cooked in their plastic packets because the melting ice within the packet produces sufficient moisture for cooking. Slit the top of the packet and shake it about half-way through the cooking to distribute the heat evenly.*

◆

*Always pierce whole vegetables with skins, such as potatoes, to prevent them bursting.*

◆

*Arrange vegetables, such as cauliflower and broccoli sprigs, with the thickest part pointing towards the edge of the dish, for even cooking.*

◆

*If cooking vegetables on their own, do not add salt directly on to them until after they have been cooked as it toughens them.*

◆

*To ensure even cooking, turn large vegetables such as potatoes and whole cauliflower over at least once during cooking.*

◆

*Dried peas and beans are not recommended for microwaving. The skins remain tough and will burst during cooking. Split lentils, however, can be successfully microwaved because they are not completely encased in a skin.*

◆

*The microwave can be used to prepare dishes using canned pulses which just require heating through or to reheat dishes containing cooked pulses.*

◆

## POTATO AND LEEK RAMEKINS

### SERVES 2 AS AN ACCOMPANIMENT

| |
|---|
| *1 large potato, weighing about 225 g ( 8 oz)* |
| *1 small leek* |
| *45 ml (3 tbsp) milk* |
| *salt and pepper* |
| *grated nutmeg to taste* |
| *1 egg yolk* |
| *15 g (½ oz) butter or margarine* |
| *5 ml (1 level tsp) poppy seeds* |

◆ Grease and line the bases of two 150 ml (¼ pint) ramekin dishes with greaseproof paper.
◆ Prick the potato all over with a fork, place on absorbent kitchen paper and microwave on HIGH for 5-6 minutes or until the potato is soft, turning over halfway through cooking.
◆ Meanwhile, finely chop the white part of the leek and slice the green part into very thin 4 cm (1½ inch) long strips. Wash separately and drain well.
◆ Put the white leek into a medium bowl with the milk, cover with cling film, pulling back one corner to allow the steam to escape and microwave on HIGH for 2-3 minutes or until the leek is very soft, stirring occasionally.
◆ Cut the potato in half, scoop out the flesh and stir into the cooked leek and milk. Mash well together and season with salt, pepper and nutmeg. Stir in the egg yolk.
◆ Spoon the mixture into the prepared ramekin dishes. Cover loosely with cling film and microwave on HIGH for 2-2½ minutes or until firm to the touch. Leave to stand.
◆ Meanwhile, put the butter into a small bowl with the strips of green leek and the poppy seeds. Cover with cling film, pulling back one corner to allow the steam to escape, and microwave on HIGH for 2-3 minutes or until the leek is tender, stirring occasionally. Season with salt and pepper.
◆ Turn the ramekins out on to a warmed serving plate and spoon over the leek and poppy seed mixture. Microwave on HIGH for 1-2 minutes to heat through, if necessary. Serve immediately.

## CHERRY TOMATOES WITH PINE NUT AND BASIL DRESSING

### SERVES 2 AS AN ACCOMPANIMENT

| |
|---|
| *15 ml (1 tbsp) olive or vegetable oil* |
| *25 g (1 oz) pine nuts* |
| *2.5 ml (½ tsp) Dijon mustard* |
| *2.5 ml (½ level tsp) brown sugar* |
| *salt and pepper* |
| *2.5 ml (½ tsp) white wine vinegar* |
| *225 g (8 oz) cherry tomatoes, cut in halves* |
| *15 ml (1 tbsp) chopped fresh basil* |

◆ Put the oil and the nuts in a medium bowl and microwave on HIGH for 2-3 minutes, or until the nuts are lightly browned, stirring frequently.
◆ Stir in the mustard, sugar, salt and pepper and whisk together with a fork. Whisk in the vinegar.
◆ Add the tomatoes and microwave on HIGH for 30 seconds or until the tomatoes are just warm. Stir in the basil and serve immediately.

## FENNEL WITH MOZZARELLA CHEESE

### SERVES 4 AS AN ACCOMPANIMENT

| |
|---|
| *2 large or 3 small heads fennel, total weight about 450 g (1 lb), trimmed* |
| *30 ml (2 tbsp) lemon juice* |
| *5 ml (1 tsp) chopped fresh marjoram* |
| *1 bay leaf* |
| *salt and pepper* |
| *200 g (7 oz) Mozzarella cheese, thinly sliced* |

◆ Cut the fennel across into 0.5 cm (¼ inch) slices, reserving the feathery leaves.
◆ Place the fennel in a shallow flameproof dish with the lemon juice, marjoram, bay leaf and 75 ml (5 tbsp) water. Three-quarters cover with cling film and microwave on HIGH for 9-10 minutes or until the fennel is tender. Stir occasionally during cooking.
◆ Drain, discarding the bay leaf, and return the vegetable to the dish. Season to taste and lay the cheese over the fennel. Grill under a hot grill until the cheese is golden brown and bubbling. Serve immediately, garnished with the reserved leaves.

## POTATO AND PARSLEY BAKE

SERVES 4 AS AN ACCOMPANIMENT

25 g (1 oz) butter or margarine

1 medium onion, skinned and thinly sliced

1 garlic clove, skinned and crushed (optional)

150 ml (¼ pint) soured cream

45 ml (3 tbsp) chopped fresh parsley

700 g (1½ lb) potatoes, peeled and very thinly sliced

salt and pepper

50 g (2 oz) Cheddar cheese, grated

chopped fresh parsley, to garnish

◆ Place the butter in a shallow heatproof dish and micro-wave on HIGH for 30 seconds or until the butter melts.

◆ Stir in the onion and garlic and microwave on HIGH for 5-7 minutes or until the onion is soft.

◆ Add the cream, parsley and potatoes and mix together well so that the potato slices are coated with the cream mixture.

◆ Three-quarters cover with cling film and microwave on HIGH for 15-17 minutes or until the potatoes are tender. Give the dish a quarter turn 3 times during cooking. Season well with salt and pepper.

◆ Sprinkle with the grated cheese and microwave on HIGH for 1-2 minutes or until the cheese is melted. Brown under a preheated grill if desired. Serve hot, garnished with chopped parsley.

## NEW POTATOES WITH SPICED HOLLANDAISE SAUCE

SERVES 4-6 AS AN ACCOMPANIMENT

25 g (1 oz) flaked almonds

900 g (2 lb) new potatoes

20 ml (4 level tsp) ground turmeric

2 egg yolks

1 garlic clove, skinned and crushed

175 g (6 oz) unsalted butter

30 ml (2 tbsp) natural yogurt

salt and pepper

◆ Spread the almonds over a large, flat ovenproof plate. Microwave on HIGH for 7-8 minutes, stirring occasionally, or until the almonds are lightly browned, then put them aside.

◆ Wash the potatoes well but do not peel them, cut them in half if they are large and put them into a large ovenproof bowl. Mix together 15 ml (3 level tsp) turmeric and 150 ml (¼ pint) water and pour this over the potatoes.

◆ Three-quarters cover the potatoes with cling film and microwave on HIGH for 8-10 minutes or until the potatoes are tender, turning frequently.

◆ Leave the potatoes to stand for 5 minutes, then drain them well. Put the potatoes into a hot serving dish, cover and keep them warm.

◆ Mix together the egg yolks and garlic in a medium ovenproof glass bowl. Cut the butter into small pieces into a small ovenproof bowl and microwave on HIGH for 1 minute until it is melted, then whisk it thoroughly into the egg yolks. Microwave on HIGH for 45 seconds until the sauce is just thick enough to coat the back of a spoon, whisking every 15 seconds – do not overcook or the sauce will curdle.

◆ Whisk the yogurt and the remaining turmeric into the sauce and microwave on HIGH for 15 seconds. Season with salt and pepper.

◆ Pour the hollandaise sauce over the potatoes, sprinkle with the toasted almonds and serve immediately.

## GLAZED VEGETABLES PROVENÇAL

SERVES 4 AS AN ACCOMPANIMENT

25 g (1 oz) butter or margarine

1 garlic clove, skinned and crushed

½ a red pepper, seeded and cut into strips

½ a yellow pepper, seeded and cut into strips

½ a green pepper, seeded and cut into strips

1 courgette, thinly sliced

50 g (2 oz) mange-tout, trimmed

1 large tomato, skinned, seeded and cut into strips

60 ml (4 tbsp) dry white wine

salt and pepper

fresh basil, to garnish

◆ Preheat a browning dish to maximum according to the manufacturer's instructions. Add the butter and garlic for the last 30 seconds of heating.

◆ Add the vegetables and stir. Microwave on HIGH for 2-3 minutes or until the vegetables are slightly softened.

◆ Stir in the white wine and season to taste with salt and pepper. Microwave on HIGH for 1 minute. Garnish with fresh basil and serve.

### ── GLAZED VEGETABLES PROVENÇAL ──

*The lightly cooked vegetables in this dish make a perfect accompaniment
for meat dishes. Shown here with Cucumber and onion mixed with
tarragon (page 142)*

SEE OPPOSITE

# CHICORY AND HAM AU GRATIN

SERVES 4 AS A MAIN DISH

| |
|---|
| 300 ml (½ pint) milk |
| 1 small onion, skinned and quartered |
| 1 small carrot, peeled and sliced |
| half a small celery stick, sliced |
| 2 cloves |
| 6 black peppercorns |
| 1 blade mace |
| 1 parsley sprig |
| 1 thyme sprig |
| 1 bay leaf |
| 25 g (1 oz) butter or margarine |
| 25 g (1 oz) plain flour |
| 4 even-sized heads chicory |
| 4 slices cooked ham |
| 50 g (2 oz) Cheddar cheese, grated |

◆ Combine the milk, onion, carrot, celery, cloves, peppercorns, mace and herbs in a large bowl. Cover the microwave on HIGH for 5 minutes or until boiling. Set aside to infuse for 30 minutes. Strain and discard vegetables, spices and herbs.

◆ Place the butter in a medium bowl and microwave on HIGH for 45 seconds or until the butter melts. Stir in the flour and microwave on HIGH for 30 seconds. Gradually whisk in the milk and microwave on HIGH for 2-3 minutes, whisking every 30 seconds, until the sauce has thickened.

◆ In a shallow flameproof dish, arrange the chicory in a single layer, add 60 ml (4 tbsp) water, cover and microwave on HIGH for 5-8 minutes or until tender. Drain well.

◆ Wrap each head of chicory in a slice of ham and place in the dish seam side down. Pour over the sauce and microwave on HIGH for 1 minute or until hot.

◆ Sprinkle with the cheese and grill under a hot grill until the cheese is golden. Serve with green salad, if liked.

# BROCCOLI WITH ALMONDS AND GARLIC

SERVES 4 AS AN ACCOMPANIMENT

| |
|---|
| 30 ml (2 tbsp) vegetable oil |
| 2 garlic cloves, skinned and crushed |
| 25 g (1 oz) flaked almonds |
| 700 g (1½ lb) broccoli, broken into small, even-sized florets |
| salt and pepper |

◆ Stir the oil, garlic and almonds together in a shallow dish large enough to hold the broccoli in a single layer. Microwave on HIGH for 2 minutes.

◆ Add the broccoli and stir until coated in the oil. Three-quarters cover with cling film and microwave on HIGH for 7 minutes or until the broccoli is tender. Stir twice during the cooking time. Season to taste with salt and pepper and serve at once.

# STUFFED COURGETTES

SERVES 4 AS A MAIN DISH

| |
|---|
| 6 medium courgettes |
| 50 g (2 oz) butter or margarine |
| 1 medium onion, skinned and chopped |
| 198 g (7 oz) can sweetcorn, drained |
| 100 g (4 oz) peeled prawns |
| 30 ml (2 level tbsp) plain flour |
| 300 ml (½ pint) milk |
| 150 g (5 oz) Cheddar cheese, grated |
| salt and pepper |

◆ Place the courgettes in a polythene bag with 60 ml (4 tbsp) water. Loosely seal the bag with an elastic band. Microwave on HIGH for 6 minutes.

◆ Drain the courgettes, then cut a thin slice off the top of each lengthways and scoop out the flesh, leaving a 0.5 cm (¼ inch) rim around the edge. Roughly chop the flesh including the top slices. Arrange the courgette shells in a large shallow heatproof dish.

◆ Place half of the butter in a large ovenproof glass bowl and microwave on HIGH for 30 seconds or until the butter melts. Add the onion and microwave on HIGH for 5-7 minutes or until the onion is soft.

◆ Stir in the chopped courgette and microwave on HIGH for 6 minutes or until soft, stirring occasionally. Add the sweetcorn and prawns.

◆ Spoon the mixture into the courgette shells spreading any excess over the top.

◆ Place the remaining butter in a large ovenproof glass bowl and microwave on HIGH for 30 seconds or until the butter melts. Next, stir in the flour and microwave on HIGH for 1 minute.

◆ Gradually whisk in the milk and microwave on HIGH for 3 minutes or until the sauce has thickened, whisking occasionally. Stir in three-quarters of the grated cheese,

◆ Pour the sauce over the stuffed courgettes and microwave on HIGH for 3 minutes or until the courgettes are heated through. Season well with salt and pepper.

◆ Sprinkle with the remaining cheese and microwave on HIGH for 1-2 minutes or until the cheese is melted.

## COURGETTES WITH TOMATOES AND CHEESE

SERVES 4 AS AN ACCOMPANIMENT
OR 2 AS A MAIN DISH

*15 g (½ oz) butter or margarine*

*1 shallot or small onion, skinned and chopped*

*1 garlic clove, skinned and crushed*

*450 g (1 lb) courgettes, trimmed and thickly sliced*

*450 g (1 lb) tomatoes, skinned, halved and quartered*

*100 g (4 oz) Cheddar cheese, grated*

*salt and pepper*

◆ Put the butter into a medium ovenproof glass bowl and microwave on HIGH for 30 seconds or until the butter melts. Stir in the onions and garlic and microwave on HIGH for 2 minutes.
◆ Mix the courgettes into the onions and three-quarters cover the vegetables with cling film. Microwave on HIGH for about 5 minutes until the courgettes are almost cooked, stirring two or three times during the cooking time.
◆ Stir the sliced tomatoes into the courgettes and continue to microwave on HIGH for 2 minutes until the tomatoes are soft.
◆ Arrange the vegetables and cheese in layers in a shallow ovenproof serving dish, ending with a layer of cheese. Season with salt and pepper. Microwave on HIGH for 3-4 minutes until the cheese melts. Brown the top under a hot grill and serve immediately.

## CABBAGE WITH SOURED CREAM AND CARAWAY

SERVES 4 AS AN ACCOMPANIMENT

*700 g (1½ lb) cabbage*

*25 g (1 oz) butter or margarine*

*10 ml (2 level tsp) caraway seeds*

*150 ml (¼ pint) soured cream*

*salt and pepper*

◆ Finely shred the cabbage, discarding any tough stalks.
◆ Place the butter in a medium casserole and microwave on HIGH for 45 seconds or until the butter melts. Add the cabbage and the caraway seeds and mix together well.
◆ Three-quarters cover with cling film and microwave on HIGH for 7 minutes, stirring twice.

◆ Stir in the soured cream and microwave on HIGH for 1 minute. Season and serve hot.

## LEEK AND BACON HOT-POT

SERVES 4 AS A MAIN DISH

*450 g (1 lb) potatoes, peeled and thickly sliced*

*700 g (1½ lb) leeks, trimmed and thinly sliced*

*90 g (3½ oz) butter or margarine*

*175 g (6 oz) streaky bacon, rinded*

*40 g (1½ oz) plain flour*

*450 ml (¾ pint) milk*

*175 g (6 oz) Cheddar cheese, grated*

*5 ml (1 level tsp) mustard powder*

*salt and pepper*

*25 g (1 oz) fresh breadcrumbs*

◆ Put the potatoes into a large ovenproof glass bowl with 60 ml (4 tbsp) water, three-quarters cover with cling film and microwave on HIGH for 8-10 minutes or until the potatoes are tender but not mushy; drain them well.
◆ Put the sliced leeks into a large ovenproof bowl and dot them with 25 g (1 oz) of the butter. Three-quarters cover with cling film and microwave on HIGH for 8-10 minutes or until the leeks are soft, stirring them once or twice during the cooking time.
◆ Place the bacon on a large plate lined with absorbent kitchen paper, and cover it with a layer of paper. Microwave on HIGH for 4-4½ minutes or until the bacon is cooked.
◆ Place the remaining butter in an ovenproof glass bowl and microwave on HIGH for 45 seconds or until it is melted, stir in the flour and microwave on HIGH for 45 seconds.
◆ Gradually stir the milk into the roux, then microwave on HIGH for 1 minute. Whisk well and then microwave on HIGH for 2-3 minutes or until the sauce is boiling and thickened, whisking every 30 seconds.
◆ Add 100 g (4 oz) of the cheese and the mustard to the sauce and stir until the cheese melts. Season the sauce with salt and pepper, then stir in the leeks.
◆ Arrange the potatoes in the bottom of a buttered, shallow ovenproof dish and arrange the bacon on the top. Pour the leek mixture over the bacon.
◆ Mix the remaining cheese with the breadcrumbs and sprinkle this over the top of the hot-pot. Microwave on HIGH for 5-6 minutes to heat through the hot-pot, then brown the top under a hot grill.

# RUNNER BEANS PROVENCAL

## SERVES 4-6 AS AN ACCOMPANIMENT

---

*30 ml (2 tbsp) olive oil*

*1 medium onion, skinned and chopped*

*1 garlic clove, skinned and crushed*

*397 g (14 oz) can tomatoes, drained*

*salt and pepper*

*700 g (1½ lb) runner or French beans, topped, tailed and cut into 5 cm (2 inch) lengths*

*15 ml (1 tbsp) chopped fresh basil*

*chopped fresh parsley or basil, to garnish*

---

◆ Put the oil into an ovenproof glass bowl with the onion and garlic and mix well. Cover with cling film, pulling back one corner to allow the steam to escape. Microwave on HIGH for 5-10 minutes or until the onion is softened.

◆ Stir the tomatoes, salt and pepper into the onions. Microwave on HIGH for 5-6 minutes or until the tomatoes are very soft and have formed a thick purée, stirring frequently. Set them aside.

◆ Put the beans into an ovenproof glass bowl with 90 ml (6 tbsp) water. Three-quarters cover the beans with cling film and microwave on HIGH for 12-14 minutes or until the beans are tender but still crisp, stirring them frequently. Allow them to stand for 3 minutes and then drain them well.

◆ Stir the tomato mixture and basil into the beans and then spoon them into an ovenproof serving dish. Cover and microwave on HIGH for 1 minute. Season with salt and pepper. Serve the beans sprinkled with parsley or basil.

# OKRA WITH COCONUT

## SERVES 4 AS AN ACCOMPANIMENT

---

*450 g (1 lb) okra*

*30 ml (2 tbsp) light sesame or vegetable oil*

*2.5 ml (½ level tsp) white mustard seeds*

*2 medium onions, skinned and thickly sliced*

*5 ml (1 level tsp) paprika*

*2.5 ml (½ level tsp) ground coriander*

*1.25 ml (¼ level tsp) cayenne pepper*

*50 g (2 oz) fresh grated or desiccated coconut*

*15 ml (1 tbsp) finely chopped fresh coriander leaves*

*salt and pepper*

---

◆ Cut off the stalk ends from the okra. Wash the okra under cold running water and dry it thoroughly.

◆ Put the oil into a shallow casserole dish and microwave on HIGH for 2 minutes or until the oil is hot, then sprinkle in the sesame seeds and stir in the onions. Cover with a lid or with cling film, pulling back one corner to allow the steam to escape.

◆ Microwave the onions on HIGH for 5-7 minutes or until they are softened, then stir in the okra and the remaining ingredients.

◆ Cover the dish with a lid or three-quarters cover with cling film. Microwave on HIGH for 6-8 minutes or until the okra is tender but still retains its shape, stirring two or three times during the cooking time. Season with salt and pepper. Serve hot.

# SPICY CAULIFLOWER WITH YOGURT

## SERVES 4-6 AS AN ACCOMPANIMENT

---

*30 ml (2 tbsp) vegetable oil*

*5 ml (1 level tsp) medium curry powder*

*2.5 ml (½ level tsp) mustard powder*

*2.5 ml (½ level tsp) ground turmeric*

*pinch of cayenne pepper*

*1 onion, skinned and finely chopped*

*1 large cauliflower, trimmed and broken into tiny florets*

*1 cooking apple, peeled, cored and chopped*

*100 g (4 oz) frozen peas*

*150 ml (¼ pint) natural yogurt*

*10 ml (2 tsp) cornflour*

*salt and pepper*

---

◆ Place the oil, curry pepper, mustard, turmeric, cayenne pepper and onion in a large bowl and microwave on HIGH for 5-7 minutes or until the onion has softened, stirring occasionally.

◆ Add the cauliflower and apple, cover with cling film, pulling back one corner to allow the steam to escape, and microwave on HIGH for 10-12 minutes until just tender.

◆ Stir in the peas. Then gradually blend the yogurt into the cornflour and stir into the cauliflower mixture.

◆ Microwave on HIGH for 2 minutes until the vegetables are heated through. Season well with salt and pepper.

—— SPICY CAULIFLOWER WITH YOGURT ——

*An Eastern presentation of cauliflower, ideal with plain meat, fish, or curry dishes*

SEE OPPOSITE

## CREAMED CARROTS AND PARSNIPS

SERVES 4 AS AN ACCOMPANIMENT

*900 g (2 lb) carrots, peeled and sliced*

*450 g (1 lb) parsnips, peeled and cut into quarters, core removed, and sliced*

*50 g (2 oz) butter or margarine*

*pinch of grated nutmeg*

*salt and pepper*

*chopped fresh parsley, to garnish*

◆ Put the carrots and the parsnips into a large ovenproof bowl and add 150 ml (¼ pint) water. Three-quarters cover with cling film and microwave on HIGH for 20-30 minutes or until the vegetables are cooked, stirring frequently. Allow them to stand for 3 minutes, then drain very well.

◆ Mash the carrots and the parsnips with a potato masher, beat in the butter and season well with nutmeg.

◆ Spoon the mixture into an ovenproof serving dish and loosely cover with cling film. Microwave on HIGH for 2-3 minutes to heat through the mixture. Season with salt and pepper. Garnish it with parsley and serve.

## RED CABBAGE BRAISED WITH ORANGE

SERVES 4-6 AS AN ACCOMPANIMENT

*25 g (1 oz) butter or margarine*

*1 medium onion, skinned and finely chopped*

*450 g (1 lb) red cabbage, trimmed and very finely shredded*

*grated rind and juice of 2 oranges*

*15 ml (1 level tbsp) demerara sugar*

*10 ml (2 tsp) lemon juice*

*15 ml (1 tbsp) red wine vinegar*

*75 ml (3 fl oz) chicken stock*

*salt and pepper*

◆ Put the butter into a large bowl and microwave on HIGH for 45 seconds or until the butter melts. Stir in the onion and microwave on HIGH for 5-7 minutes or until the onion is softened.

◆ Add the cabbage, orange rind and juice, sugar, lemon juice, vinegar, stock, salt and pepper and stir together well.

◆ Re-cover and microwave on HIGH for 15-20 minutes or until the cabbage is tender.

## SLICED POTATOES WITH MUSTARD

SERVES 6 AS AN ACCOMPANIMENT

*25 g (1 oz) butter or margarine*

*1 large onion, skinned and sliced*

*900 g (2 lb) potatoes, peeled and thinly sliced*

*150 ml (¼ pint) single cream*

*15 ml (1 level tbsp) wholegrain mustard*

*salt and pepper*

◆ Place the butter in a shallow flameproof dish and microwave on HIGH for 45 seconds or until the butter melts. Add the onion and microwave on HIGH for 3 minutes or until the onion begins to soften. Add the potato slices and toss to combine with the onion.

◆ Whisk the cream and mustard together. Season to taste with salt and pepper and add to the potatoes. Three-quarters cover with cling film and microwave on HIGH for 15 minutes or until the potatoes are tender. Leave to stand for 5 minutes, then remove the cling film.

◆ Brown under a hot grill, if liked, and serve hot.

## VEGETABLE CURRY

SERVES 6 AS A MAIN DISH

*450 g (1 lb) cauliflower, broken into florets*

*50 g (2 oz) butter or margarine*

*1 medium onion, skinned and chopped*

*15-30 ml (1-2 level tbsp) curry paste*

*30 ml (2 tbsp) tomato purée*

*90 ml (6 level tbsp) plain flour*

*15 ml (1 level tbsp) sugar*

*600 ml (1 pint) boiling chicken stock*

*450 g (1 lb) courgettes, trimmed and sliced*

*425 g (15 oz) can chick-peas, drained*

*cooked rice, to serve*

◆ Place the cauliflower in a medium bowl with 45 ml (3 tbsp) water. Cover and microwave on HIGH for 3 minutes. Leave to stand, covered.

◆ Place the butter in a large casserole and microwave on HIGH for 45 seconds or until the butter melts. Add the onion and microwave on HIGH for 5-7 minutes or until the onion has softened.

◆ Add the curry paste, tomato purée, flour and sugar and microwave on HIGH for 30 seconds. Gradually blend in the stock and microwave on HIGH for 3 minutes or until boiling and thickened, stirring once or twice.

◆ Fold in the courgettes and drained cauliflower. Cover and microwave on HIGH for 8 minutes, stirring once. Add the chick-peas and microwave on HIGH for 2 minutes. Serve with cooked rice.

## VEGETABLE HOT-POT

### SERVES 4-6 AS A MAIN DISH

| |
|---|
| 450 g (1 lb) potatoes, peeled and very thinly sliced |
| 450 g (1 lb) carrots, peeled and very thinly sliced |
| 2 leeks, trimmed and thinly sliced |
| 1 large onion, skinned and thinly sliced |
| 2 celery sticks, trimmed and thinly sliced |
| 2.5 ml (½ tsp) fresh chopped thyme or 1.25 ml (¼ level tsp) dried |
| 1 bay leaf |
| 300 ml (½ pint) boiling chicken stock |
| 10 ml (2 tsp) tomato purée |
| salt and pepper |
| 432 g (15 oz) can red kidney beans, drained and rinsed |
| 50 g (2 oz) butter or margarine |
| 75 g (3 oz) fresh breadcrumbs |
| 75 g (3 oz) rolled oats |
| 175 g (6 oz) Cheddar cheese, grated |

◆ Put the potatoes, carrots, leeks, onion, celery, thyme and bay leaf in a large casserole and mix thoroughly.

◆ Blend the chicken stock and tomato purée together, pour over the vegetables and season well with salt and pepper.

◆ Three-quarters cover with a lid or cling film and microwave on HIGH for 15-20 minutes or until the vegetables are tender, stirring occasionally. Stir in the kidney beans and set aside.

◆ Put the butter in a shallow dish and microwave on HIGH for 45 seconds or until the butter melts.

◆ Stir in the breadcrumbs and oats and mix well together. Microwave on HIGH for 1-2 minutes or until the breadcrumbs and oats are slightly brown. Stir in the cheese.

◆ Spoon the cheese mixture evenly over the vegetables and microwave on HIGH for 2 minutes or until the vegetables are hot. Brown under a hot grill, if liked.

## LEEKS IN TOMATO AND BASIL SAUCE

### SERVES 4 AS AN ACCOMPANIMENT

| |
|---|
| 30 ml (2 tbsp) olive oil |
| 1 garlic clove, skinned and crushed |
| 450 g (1 lb) large 'continental' tomatoes, skinned and coarsely chopped |
| 15 ml (1 level tbsp) soft dark brown sugar |
| 30 ml (2 tbsp) chopped fresh basil |
| salt and pepper |
| 450 g (1 lb) leeks, trimmed and thickly sliced |
| fresh basil, to garnish |

◆ Place the oil and garlic in a large bowl and microwave on HIGH for 2 minutes. Add the tomatoes, sugar, chopped basil and seasoning.

◆ Three-quarters cover with cling film and microwave on HIGH for 10 minutes or until the sauce has thickened, stirring twice.

◆ Add the leeks and stir well. Microwave on HIGH for 8 minutes or until the leeks are tender. Garnish with basil leaves and serve.

## CAULIFLOWER CHEESE

### SERVES 4 AS A MAIN DISH

| |
|---|
| 1 cauliflower, about 700 g (1½ lb), broken into florets |
| 25 g (1 oz) butter or margarine |
| 25 g (1 oz) plain flour |
| 300 ml (½ pint) milk |
| pinch of mustard powder |
| salt and pepper |
| 75 g (3 oz) Cheddar cheese, grated |

◆ Place the cauliflower in a large bowl with 60 ml (4 tbsp) water. Three-quarters cover and microwave on HIGH for 10-12 minutes or until just tender. Drain and place in a 1.1 litre (2 pint) serving dish.

◆ To make the sauce, put the butter, flour milk, mustard, salt and pepper in a medium bowl and blend well.

◆ Microwave on HIGH for about 4 minutes or until the sauce has boiled and thickened, whisking every minute. Whisk until smooth then stir in the grated cheese and pour over the cauliflower.

◆ Microwave on HIGH for 3-5 minutes or until the cauliflower cheese is heated through. Leave to stand for 2-3 minutes before serving.

## VEGETABLES WITH GINGER AND CASHEW NUTS

SERVES 2 AS AN ACCOMPANIMENT

| |
|---|
| 15 ml (1 tbsp) vegetable oil |
| 1 cm (½ inch) piece of fresh root ginger, peeled and grated |
| pinch of cayenne pepper |
| 25 g (1 oz) unsalted cashew nuts |
| 5 ml (1 level tsp) soft brown sugar |
| 15 ml (1 tbsp) soy sauce |
| 1 small red pepper, seeded and cut into 5 cm (2 inch) strips |
| 100 g (4 oz) button mushrooms, halved |
| 100 g (4 oz) beansprouts |
| salt and pepper |

◆ Put the oil, ginger, cayenne pepper and the cashew nuts in a medium bowl and microwave on HIGH for 3–4 minutes, or until lightly browned, stirring frequently.

◆ Remove the cashews from the oil with a slotted spoon and set aside. Stir in the remaining ingredients and mix together well.

◆ Microwave on HIGH for 3–4 minutes, or until the vegetables are just tender, stirring occasionally. Season with salt and pepper, sprinkle with the cashew nuts and serve hot.

## BROCCOLI WITH LEMON

SERVES 4 AS AN ACCOMPANIMENT

| |
|---|
| 700 g (1½ lb) broccoli, trimmed |
| 15 ml (1 tbsp) vegetable oil |
| 1 small onion, skinned and finely chopped |
| 1 garlic clove, skinned and crushed (optional) |
| grated rind and juice of 1 lemon |
| 150 ml (¼ pint) chicken stock |
| 1.25 ml (¼ level tsp) salt |

◆ Cut off the flower heads from the broccoli and divide them into small florets. Thinly peel the stalks and cut them into 0.5 cm (¼ inch) slices.

◆ Put the oil, onion and garlic into a casserole and mix them well. Cover with a lid or with cling film, pulling back one corner to allow steam to escape. Microwave on HIGH for 4–5 minutes until the onion softens.

◆ Place the prepared broccoli on top of the onion and sprinkle it with the lemon rind and juice. Pour in the stock.

◆ Cover with a lid or cling film, pulling back one corner to allow steam to escape. Microwave on HIGH for 7–8 minutes, carefully turning and repositioning the sprigs halfway through the cooking time. Season with salt.

## BRAISED CELERY

SERVES 4 AS AN ACCOMPANIMENT

| |
|---|
| 2 small heads celery, washed, trimmed and halved |
| 50 g (2 oz) butter or margarine |
| 1 large carrot, peeled and chopped |
| 1 medium onion, skinned and chopped |
| bouquet garni |
| 600 ml (1 pint) chicken stock |
| 45 ml (3 level tbsp) flour |
| salt and pepper |

◆ Remove the outer stalks and trim the tops off the celery heads. Reserve a few leaves as a garnish.

◆ Put 25 g (1 oz) of the butter into a shallow ovenproof dish large enough to take the celery heads in a single layer. Microwave the butter on HIGH for 45 seconds until it is melted.

◆ Stir the carrot and onion into the melted butter and cover them with cling film, pulling back one corner to allow steam to escape. Microwave on HIGH for 7 minutes until the vegetables are softened.

◆ Place the celery heads on top of the carrot and onion, add the bouquet garni and pour in the chicken stock. Cover with cling film, pulling back one corner to vent. Microwave on HIGH for 10–15 minutes until the celery heads are tender, turning them and changing their position twice during the cooking time.

◆ Carefully remove the celery and keep it warm in a heated serving dish. Reserve 450 ml (¾ pint). Discard the bouquet garni.

◆ Put the remaining butter in an ovenproof glass bowl and microwave on HIGH for 1 minute until it is melted; stir in the flour and microwave on HIGH for 1 minute. Gradually stir in the stock and microwave on HIGH for 45 seconds, then whisk well. Microwave on HIGH for 2–3 minutes until the sauce boils and thickens, whisking every 30 seconds.

◆ Pour the sauce over the celery and microwave on HIGH for 1 minute to heat it through. Season with salt and pepper. Serve the celery garnished with the reserved celery leaves.

—— LENTIL, MINT AND YOGURT SALAD ——

*An easily made, tasty salad, flavoured with allspice and mint*

SEE PAGE 143

## CUCUMBER WITH ONION AND TARRAGON

SERVES 4 AS AN ACCOMPANIMENT

*1 cucumber*

*salt and pepper*

*15 g (½ oz) butter or margarine*

*30 ml (2 tbsp) chopped fresh tarragon*

*1 bunch spring onions, trimmed and sliced*

*tarragon sprigs, to garnish*

◆ Using a sharp knife or a canelle knife, remove thin strips of skin evenly from all round the cucumber, to make a striped pattern. Quarter the cucumber lengthways and cut into 5 cm (2 inch) chunks. Place in a colander and sprinkle liberally with salt. Leave for 20 minutes, then drain and pat dry with absorbent kitchen paper.

◆ Put the cucumber, butter and tarragon into a large bowl and three-quarters cover with cling film. Microwave on HIGH for 1 minute, then add the spring onions and microwave on HIGH for 2 minutes or until the vegetables are tender. Garnish with fresh tarragon.

## STUFFED AUBERGINES

SERVES 4 AS A MAIN DISH

*2 medium aubergines*

*30 ml (2 tbsp) olive oil*

*15 ml (1 tbsp) chopped fresh parsley*

*15 ml (1 tbsp) snipped fresh chives*

*1 garlic clove, skinned and crushed*

*175 g (6 oz) button mushrooms, chopped*

*1 green pepper, cored, seeded and chopped*

*salt and pepper*

*50 g (2 oz) fresh breadcrumbs*

*15 g (½ oz) walnuts, finely chopped*

*25 g (1 oz) Cheddar cheese, grated*

◆ Cut the aubergines in half lengthways. Scoop out the insides and coarsely chop the flesh. Reserve the shells.

◆ In a medium bowl, combine the chopped aubergine with 15 ml (1 tbsp) oil, the herbs, garlic, mushrooms and green pepper. Season to taste. Microwave on HIGH for 6-7 minutes until vegetables are slightly softened, stirring occasionally.

◆ Spoon the aubergine mixture into the reserved shells and level the surface. Place in a flameproof dish, brush all over with the remaining oil and cover. Microwave on HIGH for 6-8 minutes or until the aubergines are tender.

◆ Mix the breadcrumbs, walnuts and cheese together and sprinkle over the aubergines. Place under a hot grill until browned on top. Serve with a green salad and wholemeal rolls, if liked.

## NUT CUTLETS

SERVES 4 AS A MAIN DISH

*40 g (1½ oz) butter or margarine*

*15 g (½ oz) plain flour*

*150 ml (¼ pint) milk*

*1 small onion, skinned and finely chopped*

*1 garlic clove, skinned and crushed*

*50 g (2 oz) mushrooms, chopped*

*50 g (2 oz) fresh brown breadcrumbs*

*75 g (3 oz) Cheddar cheese, grated*

*50 g (2 oz) salted peanuts, finely chopped*

*50 g (2 oz) shelled Brazil nuts, finely chopped*

*1.25 ml (¼ level tsp) vegetable extract*

*salt, pepper and lemon juice, to taste*

*15 ml (1 tbsp) chopped fresh parsley*

◆ Put 15 g (½ oz) of the butter into an ovenproof glass bowl and microwave on HIGH for 30 seconds or until the butter melts. Stir in the flour and microwave on HIGH for 30 seconds.

◆ Gradually stir the milk into the roux. Microwave on HIGH for 30 seconds, then whisk well. Microwave for 1 minute on HIGH, or until the sauce boils and thickens, whisking once. Cover the surface of the sauce with cling film to prevent a skin forming. Set aside.

◆ Put the remaining butter into an ovenproof dish and microwave on HIGH for 30 seconds or until the butter melts. Stir in the onion, garlic and mushrooms. Three-quarters cover with cling film and microwave on HIGH for 4-5 minutes until the vegetables have softened, stirring once.

◆ Stir the breadcrumbs into the onion and mushrooms, then add them and all the remaining ingredients to the thick sauce, mixing together well.

◆ Shape the mixture into a long roll about 18 cm (7 inches) long, then cut the roll into 8 even-sized pieces. Shape each piece into a neat round.

◆ Arrange 4 cutlets in a circle on a large, flat ovenproof plate lined with absorbent kitchen paper and microwave on HIGH for 4 minutes, turning them over halfway during the cooking time. Repeat with the remaining cutlets. Drain on absorbent kitchen paper and serve with baked potatoes and salad, if liked.

## LENTIL, MINT AND YOGURT SALAD

SERVES 2 AS AN ACCOMPANIMENT

*100 g (4 oz) green lentils*

*bouquet garni*

*60 ml (4 tbsp) olive or vegetable oil*

*30 ml (2 tbsp) lemon juice*

*large pinch of ground allspice*

*salt and pepper*

*45 ml (3 tbsp) chopped fresh mint*

*3 spring onions, trimmed and chopped*

*3 large tomatoes, skinned and cut into small wedges*

*30 ml (2 tbsp) Greek strained yogurt*

*lemon wedges and mint sprigs, to garnish*

◆ Put the lentils into a large bowl and pour over 900 ml (1½ pints) boiling water. Add the bouquet garni and cover with cling film, pulling back one corner to allow the steam to escape. Microwave on HIGH for 10-12 minutes or until the lentils are just tender.

◆ Meanwhile, mix together the olive oil and lemon juice and season with allspice, salt and pepper. Stir in the mint.

◆ Drain the lentils and stir in the dressing. Chill in the refrigerator for about 30 minutes

◆ Stir the onions and tomatoes into the lentils and mix together well. Stir in the yogurt. Season if necessary. Serve chilled, garnished with lemon wedges and mint sprigs.

## MIXED VEGETABLES JULIENNE

SERVES 2 AS AN ACCOMPANIMENT

*2 spring onions, trimmed*

*2 medium carrots, peeled*

*1 large courgette, trimmed*

*1 small red, green or yellow pepper, cored and seeded*

*15 g (½ oz) butter or margarine, cut into pieces*

*5 ml (1 tsp) chopped fresh oregano or 2.5 ml (½ level tsp) dried*

*2.5 ml (½ tsp) lemon juice*

*salt and pepper*

◆ Cut the vegetables into neat strips 5 cm (2 inches) long and 0.5 cm (¼ inch) wide.

◆ Put the butter into a medium ovenproof serving dish and microwave on HIGH for 30 seconds or until the butter melts.

◆ Stir in the vegetables, oregano, lemon juice, salt and pepper and mix together. Cover with cling film, pulling back one corner to allow the steam to escape, and microwave on HIGH for 2-3 minutes or until the vegetables are just tender. Serve immediately.

## DHAL

SERVES 4 AS AN ACCOMPANIMENT

*30 ml (2 tbsp) vegetable oil*

*1 medium onion, skinned and finely chopped*

*3 garlic cloves, skinned and crushed*

*1 green chilli, seeded and thinly sliced*

*100 g (4 oz) red lentils*

*600 ml (1 pint) boiling chicken stock*

*5 ml (1 level tsp) salt*

*1.25 ml (¼ level tsp) ground turmeric*

*1.25 ml (¼ level tsp) chilli powder*

*1.25 ml (¼ level tsp) ground cumin*

*fresh coriander, to garnish*

◆ Place the oil, onion, garlic and chilli in a large bowl and microwave on HIGH for 5-7 minutes or until the onion is softened, stirring once.

◆ Stir in the lentils, stock, salt and spices. Cover and microwave on HIGH for 20 minutes, stirring once.

◆ Beat well with a wooden spoon or, for a smoother texture, liquidise in a blender or food processor. Garnish with fresh coriander and serve.

## MINTED CARROTS AND
—— BRUSSELS SPROUTS ——

*The textures of these two vegetables complement each other well. Shown
here with an Okra and coconut dish (page 136)*

SEE OPPOSITE

## MINTED CARROTS AND BRUSSELS SPROUTS

SERVES 4 AS AN ACCOMPANIMENT

| |
|---|
| 450 g (1 lb) Brussels sprouts, trimmed |
| 225 g (8 oz) carrots, peeled and sliced |
| 50 g (2 oz) butter or margarine |
| 30 ml (2 tbsp) chopped fresh mint |
| salt and pepper |

◆ Put the sprouts and carrots in a large casserole. Add 45 ml (3 tbsp) water and three-quarters cover with cling film. Microwave on HIGH for 9-12 minutes or until tender. Shake the casserole once during the cooking time.
◆ Drain the vegetables and return to the casserole.
◆ Place the butter and mint in a small measuring jug and microwave on HIGH for 1 minute or until the butter is melted and foaming. Pour the butter over the vegetables and toss until well coated.
◆ Microwave on HIGH for 1 minute to reheat if necessary. Season to taste with salt and pepper and serve.

## SPINACH AND POTATO BAKE

SERVES 4 AS AN ACCOMPANIMENT

| |
|---|
| 700 g (1½ lb) potatoes, peeled and thinly sliced |
| 25 g (1 oz) butter or margarine |
| 60 ml (4 tbsp) double cream |
| pinch of grated nutmeg |
| salt and pepper |
| 450 g (1 lb) fresh spinach, trimmed and finely chopped |
| 45 ml (3 level tbsp) fresh breadcrumbs |
| 45 ml (3 level tbsp) grated Parmesan cheese |

◆ Place the potatoes and half the butter in a shallow flameproof dish. Microwave on HIGH for 5 minutes, stirring twice.
◆ Stir in the cream, nutmeg and seasoning. Spread the spinach evenly over the top of the potatoes.
◆ Cover and microwave on HIGH for 12 minutes or until the potatoes are tender. Give the dish a half-turn once during cooking. Leave to stand for 5 minutes.
◆ Mix the breadcrumbs and cheese together and sprinkle the mixture over the spinach. Dot with the remaining butter or margarine. Brown under a hot grill.

## BRUSSELS SPROUTS WITH HAZELNUT BUTTER

SERVES 2 AS AN ACCOMPANIMENT

| |
|---|
| 25 g (1 oz) hazelnuts |
| 1 shallot or ½ small onion, skinned and finely chopped |
| 25 g (1 oz) butter or margarine |
| salt and pepper |
| large pinch of ground cumin |
| 225 g (8 oz) small Brussels sprouts, trimmed |

◆ Spread the hazelnuts out evenly on a large flat plate and microwave on HIGH for 2-3 minutes or until the skins 'pop', stirring occasionally. Rub the skins off, using a clean teatowel, and chop the nut finely.
◆ Put the shallot and the butter in a medium bowl and microwave on HIGH for 3-4 minutes or until the shallot is softened, stirring occasionally.
◆ Stir in the hazelnuts and season with salt, pepper and cumin. Microwave on HIGH for 1 minute, then stir in the Brussels sprouts.
◆ Cover with cling film, pulling back one corner to allow the steam to escape, and microwave on HIGH for 4-5 minutes or until the sprouts are just tender, stirring occasionally.

## CHINESE FRIED VEGETABLES

SERVES 4 AS A MAIN DISH

| |
|---|
| 2.5 cm (1 inch) piece of fresh root ginger, peeled and thinly sliced |
| 30 ml (2 tbsp) vegetable oil |
| 50 g (2 oz) mange-tout, trimmed |
| 50 g (2 oz) mushrooms, sliced |
| 75 g (3 oz) beansprouts |
| 227 g (8 oz) can sliced bamboo shoots, drained |
| 50 g (2 oz) cashew nuts |
| 15 ml (1 tbsp) soy sauce |
| pepper to taste |
| cooked rice, to serve |

◆ Place the thinly sliced ginger in a large shallow dish along with the oil. Microwave on HIGH for 1 minute to heat the oil.
◆ Stir in the mange-tout, mushrooms and beansprouts. Microwave on HIGH for 2 minutes, stirring once.
◆ Add the bamboo shoots, cashew nuts and soy sauce. Microwave on HIGH for 2 minutes or until the vegetables are hot. Season with pepper and serve with rice.

## CHICK-PEAS WITH TOMATOES AND CHILLI

SERVES 2 AS A MAIN DISH

30 ml (2 tbsp) vegetable oil, plus extra for brushing

1 medium onion, skinned and chopped

1 garlic clove, skinned and crushed

1 green chilli, seeded and finely chopped

1.25 ml (¼ level tsp) mild chilli powder

2.5 ml (½ level tsp) ground turmeric

2.5 ml (½ level tsp) paprika

2.5 ml (½ level tsp) ground cumin

5 ml (1 level tsp) ground coriander

3 tomatoes, skinned and coarsely chopped

425 g (15 oz) can chick-peas, drained

15 ml (1 tbsp) chopped fresh coriander

salt and pepper

4-6 poppadums, to serve

fresh coriander, to garnish

◆ Put the oil, onion, and garlic in a medium bowl and cover with cling film, pulling back one corner to allow the steam to escape. Microwave on HIGH for 5-7 minutes or until the onion is softened.

◆ Stir in the chilli, chilli powder, turmeric, paprika, cumin and ground coriander and microwave on HIGH for 1 minute, stirring once.

◆ Stir in the tomatoes and microwave on HIGH for 3-5 minutes or until the tomatoes reduce to a thick purée, stirring occasionally.

◆ Stir in the chick-peas, fresh coriander, salt and pepper. Re-cover and microwave on HIGH for 2-3 minutes, or until heated through, stirring occasionally.

◆ Brush one side of each poppadum lightly with oil. Stand, one at a time, oiled side up on absorbent kitchen paper in the microwave and cook on HIGH for 45 seconds to 1 minute until puffed all over. Leave to stand for 30 seconds.

◆ Garnish the chick-peas with coriander and serve with the poppadums.

## SPICY RED LENTILS WITH COCONUT

SERVES 2 AS AN ACCOMPANIMENT

15 ml (1 tbsp) vegetable oil

1 medium onion, skinned and finely chopped

1 garlic clove, skinned and crushed

1.25 ml (¼ level tsp) cayenne pepper

5 ml (1 level tsp) paprika

10 ml (2 level tsp) ground cumin

5 ml (1 level tsp) fennel seeds

75 g (3 oz) red split lentils

50 g (2 oz) creamed coconut

salt and pepper

15 ml (1 tbsp) chopped fresh coriander (optional)

15 ml (1 level tbsp) desiccated coconut

◆ Put the oil, onion and garlic in a large bowl and cover with cling film, pulling back one corner to allow the steam to escape. Microwave on HIGH for 5-7 minutes or until the onion is softened, stirring occasionally.

◆ Stir in the cayenne pepper, paprika, cumin and the fennel seeds and microwave on HIGH for 1-2 minutes stirring frequently. Stir in the lentils.

◆ Mix the creamed coconut with 450 ml (¾ pint) boiling water and stir until the coconut dissolves.

◆ Stir into the spice and lentil mixture. Mix well and microwave on HIGH for 10-15 minutes, stirring occasionally, until the lentils are tender. Add a little extra boiling water during cooking, if needed.

◆ Season with salt and pepper and stir in the coriander, if using. Leave to stand for 5 minutes.

◆ Meanwhile, put the desiccated coconut on a large flat plate and microwave on HIGH for 3-4 minutes or until it feels slightly crispy, stirring frequently.

◆ Reheat the lentils on HIGH for 1-1½ minutes or until warmed through, then turn into a warmed serving dish and sprinkle with the coconut.

# CURRIED CARROTS AND LENTILS

### SERVES 4 AS AN ACCOMPANIMENT

| |
|---|
| 25 g (1 oz) flaked almonds |
| 30 ml (2 tbsp) vegetable oil |
| 1 medium onion, skinned and very finely chopped |
| 225 g (8 oz) carrots, peeled and thinly sliced |
| 1 garlic clove, skinned and crushed |
| 1.25 ml (¼ level tsp) ground cumin |
| 1.25 ml (¼ level tsp) ground coriander |
| 1.25 ml (¼ level tsp) ground cinnamon |
| 175 g ( 6 oz) red lentils, rinsed and drained |
| salt and pepper |
| 1 litre (1¾ pints) boiling chicken stock |

◆ Place the almonds on a large ovenproof plate and microwave on HIGH for 8-10 minutes, stirring frequently until the almonds are brown, then reserve.
◆ Put the oil in a large ovenproof glass bowl and stir in the onion, carrots and garlic. Microwave on HIGH for 5-6 minutes, or until the vegetables soften. Stir them occasionally during cooking.
◆ Stir in the spices and lentils and then microwave on HIGH for 3 minutes, stirring occasionally.
◆ Add salt and pepper and the boiling stock and stir well. Microwave on HIGH for 25 minutes or until the lentils are just tender, stirring occasionally during cooking. Serve hot, garnished with the toasted almonds.

# VEGETABLE GOULASH

### SERVES 2

| |
|---|
| 30 ml (2 tbsp) vegetable oil |
| 1 medium onion, skinned and chopped |
| 1 small green pepper, seeded and chopped |
| 15 ml (1 tbsp) sweet paprika |
| 2.5 ml (½ tsp) caraway seeds |
| 30 ml (2 tbsp) medium oatmeal |
| 450 ml (¾ pint) tomato juice |
| 2 medium carrots |
| 2 medium courgettes |
| freshly grated nutmeg |
| salt and pepper |
| 30 ml (2 tbsp) soured cream or natural yogurt |
| chopped fresh parsley, to garnish |

◆ Put the oil, onion and pepper in a medium bowl. Cover with cling film, pulling back one corner to let steam escape, and microwave on HIGH for 5-7 minutes or until softened, stirring occasionally.
◆ Stir in the paprika and caraway seeds and microwave on HIGH for 1 minute. Stir in the oatmeal and gradually stir in the tomato juice.
◆ Cut the carrot into 0.5 cm (¼ in) slices and the courgette into 2.5 cm (1 inch) slices. Stir into the paprika mixture and mix well. Season with nutmeg and salt and pepper to taste.
◆ Re-cover and microwave on HIGH for 15-20 minutes or until the vegetables are tender. Serve with the soured cream or yogurt spooned on top, garnished with chopped parsley.

# PASTA & GRAINS

## ——— PASTA IN SOURED CREAM SAUCE ———

*The sour cream in this dish provides a less heavy sauce than the single
cream frequently used for pasta*

SEE PAGE 151

# Cooking Tips

◆

*Boil the water for cooking pasta and grains in a kettle to save time.*

◆

*Remove the pasta or grains from the oven when it is still slightly undercooked otherwise prolonged microwaving will cause it to become soggy. Part of the cooking occurs during the standing time.*

◆

*Pasta and grains should be covered and left to stand in their cooking liquid for 5-10 minutes, depending on the type of pasta shape. If you are making a sauce, do this during standing time.*

◆

*Frozen pasta and grains can be cooked directly from frozen on the HIGH setting unless combined with a sauce which might spoil or curdle.*

◆

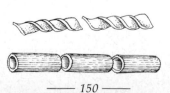

## PASTA IN SOURED CREAM SAUCE

### SERVES 4

| |
|---|
| 10 ml (2 tsp) vegetable oil |
| 350 g (12 oz) pasta shapes, such as cartwheels, twists or bows |
| 100 g (4 oz) butter or margarine |
| 2 shallots, skinned and chopped |
| 30 ml (2 level tbsp) plain flour |
| 150 ml (¼ pint) chicken stock |
| 150 ml (¼ pint) dry white wine |
| 150 ml (¼ pint) soured cream or natural yogurt |
| salt and pepper |
| 100 g (4 oz) button mushrooms, quartered |
| 100 g (4 oz) Cheddar cheese, grated |
| 50 g (2 oz) black olives |
| 200 g (7 oz) can tuna, drained |
| chopped fresh parsley, to garnish |

◆ Boil 2 litres (3½ pints) water in a kettle and pour into a 2.8 litre (5 pint) ovenproof glass bowl. Add 10 ml (2 level tsp) salt and half of the vegetable oil.

◆ Bring the water back to a full rolling boil in the microwave oven set on HIGH. Quickly lower the pasta into the water, stir once and cover with cling film. Microwave on HIGH for 7 minutes.

◆ Remove the bowl from the oven, leave the pasta to stand for 5 minutes until it is cooked firm to the bite. Drain well.

◆ Put 50 g (2 oz) of the butter into a large ovenproof serving dish and microwave on HIGH for 45 seconds until melted. Stir in the shallots and cover the bowl with cling film, pulling back one corner to allow the steam to escape. Microwave on HIGH for 4-5 minutes or until the shallots are soft.

◆ Stir the flour into the shallots and microwave on HIGH for 1 minute. Gradually stir in the stock and the wine and microwave on HIGH for 45 seconds, then whisk well. Microwave on HIGH for 2 minutes until the sauce is boiling and has thickened. Continue to microwave further on HIGH for 1 minute.

◆ Stir the soured cream and pasta into the sauce and season it well with salt and pepper. Add the mushrooms, cheese, olives and tuna and mix gently together.

◆ Cover with cling film and microwave on HIGH for 2 minutes or until hot. Serve immediately, garnished with parsley.

## TUNA AND TOMATO PASTA

### SERVES 4

| |
|---|
| 225 g (8 oz) pasta shapes, such as bows |
| salt and pepper |
| 45 ml (3 tbsp) vegetable oil |
| 2 medium onions, skinned and sliced |
| 1 garlic clove, skinned and crushed |
| 397 g (14 oz) can tomatoes, drained and chopped |
| 198 g (7 oz) can tuna, drained and flaked |
| 45 ml (3 tbsp) chopped fresh parsley |
| 150 ml (¼ pint) soured cream |
| For the topping: |
| 50 g (2 oz) can anchovies |
| 75 g (3 oz) fresh bread |
| 25 g (1 oz) butter or margarine |

◆ Place the pasta and salt to taste in a 2.6 litre (4½ pint) bowl. Pour over 1.4 litres (2½ pints) boiling water. Stir once, cover and microwave on HIGH for 7 minutes. Leave to stand, covered.

◆ Mix the oil, onion and garlic together in a medium bowl and microwave on HIGH for 5-7 minutes or until the onion is softened.

◆ Stir in the tomatoes and tuna and microwave on HIGH for 3 minutes until the sauce is bubbling. Add the parsley and season with pepper.

◆ Drain the pasta and return to the bowl. Pour over the tomato sauce and toss lightly together. Set aside.

◆ Drain the anchovy oil into a frying pan and place the bread and anchovies in a food processor or blender. Liquidise well.

◆ Heat the butter with the anchovy oil, add the anchovy crumbs and stir over a high heat until crisp.

◆ Spoon the soured cream over the pasta and gently mix in. Microwave on HIGH for 1 minute to heat through. Sprinkle with the anchovy crumbs and serve.

## Tagliatelle with Fresh Figs

*An imaginative combination of tastes, textures and colours is used
in this recipe*

SEE PAGE 156

## TAGLIATELLE WITH SMOKED HAM AND PEAS

### SERVES 4

225 g (8 oz) dried tagliatelle

salt and pepper

1 medium onion, skinned and thinly sliced

30 ml (2 tbsp) vegetable oil

100 g (4 oz) fresh shelled or frozen peas

225 g (8 oz) piece smoked ham

150 ml (¼ pint) double cream

50 g (2 oz) freshly grated Parmesan cheese

◆ Place the tagliatelle in a 2.6 litre (4½ pint) bowl and pour over 1.7 litres (3 pints) boiling water. Add salt to taste and stir once. Cover and microwave on HIGH for 7 minutes. Leave to stand, covered.
◆ Mix the onion and oil together in a medium bowl and microwave on HIGH for 2 minutes. Stir in the peas, cover and microwave on HIGH for 5 minutes or until the onion and peas are tender.
◆ Meanwhile, cut the ham into ribbons. Add to the onion and peas along with the cream. Season to taste with salt and pepper and microwave on HIGH for 3 minutes or until hot, stirring once or twice.
◆ Drain the pasta and tip into a warmed serving dish. Pour over the sauce and toss lightly. Sprinkle with the freshly grated Parmesan cheese and serve.

## HAM AND MUSHROOM BAKE

### SERVES 4

225 g (8 oz) pasta shapes, such as twirls, small shells or quills

salt and pepper

30 ml (2 tbsp) vegetable oil

2 medium onions, skinned and chopped

2 garlic cloves, skinned and crushed

225 g (8 oz) ham, diced

100 g (4 oz) button mushrooms

1 red pepper, cored, seeded and chopped

30 ml (2 level tbsp) plain flour

30 ml (2 tbsp) tomato purée

30 ml (2 tbsp) chopped fresh oregano or 15 ml (1 level tbsp) dried

397 g (14 oz) can chopped tomatoes

100 g (4 oz) Cheddar cheese, grated

◆ Place the pasta in a 2.6 litre (4½ pint) bowl and add 1.4 litre (2½ pints) boiling water. Add salt to taste and stir once. Cover and microwave on HIGH for 7 minutes. Leave to stand, covered.
◆ Mix the oil, onion and garlic together in a large flameproof casserole and microwave on HIGH for 5-7 minutes, or until the onion is softened, stirring once.
◆ Stir in the ham, mushrooms, red pepper, flour, tomato purée, oregano and tomatoes with their juice and season to taste with salt and pepper. Pour over 300 ml (½ pint) boiling water. Microwave on HIGH for 8 minutes, stirring once or twice.
◆ Drain the pasta and stir into the sauce. Microwave on HIGH for 5 minutes. Sprinkle with the cheese and brown under a hot grill.

## LEEK AND MACARONI AU GRATIN

### SERVES 4

125 g (4 oz) short-cut macaroni

salt and pepper

50 g (2 oz) butter or margarine

275 g (10 oz) leeks, trimmed and thinly sliced

50 g (2 oz) plain flour

568 ml (1 pint) milk

225 g (8 oz) Cheddar cheese, grated

25 g (1 oz) fresh breadcrumbs

◆ Place the macaroni in a medium bowl and pour over 900 ml (1½ pints) boiling water. Season with salt, cover and microwave on HIGH for 5 minutes. Leave to stand, covered.
◆ Microwave the butter in a medium flameproof casserole on HIGH for 45 seconds or until the butter melts. Stir in the leeks and microwave on HIGH for 5 minutes or until the leeks are soft.
◆ Stir in the flour and microwave on HIGH for 30 seconds. Gradually stir in the milk. Microwave on HIGH for 5 minutes or until the sauce boils and thickens, stirring occasionally. Stir in two thirds of the cheese and season to taste.
◆ Drain the pasta, add to the cheese sauce and mix lightly together.
◆ Combine the reserved cheese with the breadcrumbs and sprinkle evenly over the dish. Grill under a preheated grill until golden brown.

## MACARONI CHEESE

### SERVES 4

*100 g (4 oz) butter or margarine*

*225 g (8 oz) short-cut macaroni*

*1 small onion, skinned and finely chopped*

*½ green pepper, seeded and finely chopped*

*2.5 ml (½ level tsp) salt*

*1.25 ml (¼ level tsp) mustard powder*

*450 ml (¾ pint) boiling water*

*225 g (8 oz) Cheddar cheese, grated*

◆ Put the butter into a large casserole dish and microwave on HIGH for 1 minute or until the butter melts.

◆ Add the macaroni, onion and pepper to the butter and stir well. Cover the dish with a lid or three-quarters cover with cling film and microwave on HIGH for 4-5 minutes, stirring once or twice.

◆ Add the salt, mustard and water to the macaroni. Re-cover and microwave on HIGH for about 5 minutes or until the macaroni is almost cooked, stirring once.

◆ Remove the macaroni from the oven and cover it tightly. Leave to stand for 5 minutes, until the macaroni is completely cooked.

◆ Add the grated cheese to the macaroni and stir until the cheese melts. Serve immediately.

## TARRAGON EGG ON A PASTA NEST

*15 g (½ oz) butter or margarine*

*½ small onion, skinned and chopped*

*1 small garlic clove, skinned and crushed*

*60 ml (4 tbsp) double cream*

*2.5 ml (½ tsp) chopped fresh tarragon, or 1.25 ml (¼ level tsp) dried*

*salt and pepper*

*50 g (2 oz) green tagliatelle*

*1 egg*

*fresh tarragon, to garnish*

◆ Put the butter, onion and garlic in a small bowl and cover with cling film, pulling back one corner to allow the steam to escape. Microwave on HIGH for 3-4 minutes or until the onion is softened

◆ Stir in the cream, tarragon and lots of salt and pepper and microwave on HIGH for 1 minute. Set aside.

◆ Put the pasta into a medium bowl with salt to taste and pour over 600 ml (1 pint) boiling water. Cover with cling film, pulling back one corner to allow the steam to escape, and microwave on HIGH for 3-4 minutes or until the pasta is almost tender. Leave to stand, covered. Do not drain.

◆ Meanwhile, put 30 ml (2 tbsp) water and a large pinch of salt into a 150 ml (¼ pint) ramekin dish. Microwave on HIGH for 1 minute or until boiling.

◆ Break the egg into the ramekin and carefully prick the yolk with a cocktail stick or fine skewer.

◆ Cover loosely with cling film or a double thickness of greaseproof paper and microwave on MEDIUM for 1-1½ minutes or until the white is almost set. Leave to stand.

◆ Meanwhile, reheat the tarragon sauce on HIGH for 1-2 minutes, or until heated through.

◆ Drain the pasta and toss with half of the sauce. Season with salt and pepper. Arrange on a large serving plate to make a 'nest' for the egg.

◆ Drain the egg and put on top of the pasta. Spoon over the remaining sauce, garnish with fresh tarragon and serve immediately.

## SPAGHETTI WITH MUSSELS

### SERVES 4

*75 ml (5 tbsp) vegetable oil*

*1 garlic clove, skinned and crushed*

*60 ml (4 tbsp) chopped fresh parsley*

*397 g (14 oz) can tomatoes*

*15 ml (1 tbsp) red wine vinegar*

*salt and pepper*

*400 g (14 oz) spaghetti*

*450 g (1 lb) frozen shelled mussels, thawed*

◆ Mix 45 ml (3 tbsp) oil, the garlic and 30 ml (2 tbsp) parsley together in a medium bowl and microwave on HIGH for about 2 minutes or until the garlic is soft.

◆ Place the tomatoes and vinegar in a food processor or blender and liquidise until smooth. Add to the garlic and parsley and season to taste. Microwave on HIGH for 5 minutes.

◆ Place the pasta in a 2.6 litre (4½ pint) bowl. Pour over 1.7 litres (3 pints) boiling water, add salt to taste, cover and microwave on HIGH for 7 minutes. Leave to stand, covered.

◆ Rinse the mussels, removing any broken shell, and add to the sauce. Microwave on HIGH for 5 minutes, stirring once. Check that the mussels are heated through.

◆ Drain the pasta, tip into a heated serving bowl and toss with the remaining oil. Pour over the sauce and serve immediately, sprinkled with the reserved parsley.

# MACARONI WITH CHEESE AND GREEN PEPPER

### SERVES 2-3

| |
|---|
| *50 g (2 oz) butter or margarine, diced* |
| *1 small onion, skinned and finely chopped* |
| *½ green pepper, seeded and finely chopped* |
| *5 ml (1 tsp) prepared mustard* |
| *salt and pepper* |
| *225 g (8 oz) short-cut macaroni* |
| *225 g (8 oz) Cheddar cheese, grated* |
| *10 stuffed green olives, sliced (optional)* |

◆ Put the butter in a large bowl and microwave on HIGH for 45 seconds or until the butter melts. Stir in the onion and green pepper and three-quarters cover with cling film or a lid. Microwave on HIGH for 5-7 minutes or until the vegetables are softened, stirring occasionally.
◆ Stir in the mustard, salt and pepper and macaroni and mix together well. Pour 450 ml (¾ pint) boiling water over, cover and microwave on HIGH for 7 minutes.
◆ Stir in the cheese and the olives, if using, and leave to stand, covered, for 5 minutes.

# SPAGHETTI CARBONARA

### SERVES 4

| |
|---|
| *225 g (8 oz) spaghetti* |
| *salt and pepper* |
| *2 eggs* |
| *100 g (4 oz) Cheddar cheese, finely grated* |
| *45 ml (3 level tbsp) freshly grated Parmesan cheese* |
| *225 g (8 oz) streaky bacon, rinded and chopped* |
| *150 ml (¼ pint) double cream* |
| *chopped fresh parsley, to garnish* |
| *freshly grated Parmesan cheese, to serve* |

◆ Place the spaghetti in a 2.6 litre (4½ pint) bowl, pour over 1.4 litres (2½ pints) boiling water. Add salt to taste, and stir once. Cover and microwave on HIGH for 7 minutes. Leave to stand, covered.
◆ Beat together the eggs and cheeses. Place the bacon in a medium bowl, cover with absorbent kitchen paper, and microwave on HIGH for 5 minutes.
◆ Stir in the cream and season to taste. Microwave on HIGH for 2 minutes or until the cream is heated through.
◆ Drain the pasta and tip into a warmed serving dish. Pour over the egg and cheese mixture and mix well. Add the bacon and cream mixture. Mix well and sprinkle with parsley. Serve at once with Parmesan cheese.

# SEAFOOD PASTA

### SERVES 2

| |
|---|
| *25 g (1 oz) butter, cut into pieces* |
| *15 ml (1 tbsp) vegetable oil* |
| *6 medium fresh scallops, shelled* |
| *1 medium onion, skinned and finely chopped* |
| *1 small garlic clove, skinned and crushed* |
| *175 g (6 oz) fresh tagliatelle* |
| *salt and pepper* |
| *175 g (6 oz) peeled prawns* |
| *30 ml (2 tbsp) chopped fresh parsley* |
| *150 ml (¼ pint) soured cream* |
| *2 whole prawns, lemon or lime slices and parsley sprigs, to garnish* |

◆ Put the butter and oil in a medium bowl and microwave on HIGH for 45 seconds or until the butter melts.
◆ Pierce each scallop with the point of a knife and stir into the bowl. Cover with cling film, pulling back one corner to allow the steam to escape, and microwave on HIGH for 1 minute, turning once during cooking.
◆ Remove the scallops from the bowl. Separate the coral from the white flesh and cut the white part into slices.
◆ Add the onion and garlic to the fat remaining in the bowl and microwave on HIGH for 5-7 minutes, or until the onion is softened.
◆ Put the tagliatelle and salt to taste in a large bowl. Pour over 1.1 litre (2 pints) boiling water and microwave on HIGH for 3-4 minutes or until the pasta is almost tender, stirring frequently.
◆ Leave to stand for 2 minutes then drain and transfer to an ovenproof serving dish. Add the onion mixture, sliced scallops and corals, prawns, parsley, soured cream, salt and pepper.
◆ Toss gently together and microwave on HIGH for 2-3 minutes until the seafood pasta is hot. Serve immediately, garnished with the whole prawns, lemon or lime slices and parsley.

## PAPRIKA PASTA

### SERVES 4

*255 g (8 oz) pasta shapes, such as twirls*

*salt and pepper*

*75 g (3 oz) butter or margarine*

*2 medium onions, skinned and thinly sliced*

*150 ml (¼ pint) soured cream*

*15 ml (1 level tbsp) paprika*

◆ Place the pasta in a 2.6 litre (4½ pint) bowl and pour over 1.4 litres (2½ pints) boiling water. Add salt to taste, stir, cover and microwave on HIGH for 7 minutes. Leave to stand.
◆ Place the butter in a medium bowl and microwave on HIGH for 45 seconds or until the butter melts. Stir in the onions and microwave on HIGH for 5-7 minutes, or until soft, stirring once.
◆ Stir in the soured cream and paprika. Season to taste with salt and pepper.
◆ Drain the pasta and return to the bowl. Pour over the onion and soured cream mixture and toss lightly together. Microwave on HIGH for 1-2 minutes or until the pasta is heated through.

## PASTA, TUNA AND LEMON SALAD

### SERVES 1

*100 g (4 oz) small pasta shapes*

*salt and pepper*

*100 g (4 oz) can tuna in vegetable oil*

*1 small onion, skinned and sliced into rings*

*45 ml (3 tbsp) double cream*

*pinch of ground turmeric*

*finely grated rind and juice of ½ lemon*

*25 g (1 oz) black or green olives*

*15 ml (1 tbsp) chopped fresh parsley*

*a few lettuce leaves, to serve*

◆ Put the pasta and salt to taste in a medium bowl and pour over 600 ml (1 pint) boiling water. Stir, then cover with cling film, pulling back one corner to allow the steam to escape. Microwave on HIGH for 6-8 minutes, or until the pasta is almost tender, stirring occasionally. Leave to stand, covered. Do not drain.
◆ Meanwhile, drain the tuna and put the oil into a medium bowl with the onion. Flake the fish and set aside.

◆ Cover the bowl with cling film, pulling back one corner to allow the steam to escape, and microwave on HIGH for 4-5 minutes, or until the onion is softened, stirring occasionally.
◆ Stir in the cream and the turmeric and microwave on HIGH, uncovered, for 2-3 minutes, until the cream has thickened and reduced.
◆ Stir in the lemon rind and juice and season well with salt and pepper.
◆ Drain the pasta, rinse with boiling water and stir into the dressing. Mix thoroughly together, then stir in the tuna, olives and the parsley. Cover and chill for at least 30 minutes. To serve, arrange the lettuce on a serving plate and spoon over the salad.

*To serve 2:* double the ingredients, using a 198 g (7 oz) can tuna, then follow the recipe above, but in point 1 microwave on HIGH for 8-10 minutes; in point 3 microwave on HIGH for 5-7 minutes; in point 4 microwave on HIGH for 3½-4 minutes.

## TAGLIATELLE WITH FRESH FIGS

### SERVES 1

*75 g (3 oz) tagliatelle*

*salt and pepper*

*3 large ripe fresh figs*

*15 (½ oz) butter or margarine*

*1.25 ml (¼ level tsp) medium curry powder*

*30 ml (2 tbsp) soured cream*

*30 ml (2 level tbsp) freshly grated Parmesan cheese*

*fresh herbs, to garnish (optional)*

◆ Put the tagliatelle and salt to taste in a medium bowl and pour over 600 ml (1 pint) boiling water. Stir and cover with cling film, pulling back one corner to allow the steam to escape. Microwave on HIGH for 3-4 minutes or until the pasta is almost tender, stirring frequently. Leave to stand, covered (do not drain).
◆ Meanwhile, cut one of the figs in half lengthways. Reserve one of the halves to garnish, peel and roughly chop the remainder.
◆ Put the butter, chopped figs and curry powder in a shallow dish and microwave on HIGH for 2 minutes, stirring occasionally.
◆ Drain the pasta and stir into the fig mixture with the soured cream and Parmesan cheese. Season well with salt and pepper. Carefully mix together with 2 forks and microwave on HIGH for 1-2 minutes or until hot.
◆ Garnish with fresh herbs, if using, and the reserved fig half and serve immediately.

## TAGLIATELLE WITH SMOKED HAM
### —— AND PEAS ——

*A rich and filling pasta dish with the ham and peas adding colour
and texture*

SEE PAGE 153

# CANNELLONI

SERVES 6

| |
|---|
| 750 ml (1¼ pints) milk |
| 1 small onion, skinned and sliced |
| 1 small carrot, peeled and sliced |
| 2 bay leaves |
| 8 peppercorns |
| 1 parsley sprig |
| 50 g (2 oz) breadcrumbs |
| 50 g (2 oz) freshly grated Parmesan cheese |
| 150 ml (¼ pint) strong beef stock |
| 1 egg, beaten |
| grated nutmeg to taste |
| salt and pepper |
| 10 ml (2 tsp) vegetable oil |
| 18 cannelloni tubes |
| 100 g (4 oz) butter or margarine |
| 60 g (2½ oz) plain flour |
| 1 quantity of basic meat sauce (see p. 213) |

◆ Put the milk into a large ovenproof glass bowl with the onion, carrot, bay leaves, peppercorns and parsley. Microwave on HIGH for 4-5 minutes or until the milk comes just to the boil.

◆ Remove the milk from the oven, cover and leave it to infuse for 30-40 minutes.

◆ Put the breadcrumbs and 30 ml (2 level tbsp) Parmesan cheese into a small mixing bowl, pour in the beef stock, stir well and leave the mixture to stand for 10 minutes.

◆ Mix the breadcrumb mixture and egg into the ragù. Season well with freshly grated nutmeg, salt and pepper.

◆ Boil 2.3 litres (4 pints) water in a kettle and pour it into a deep casserole dish or a 2.8 litre (5 pint) ovenproof glass bowl. Add 10 ml (2 level tsp) salt and 5 ml (1 tsp) oil.

◆ Bring the water back to a full rolling boil in a microwave oven set on HIGH. Quickly lower cannelloni tubes into the water, cover and microwave on HIGH for 5 minutes.

◆ Remove the bowl from the oven and cover tightly with foil. Leave the cannelloni to stand for about 3 minutes until it is cooked and is firm to the bite.

◆ Drain the cannelloni well and then lay them on clean tea-towels to absorb the excess moisture. Strain the milk and discard the vegetables.

◆ Put 75 g (3 oz) butter into a large ovenproof glass bowl and microwave on HIGH for 1 minute until the butter melts. Stir in the flour and microwave on HIGH for 45 seconds.

◆ Gradually stir the flavoured milk into the roux and microwave on HIGH for 1 minute, then whisk well. Microwave on HIGH for 4-5 minutes until the sauce is boiling and

thickened, stirring with a whisk every 30 seconds. Season the sauce well with salt, pepper and freshly grated nutmeg.

◆ Fill the cannelloni tubes with the meat sauce and place them side by side in a large, shallow buttered ovenproof dish.

◆ Pour the sauce over the cannelloni, sprinkle it with the remaining cheese and dot with the remaining butter. Microwave on HIGH for 5 minutes until well heated through and the sauce is bubbling hot. Brown the top under a hot grill and serve immediately.

# CANNELLONI WITH BROCCOLI AND MIXED NUTS

SERVES 2

| |
|---|
| 6 cannelloni tubes |
| salt and pepper |
| 1 small onion, skinned and chopped |
| 15 ml (1 tbsp) vegetable oil |
| 275 g (10 oz) broccoli, trimmed and finely chopped |
| finely grated rind and juice of ½ small lemon |
| 50 g (2 oz) chopped mixed nuts, such as Brazils and walnuts |
| 50 g (2 oz) fresh wholemeal breadcrumbs |
| 30 ml (2 level tbsp) freshly grated Parmesan cheese |
| 5 ml (1 tsp) chopped fresh marjoram, or 2.5 ml (½ level tsp) dried |
| grated nutmeg to taste |
| 1 egg yolk |
| 15 ml (1 level tbsp) plain flour |
| 25 g (1 oz) butter or margarine, cut into pieces |
| 300 ml (½ pint) milk |

◆ Put the cannelloni and salt to taste into a large bowl and pour over enough boiling water to cover.

◆ Microwave on HIGH for 5 minutes or until just tender, stirring occasionally. Leave to stand.

◆ Meanwhile, put the onion and oil into a medium bowl, cover with cling film, pulling back one corner to allow the steam to escape, and microwave on HIGH for 3-4 minutes or the onion is softened.

◆ Drain the pasta and spread out on a clean tea-towel, cover with a second tea-towel or absorbent kitchen paper.

◆ Stir the broccoli and half of the lemon rind and juice into the onion, cover again and microwave on HIGH for 10-12 minutes or until the broccoli is quite soft.

◆ Stir in the nuts, 40 g (1½ oz) breadcrumbs, half of the cheese, and the marjoram. Season well with salt, pepper and nutmeg. Stir in the egg yolk.

◆ Use this mixture to stuff the cannelloni, then arrange in 2 individual shallow gratin dishes. Set aside.

◆ To make the sauce, put the flour, butter, milk and remaining lemon rind and juice in a medium bowl and microwave on HIGH for 5-6 minutes, whisking every 30 seconds, until the sauce thickens.

◆ Season with salt, pepper and nutmeg and pour over the cannelloni. Microwave on HIGH for 4-5 minutes or until thoroughly heated through.

◆ Sprinkle with the remaining breadcrumbs and cheese and brown under a preheated grill.

# TAGLIATELLE WITH CREAM AND MUSHROOM SAUCE

### SERVES 4

| |
|---|
| 400 g (14 oz) tagliatelle |
| salt and pepper |
| 25 g (1 oz) butter or margarine |
| 175 g (6 oz) mushrooms, sliced |
| 1 garlic clove, skinned and crushed |
| 30 ml (2 tbsp) dry white wine (optional) |
| 300 ml (½ pint) double cream |
| 30 ml (2 level tbsp) freshly grated Parmesan cheese |
| 30 ml (2 tbsp) chopped fresh parsley |

◆ Place the pasta in a 2.6 litre (4½ pint) ovenproof glass bowl. Pour over 1.7 litres (3 pints) boiling water, add salt to taste. Cover with cling film and microwave on HIGH for 7 minutes. Leave to stand, covered.

◆ Place the butter in a large bowl and microwave on HIGH for 30 seconds or until the butter melts. Add the mushrooms and garlic and microwave on HIGH for 2 minutes.

◆ Add the wine and cream and mix thoroughly. Microwave on HIGH for 5-6 minutes or until the sauce is boiling and slightly reduced, stirring occasionally.

◆ Stir in the cheese and parsley and season well with salt and pepper.

◆ Drain the pasta and carefully mix with the sauce. Microwave on HIGH for 1 minute. Serve with extra Parmesan cheese.

# LASAGNE

### SERVES 4

| |
|---|
| 175 g (6 oz) lasagne |
| 45 ml (3 tbsp) vegetable oil |
| salt and pepper |
| 1 medium onion, skinned and finely chopped |
| 450 g (1 lb) lean minced beef |
| 30 ml (2 level tbsp) plain flour |
| 20 ml (4 tsp) chopped fresh basil or 10 ml (2 level tsp) dried |
| 397 g (14 oz) can chopped tomatoes |
| 150 ml (¼ pint) hot beef stock |
| 175 g (6 oz) mushrooms, sliced |
| 300 ml (½ pint) one-stage white sauce (see p. 211) |
| 100 g (4 oz) Cheddar cheese, grated |

◆ Place the lasagne in a 5 cm (2 inch) deep rectangular casserole. Spoon 5 ml (1 tsp) oil over and add 900 ml (1½ pints) boiling water and a pinch of salt. Cover with the casserole lid or cling film and microwave on HIGH for 9 minutes. Leave to stand for 15 minutes, then drain well and rinse.

◆ Mix the remaining oil and the onion in a medium bowl. Microwave on HIGH for 3 minutes, stirring once. Add the meat, breaking up any large pieces, and microwave on HIGH for 5 minutes, stirring once.

◆ Sprinkle the flour over, then stir in with the basil, tomatoes, stock and mushrooms. Season with salt and pepper. Microwave on HIGH for 20 minutes, stirring once.

◆ Layer the lasagne and meat sauce in the casserole dish, finishing with a layer of sauce. Pour the white sauce over the microwave on HIGH for 2 minutes or until heated through.

◆ Sprinkle the cheese over, and place under a hot grill until the cheese is bubbling and has melted.

## NOODLES IN WALNUT SAUCE

### SERVES 4

| |
|---|
| 100 g (4 oz) walnut pieces |
| 50 g (2 oz) butter, softened |
| 1 garlic clove, skinned and crushed |
| 150 ml (¼ pint) soured cream |
| salt and pepper |
| 5 ml (1 tsp) vegetable oil |
| 275 g (10 oz) green tagliatelle |
| freshly grated Parmesan cheese, to serve |

◆ In a blender or food processor liquidise the walnuts, butter, garlic, soured cream and seasoning.
◆ Boil 2 litres (3½ pints) water in a kettle and pour it into either a deep casserole dish or a 2.8 litre (5 pint) ovenproof glass bowl. Add 10 ml (2 level tsp) salt and vegetable oil.
◆ Bring the water back to a full rolling boil in the microwave oven set on HIGH. Quickly lower the tagliatelle into the water, three-quarters cover with cling film and microwave on HIGH for 5 minutes until it is partially cooked.
◆ Remove the bowl from the oven and leave the tagliatelle to stand, covered, for about 2 minutes until it is cooked and firm to the bite. Drain well.
◆ Place the tagliatelle in a large ovenproof serving dish and add the nut mixture. Toss gently until the tagliatelle is well coated. Microwave on HIGH for 1-2 minutes until it is hot. Sprinkle the tagliatelle with Parmesan cheese before serving.

## MACARONI AND TUNA BAKE

### SERVES 4

| |
|---|
| 225 g (8 oz) short-cut macaroni |
| salt and pepper |
| 198 g (7 oz) can tuna, drained and flaked |
| 225 g (8 oz) cottage cheese |
| 75 g (3 oz) Cheddar cheese, grated |
| 225 g (8 oz) courgettes, trimmed and thinly sliced |
| 397 g (14 oz) can chopped tomatoes with their juice |

◆ Place the macaroni in a 2.6 litre (4½ pint) ovenproof glass bowl and pour over 1.7 litres (3 pints) boiling water; add salt to taste. Cover with cling film and microwave on HIGH for 7 minutes. Leave to stand, covered
◆ Mix the tuna, cottage cheese and two thirds of the Cheddar together. Season well with salt and pepper.

◆ Line the bottom of a heatproof casserole dish with one third of the courgettes. Spread with half of the tuna mixture.
◆ Drain the macaroni and spread half on top of the tuna mixture. Repeat the layers, finishing with a layer of courgettes.
◆ Pour over the can of tomatoes, spreading the tomatoes evenly over the courgettes.
◆ Three-quarters cover with cling film and microwave on HIGH for 12-15 minutes or until the courgettes are tender.
◆ Sprinkle with the remaining cheese and microwave on HIGH for 1-2 minutes or until the courgettes are tender.
◆ Sprinkle with the remaining cheese and microwave on HIGH for 1-2 minutes or until the cheese is melted. Brown under a preheated grill if liked.

## SPAGHETTI WITH ANCHOVY AND TOMATO SAUCE

### SERVES 4

| |
|---|
| 400 g (14 oz) spaghetti |
| salt and pepper |
| 50 g (2 oz) can anchovies |
| 30 ml (2 tbsp) vegetable oil |
| 1 medium onion, skinned and thinly sliced |
| 397 g (14 oz) can tomatoes with their juice |
| 10 ml (2 tsp) tomato purée |
| 1 garlic clove, skinned and crushed |
| 30 ml (2 tbsp) chopped fresh parsley |
| 30 ml (2 level tbsp) drained capers |
| chopped fresh parsley, to garnish |

◆ Place the pasta in a 2.6 litre (4½ pint) ovenproof glass bowl. Pour over 1.7 litres (3 pints) boiling water and add salt to taste. Cover with cling film and microwave on HIGH for 7 minutes. Leave to stand, covered.
◆ To make the sauce, place the oil from the can of anchovies and 15 ml (1 tbsp) of the vegetable oil in a large ovenproof glass bowl. Stir in the onion and microwave on HIGH for 5-7 minutes or until the onion is softened.
◆ Add the rest of the ingredients except for the remaining vegetable oil and mix thoroughly. Microwave on HIGH for 5-6 minutes, until the sauce is slightly reduced, stirring occasionally.
◆ Drain the pasta, tip it into a heated serving bowl and toss it with the remaining oil. Microwave on HIGH for 1 minute.
◆ Pour over the sauce and serve immediately, garnished with chopped parsley.

# RICE WITH LENTILS

SERVES 8 AS AN ACCOMPANIMENT

*50 g (2 oz) flaked almonds*

*50 g (2 oz) butter or margarine*

*50 g (2 oz) piece of fresh ginger, scraped and finely chopped*

*1 large onion, skinned and finely chopped*

*2 garlic cloves, skinned and crushed*

*2.5 ml (½ level tsp) ground turmeric*

*2.5 ml (½ level tsp) chilli powder*

*5 ml (1 tsp) cumin seeds*

*3 large tomatoes, skinned, seeded and chopped*

*275 g (10 oz) long grain rice*

*175 g (6 oz) green lentils*

*salt and pepper*

*30 ml (2 tbsp) chopped fresh coriander or parsley*

*750 ml (1¼ pints) boiling chicken stock*

*3 tomato slices, to garnish*

*1 coriander sprig, to garnish*

◆ Place the almonds on a large ovenproof plate or baking tray and microwave on HIGH for 8-10 minutes, stirring occasionally, until browned.

◆ Put the butter into a large casserole dish and microwave on HIGH for 45 seconds or until the butter melts.

◆ Add the ginger, onion and garlic. Cover with cling film and microwave on HIGH for 5-6 minutes or until the onion softens. Stir in the spices and microwave on HIGH for 2 minutes.

◆ Add the tomatoes, rice, lentils, salt and pepper to the spice mixture and stir well to coat. Microwave on HIGH for 3 minutes, stirring once.

◆ Add half of the coriander and the stock to the casserole and stir well. Three-quarters cover with cling film and microwave on HIGH for about 10-12 minutes, or until the rice and lentils are just tender and most of the stock has been absorbed. Using a fork, stir once during the cooking time.

◆ Stir the rice and the lentils once again and cover them tightly with a lid. Leave them to stand for about 5 minutes, during which time all the liquid should be absorbed.

◆ Fluff up the rice with a fork and garnish it with the tomato slices and coriander. Serve immediately.

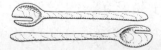

# EASTERN PILAU RICE

SERVES 4 AS AN ACCOMPANIMENT

*50 g (2 oz) butter or margarine*

*2 medium onions, skinned and thinly sliced*

*4 cloves*

*5 ml (1 level tsp) cardamom seeds*

*5 ml (1 level tsp) ground cinamon*

*225 g (8 oz) basmati or other long grain white rice*

*50 g (2 oz) seedless raisins*

*salt and pepper*

◆ Place the butter in a large casserole and microwave on HIGH for 45 seconds or until the butter melts. Stir in the onion and microwave on HIGH for 5-7 minutes or until the onion is softened, stirring once. Add the spices, stir well, and microwave on HIGH for 1 minute.

◆ Add the rice and raisins to the casserole and mix well. Pour over 600 ml (1 pint) boiling water, stir once, then cover and microwave on HIGH for 12 minutes. Leave to stand, covered, for 10 minutes.

◆ Season to taste, mix lightly with a fork and serve immediately.

# GREEN RICE

SERVES 6 AS AN ACCOMPANIMENT

*75 g (3 oz) butter or margarine*

*450 g (1 lb) long grain white rice*

*30 ml (2 tbsp) chopped fresh marjoram or 15 ml (1 level tbsp) dried*

*900 ml (1½ pints) boiling chicken stock*

*225 g (8 oz) broccoli, broken into small florets*

*salt and pepper*

*25 g (1 oz) flaked almonds, toasted, to garnish*

◆ Place 50 g (2 oz) butter in a large casserole and microwave on HIGH for 1 minute until the butter is foaming.

◆ Stir in the rice and marjoram. Pour over the boiling stock and stir well. Cover and microwave on HIGH for 13 minutes. Leave to stand, covered, for 10 minutes.

◆ Place the broccoli florets in a roasting bag with the remaining butter and 30 ml (2 tbsp) water. Fasten the top and pierce the bag with a fork. Microwave on HIGH for 3 minutes. Tip the broccoli florets into the rice and mix carefully with a fork. Garnish with the almonds and serve.

## ORANGE RICE

SERVES 6 AS AN ACCOMPANIMENT

| |
| --- |
| *50 g (2 oz) butter or margarine* |
| *1 small onion, skinned and finely chopped* |
| *3 celery sticks, trimmed and thinly sliced* |
| *450 g (1 lb) long grain white rice* |
| *finely grated rind and juice of 2 oranges* |
| *30 ml (2 tbsp) chopped fresh mint* |
| *salt and pepper* |
| *100 g (4 oz) Brazil nuts, shredded* |

◆ Place the butter in a large casserole and microwave on HIGH for 45 seconds or until the butter melts.
◆ Stir in the onion and celery and microwave on HIGH for 5-7 minutes or until the onion is softened, stirring once. Stir in the rice, orange rind and mint.
◆ Make up the orange juice to 600 ml (1 pint) with boiling water and add to the rice. Microwave on HIGH for 5 minutes or until boiling. Stir well, cover and microwave on HIGH for 13 minutes. Leave to stand for 5 minutes.
◆ Season to taste and stir in the Brazil nuts with a fork. Serve immediately.

## COUNTRY-STYLE RISOTTO

SERVES 4

| |
| --- |
| *45 ml (3 tbsp) vegetable oil* |
| *2 medium onions, skinned and chopped* |
| *2 celery sticks, trimmed and thinly sliced* |
| *100 g (4 oz) courgettes, trimmed and sliced* |
| *100 g (4 oz) shelled broad beans* |
| *350 g (12 oz) Italian arborio or long grain white rice* |
| *600 ml (1 pint) boiling chicken stock* |
| *salt and pepper* |
| *100 g (4 oz) garlic sausage, thinly sliced* |
| *45 ml (3 tbsp) chopped fresh parsley* |
| *25 g (1 oz) freshly grated Parmesan cheese* |

◆ Place the oil, onion and celery in a large bowl and microwave on HIGH for 5-7 minutes or until the vegetables are softened, stirring once.
◆ Stir in the courgettes, beans, rice and stock. Cover and microwave on HIGH for 13 minutes. Leave to stand, covered, for 10 minutes.
◆ Carefully toss with a fork, season to taste and mix in the sausage, parsley and Parmesan cheese. Serve immediately.

## CHICKEN RISOTTO

SERVES 4

| |
| --- |
| *30 ml (2 tbsp) vegetable oil* |
| *1 large onion, skinned and chopped* |
| *1 leek, trimmed and sliced* |
| *1 green pepper, cored, seeded and sliced* |
| *2.5 ml (1 level tsp) ground cumin* |
| *350 g (12 oz) cooked chicken, diced* |
| *finely grated rind and juice of 1 lemon* |
| *25 g (1 oz) stoned black or green olives* |
| *900 ml (1½ pints) boiling chicken stock* |
| *450 g (1 lb) long grain white rice* |
| *salt and pepper* |
| *chopped fresh parsley, to garnish* |

◆ Place the oil, onion, vegetables and spices in a large casserole dish and microwave on HIGH for 5-7 minutes or until the vegetables are softened, stirring once.
◆ Stir in the chicken, lemon rind and juice, olives, stock, rice and seasoning. Mix well, cover and microwave on HIGH for 13 minutes. Leave to stand, covered, for 10 minutes.
◆ Mix lightly with a fork and serve hot, garnished with chopped parsley.

## SPAGHETTI BOLOGNESE

SERVES 2

| |
| --- |
| *5 ml (1 tsp) vegetable oil* |
| *1 shallot or ½ small onion, skinned and chopped* |
| *3 rashers smoked and streaky bacon, rinded and chopped* |
| *1 garlic clove, skinned and crushed* |
| *225 g (8 oz) lean minced beef* |
| *1 medium carrot, peeled and grated* |
| *1 bay leaf* |
| *2.5 ml (½ level tsp) dried oregano* |
| *15 ml (1 level tbsp) tomato purée* |
| *200 g (7 oz) can tomatoes* |
| *150 ml (¼ pint) dry red wine* |
| *100 ml (4 fl oz) beef stock* |
| *salt and pepper* |
| *225 g (4 oz) dried spaghetti* |

◆ Put the oil, shallot bacon, garlic and beef in a medium bowl. Microwave on HIGH for 5-7 minutes or until the onion is soft, and the meat has changed colour, stirring occasionally. Drain off any excess fat.

◆ Stir in the remaining ingredients and cover with cling film, pulling back one corner to let steam escape. Microwave on HIGH for 20-30 minutes or until the meat is tender and the sauce is slightly reduced. Leave to stand.

◆ Meanwhile, put the spaghetti into a large bowl and pour over 1.1 litre (2 pints) boiling water. Stir, cover with cling film, pulling back one corner to allow the steam to escape and microwave on HIGH for 5-6 minutes until almost tender. Leave to stand, covered, for 5 minutes. Do not drain.

◆ Microwave the sauce on HIGH for 1-2 minutes until hot. Drain the spaghetti and turn into a warmed serving dish. Pour over the sauce and serve immediately.

## BASMATI RICE WITH PISTACHIO NUTS

### SERVES 2 AS AN ACCOMPANIMENT

| |
|---|
| 100 g (4 oz) Basmati rice |
| salt and pepper |
| finely grated rind and juice of 1 lemon |
| 15 g (½ oz) butter or margarine, cut into pieces |
| 15 g (½ oz) blanched pistachio nuts, chopped |
| 15 ml (1 tbsp) chopped fresh parsley |

◆ Put the rice, salt to taste, the lemon rind and juice and 300 ml (½ pint) boiling water in a medium bowl. Cover with cling film, pulling back one corner to allow the steam to escape, and microwave on HIGH for 7 minutes.

◆ Leave to stand, covered, for 5 minutes, by which time the rice should be tender and the liquid absorbed.

◆ While the rice is still standing, put the butter into an ovenproof serving dish and microwave on HIGH for 45 seconds or until the butter melts.

◆ Stir the nuts into the butter and microwave on HIGH for 2 minutes, stirring occasionally. Stir in the parsley and season well with salt and pepper.

◆ Gradually stir in the rice, turning carefully with a fork to ensure that all the grains are coated in butter. Add more seasoning, if necessary, and serve hot.

## NOODLES WITH GOAT'S CHEESE AND CHIVES

### SERVES 1

| |
|---|
| 100 g (4 oz) dried egg noodles |
| salt and pepper |
| 15 g (½ oz) butter or margarine |
| 30 ml (2 tbsp) double cream |
| 40 g (1½ oz) fresh goat's cheese, crumbled |
| 15 ml (1 tbsp) snipped fresh chives |
| snipped fresh chives, to garnish |

◆ Put the noodles and salt to taste in a medium bowl. Pour over 600 ml (1 pint) boiling water. Stir and cover with cling film, pulling back one corner to allow the steam to escape. Microwave on HIGH for 2-3 minutes or until almost tender. Leave to stand (do not drain).

◆ Meanwhile, put the butter and cream in a medium bowl and microwave on HIGH for 1-2 minutes, or until very hot. Stir in cheese, season and microwave on HIGH for 1 minute.

◆ Drain the noodles and stir into the cheese mixture with the chives. Microwave on HIGH for 1-2 minutes. Garnish with chives and serve immediately.

## BURGHAL PILAU

### SERVES 2 AS AN ACCOMPANIMENT

| |
|---|
| 15 g (½ oz) flaked almonds |
| 15 g (½ oz) butter or margarine |
| 1 medium onion, skinned and finely chopped |
| 1 garlic clove, skinned and crushed |
| 100 g (4 oz) large grained burghal wheat |
| 200 ml (7 fl oz) boiling chicken stock |
| salt and pepper |
| 30 ml (2 tbsp) natural yogurt |
| 15 ml (1 tbsp) snipped fresh chives or parsley |

◆ Put the almonds and butter in a medium bowl and microwave on HIGH for 1-2 minutes or until the almonds are golden brown, stirring occasionally.

◆ Stir in the onion and garlic, cover with cling film, pulling back one corner to allow the steam to escape, and microwave on HIGH for 4-5 minutes.

◆ Meanwhile, wash the burghal in several changes of water. Drain and then stir into the cooked onion and garlic. Stir in the stock, cover again and microwave on HIGH for 6-8 minutes, stirring occasionally.

◆ Season, stir in yogurt and chives and serve.

# BREADS & BAKING

## DATE AND WALNUT FLAPJACKS AND BRAN
### TEA BREAD
*Two delicious tea-time fillers, both of which use healthier wholemeal flour
or bran*

SEE PAGE 167

# Cooking Tips

◆

*Even if your oven has a turntable, it is advisable to turn cakes to ensure even cooking.*

◆

*Underbake a mixture if you are not sure about timing. You can always put it back to bake for a few seconds, if necessary.*

◆

*Remove cakes from the oven after the time recommended even if the mixture looks wet. Standing time will complete the baking process.*

◆

*Mixtures should be of a softer consistency than when baked conventionally. Add an extra 15 ml (1 tbsp) milk for each egg used.*

◆

*Use adequately large baking containers as mixtures rise up during microwave cooking. Containers should not be more than half full of uncooked mixture.*

◆

*Reheat baked goods and pastry on kitchen paper which will absorb steam and prevent sogginess.*

◆

*Cook small cakes in small paper cases – use 2 per cake for extra support and stand in a muffin pan, ramekins or cups to support the paper cups.*

◆

*When cooking a number of small cakes arrange them in a circle in the oven about 5 cm (2 inches) apart.*

◆

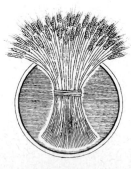

# DATE AND WALNUT FLAPJACKS

### MAKES 8

225 g (8 oz) dates, stoned and finely chopped

30 ml (2 tbsp) clear honey

100 g (4 oz) butter or margarine, chopped

75 g (3 oz) wholemeal flour

100 g (4 oz) soft dark brown sugar

pinch of salt

75 g (3 oz) rolled oats

50 g (2 oz) finely chopped walnuts

◆ Put the dates in a medium bowl, add the honey and 75 ml (3 fl oz) water and microwave on HIGH for 5 minutes. Cover and leave to stand.

◆ Rub the butter into the flour until the mixture resembles fine breadcrumbs. Stir in the sugar, salt, oats and walnuts.

◆ Press half the mixture into the base of a 20.5 cm (8 inch) shallow glass dish. Microwave on MEDIUM for 4 minutes.

◆ Spoon the dates evenly over the cooked mixture and sprinkle with the remaining oat mixture. Microwave on HIGH for 6 minutes.

◆ Mark into 8 wedges while warm and leave to cool in the dish. When cold turn out and cut into wedges.

# BRAN TEA BREAD

### MAKES ONE 20 × 12.5 CM (8 × 5 INCH) LOAF

100 g (4 oz) bran breakfast cereal (not flaked)

75 g (3 oz) soft dark brown sugar

225 g (8 oz) mixed dried fruit

50 g (2 oz) chopped nuts

300 ml (½ pint) milk

100 g (4 oz) self raising flour

5 ml (1 level tsp) mixed spice

◆ Grease a 20 × 12.5 × 6 cm (8 × 5 × 2½ inch) loaf dish and line the base with greaseproof paper.

◆ Put the bran cereal, sugar, fruit and nuts in a bowl. Pour the milk over and leave to soak for 1½-2 hours, until the liquid has been absorbed.

◆ Stir in the flour and spice, mixing all the ingredients together well.

◆ Turn the mixture into the prepared dish. Press down firmly and level the surface.

◆ Microwave on LOW for 14-16 minutes until the bread is cooked and a wooden cocktail stick inserted into the centre of the bread comes out clean. Give the dish a quarter turn 4 times during cooking if the oven is not fitted with a turntable.

◆ Leave to stand for 5 minutes before turning out to cool on a wire rack.

◆ When cold, wrap and store for 1-2 days. Serve sliced and buttered.

# WHOLEMEAL SESAME ROLLS

### MAKES 36

1 quantity of wholemeal bread dough (see p. 169)

a little milk, for brushing

sesame seeds

◆ Make up the bread dough as instructed in the recipe for wholemeal bread (p. 169), following the directions to the end of point 4.

◆ Cut off 50 g (2 oz) pieces of dough and shape them into neat rolls.

◆ Place the rolls on large, greased, flat ovenproof plates, 4 to 6 rolls to a plate. Loosely cover the rolls with a clean tea-towel and leave them in a warm place for about 1 hour until they double in size.

◆ Brush the rolls with a little milk, then sprinkle them with sesame seeds.

◆ Microwave the rolls one plate at a time on HIGH for 3 minutes or until they sound hollow when tapped on the base. Cool the rolls on a wire cooling rack.

# GARLIC BREAD

### SERVES 6

100 g (4 oz) butter or margarine

1 garlic clove, skinned and crushed

salt and pepper

1 small French loaf, about 43 cm (17 inches) long

◆ Put the butter into a small ovenproof glass bowl and microwave on LOW for about 1 minute to soften it. Beat in the crushed garlic and season very well with salt and pepper.

◆ Cut the bread into diagonal slices about 2.5 cm (1 inch) thick. Spread the slices with the garlic butter, then sandwich the loaf together again.

◆ Divide the loaf into 2 and wrap each piece in absorbent kitchen paper.

◆ Microwave on HIGH for 50-60 seconds or until warm. Do not over-heat the bread as it will become tough. Serve immediately while the bread is still hot.

— OATY APRICOT FLAPJACKS —

*The apricot provides a perfect fruity filling in these tea-time treats*

SEE OPPOSITE

## OATY APRICOT FLAPJACKS

MAKES 8

| |
|---|
| 175 g (6 oz) dried apricots, finely chopped |
| 30 ml (2 level tbsp) clear honey |
| 100 g (4 oz) butter or margarine |
| 100 g (4 oz) plain flour |
| 100 g (4 oz) soft light brown sugar |
| pinch of salt |
| 100 g (4 oz) rolled oats |

◆ Place the apricots in a medium bowl, add the honey and 75 ml (3 fl oz) water and microwave on HIGH for 5 minutes. Cover and leave to stand.
◆ Rub the butter into the flour until the mixture resembles fine breadcrumbs. Stir in the sugar, salt and oats.
◆ Press two thirds of the mixture into the base of a 20.5 cm (8 inch) soufflé dish. Microwave on MEDIUM for 5 minutes.
◆ Spoon the apricots evenly over the oats, and sprinkle with the reserved oat mixture. Microwave on HIGH for 6 minutes. Mark into 8 wedges while warm and leave to cool in the dish. When cold turn out and cut into wedges.

## QUICK ROLLS

MAKES 10

| |
|---|
| 225 g (8 oz) plain wholemeal flour |
| 10 ml (2 level tsp) baking powder |
| 2.5 ml (½ level tsp) salt |
| 25 g (1 oz) butter or margarine |
| about 150 ml (¼ pint) milk |
| 45 ml (3 tbsp) coarse oatmeal or cracked wheat |

◆ Put the flour, baking powder and salt into a large bowl. Rub in the butter until the mixture resembles fine breadcrumbs.
◆ Make a well in the centre, add the milk and mix with a round-bladed knife to give a fairly soft dough. Add a little extra milk if necessary.
◆ Draw the mixture together and turn on to a lightly floured board. Divide into 10 portions and shape into rolls.
◆ Flatten the top of each roll then brush with water and sprinkle with the coarse oatmeal or cracked wheat.
◆ Place the rolls on 2 large, flat plates, 5 to a plate. Microwave one plate at a time on HIGH for 3 minutes or until risen.
◆ Cool on a wire cooling rack. There are best eaten while still warm.

## WHOLEMEAL BREAD

MAKES FOUR 450 G (1 LB) LOAVES

| |
|---|
| 900 ml (1½ pints) tepid water |
| 50 g (2 oz) fresh yeast or 30 ml (2 level tbsp) dried yeast and 5 ml (1 tsp) honey |
| 1.4 kg (3 lb) plain wholemeal flour |
| 30 ml (2 level tbsp) demerara sugar |
| 20 ml (4 level tsp) salt |
| 25 g (1 oz) margarine, for greasing |
| cracked wheat, for sprinkling |

◆ Put 300 ml (½ pint) tepid water in a measuring jug or bowl and stir in the fresh yeast until it is dissolved. Or, if using dried yeast, stir the honey into 300 ml (½ pint) of the water, sprinkle in the yeast and leave it in a warm place for about 15 minutes until it becomes frothy.
◆ Mix the flour, sugar and salt together in a large mixing bowl and make a well in the centre. Pour in the yeast liquid and the remaining water. Mix together to make a firm dough, adding a little more water if necessary.
◆ Knead the dough on a very lightly floured work surface and knead it for at least 10 minutes until it is very smooth and elastic and no longer sticky.
◆ Place the dough in a bowl, cover it with a clean tea-towel and leave it in a warm place until it has doubled in size — about 1 hour, depending on room temperature.
◆ Grease four 450 g (1 lb) ovenproof glass or plastic loaf dishes.
◆ Turn the risen dough on to a lightly floured work surface and knead it with clenched fists to 'knock back' the dough, to remove all the large air bubbles. Knead the dough once again for about 5 minutes until it is smooth.
◆ Divide the dough into 4 equal-sized pieces, shape and press these into the prepared dishes, pressing the dough well into the corners.
◆ Loosely cover the loaves with a clean tea-towel and leave them in a warm place to double in size and to rise almost to the top of the dishes.
◆ Brush the tops of the loaves with a little salted water and sprinkle them with the cracked wheat.
◆ Microwave the loaves one at a time on HIGH for 5 minutes. Next, turn out each loaf upside down on to a double thickness of absorbent kitchen paper and microwave on HIGH for 1 minute until they sound hollow when they are tapped on the base, or until a wooden cocktail stick or skewer inserted in them comes out clean. Cool on a wire rack.

## IRISH SODA BREAD

MAKES ONE 450 G (1 LB) LOAF

| |
|---|
| 450 g (1 lb) wholemeal flour, plus extra for sifting |
| 5 ml (1 level tsp) salt |
| 5 ml (1 level tsp) bicarbonate of soda |
| 15 g (½ oz) butter or margarine |
| 10 ml (2 level tsp) cream of tartar |
| 5 ml (1 level tsp) Barbados sugar |
| 300 ml (½ pint) milk |

◆ Lightly grease a large, flat ovenproof plate or microwave baking tray. Mix the flour, salt and bicarbonate of soda in a mixing bowl and rub in the butter until the mixture resembles fine breadcrumbs.

◆ Dissolve the cream of tartar and sugar into the milk and use this to bind the flour together, adding a little more milk if necessary.

◆ Knead the dough on a lightly floured work surface until it is firm and smooth and there are no cracks.

◆ Flatten out the dough to a round about 18 cm (7 inches) in diameter and place it on the prepared plate or tray.

◆ Brush the surface of the dough with a little milk and mark a deep cross on the top with a knife. Sift a little flour on top.

◆ Microwave on HIGH for 9 minutes, giving the dish a quarter turn 3 times during the cooking time, until the bread is well risen and dry on top, then turn it over and microwave on HIGH for 1-1½ minutes or until the surface looks cooked. Cool on a wire rack for 5 minutes, then serve warm.

## HERBED CHEESE BREAD

MAKES ONE 450 G (1 LB) LOAF

| |
|---|
| 225 g (8 oz) self-raising wholemeal flour |
| salt and pepper |
| 5 ml (1 level tsp) mustard powder |
| 15 ml (1 tbsp) snipped fresh chives |
| 30 ml (2 tbsp) chopped fresh parsley |
| 150 g (5 oz) Cheddar cheese, grated |
| 25 g (1 oz) butter or margarine |
| 1 egg, size 2, beaten |
| 225 ml (8 fl oz) milk |

◆ Grease 1.1 litre (2 pint) ovenproof loaf dish and line the base with greaseproof paper.

◆ Mix the flour, salt, pepper, mustard, fresh herbs and 100 g (4 oz) of the cheese together in a mixing bowl.

◆ Put the butter into a small ovenproof mixing bowl and microwave on HIGH for 45 seconds or until the butter melts.

◆ Mix together the butter, the egg and milk, pour this into the flour and mix well to form a soft dropping consistency. Spoon the mixture into the prepared dish, smooth the top and shield the ends of the dish with small pieces of smooth foil, shiny side in.

◆ Cover with cling film and microwave on HIGH for 6 minutes or until the bread is well risen, remove the cling film and foil, sprinkle with the remaining cheese and microwave on HIGH for 2 minutes or until the bread is cooked and a wooden cocktail stick or skewer inserted in the centre comes out clean. Give the dish a quarter turn 3 times during the cooking time.

◆ Leave the bread to stand for 10 minutes before turning it out on to a rack to cool.

## MOIST CHOCOLATE SANDWICH CAKE

MAKES ONE 23 CM (9 INCH)

LOAF-SHAPED CAKE

| |
|---|
| 100 g (4 oz) golden syrup |
| 100 g (4 oz) soft dark brown sugar |
| 100 g (4 oz) butter or margarine |
| 175 g (6 oz) self raising flour |
| 50 g (2 oz) cocoa powder |
| 1 egg, beaten |
| 150 ml (¼ pint) milk |
| 100 g (4 oz) plain chocolate, broken into small pieces |
| 25 g (1 oz) flaked almonds |

◆ Grease a 23 cm (9 inch) loaf dish and line with grease-proof paper.

◆ Put the syrup, brown sugar and butter in a large bowl and microwave on HIGH for 2 minutes or until the butter has melted and the sugar dissolved, stirring occasionally.

◆ Sift in the flour and cocoa and mix together well. Beat in the eggs then stir in the milk.

◆ Turn the mixture into the prepared dish and microwave on HIGH for 5 minutes until the cake is cooked and a wooden cocktail stick or skewer inserted into the centre of the cake comes out clean.

◆ Leave to stand for 5 minutes before turning out to cool completely.

◆ Put the chocolate into a small bowl and microwave on HIGH for about 1 minute until melted, stirring occasionally.

◆ Spread the melted chocolate over the top of the cake, allowing it to trickle over the edges and sides. Leave to set, then sprinkle the flaked almonds over the top.

# VICTORIA SANDWICH CAKE

### SERVES 6-8

175 g (6 oz) self raising flour

175 g (6 oz) butter or margarine, softened

175 g (6 oz) caster sugar

3 eggs

30-40 ml (2-3 tbsp) milk

jam, to fill

icing sugar, for dusting

◆ Grease a 19 cm (7½ inch) deep soufflé dish and line the base with greased greaseproof paper.
◆ Mix the flour, butter, sugar, eggs and 30 ml (2 tbsp) milk together in a medium bowl. Beat until smooth. If necessary, add an extra 15 ml (1 tbsp) milk to give a soft dropping consistency.
◆ Spoon the mixture into the prepared dish and microwave on HIGH for 5½-7½ minutes until the cake is cooked and a wooden cocktail stick or skewer inserted into the centre of the cake comes out clean.
◆ Leave to stand for 10 minutes then turn out on to a wire rack, remove the lining paper and leave to cool.
◆ When the cake is completely cold, split it in half and sandwich together with jam. Sift icing sugar over the top of the cake.

VARIATIONS
*Orange or lemon:* Replace the milk with the juice and the grated rind of 1 orange or 1 lemon and proceed as above. When cold, split and fill with orange- or lemon-flavoured butter cream.
*Chocolate:* Replace 45 ml (3 level tbsp) of flour with 45 ml (3 level tbsp) of cocoa powder. Sandwich together with vanilla or chocolate butter cream. For a more moist cake, blend the cocoa powder with water to give a thick paste. Mix into the beaten ingredients.
*Coffee:* Dissolve 10 ml (2 level tsp) instant coffee in a little warm water and the milk, then add to the remaining ingredients. Or use 10 ml (2 tsp) coffee essence.
*Vanilla butter cream:* Sift 225 g (8 oz) icing sugar into a bowl then gradually beat in 100 g (4 oz) softened butter, adding a few drops of vanilla essence and 15-30 ml (1-2 tbsp) milk.
**For chocolate butter cream**, beat in 15 ml (1 level tsp) cocoa powder dissolved in a little hot water then left to cool. Omit the milk.
**For coffee butter cream**, omit the vanilla essence but add 10 ml (2 tsp) instant coffee powder dissolved in a little of the milk.

# GRANARY TEA-CAKES

### MAKES 16

100 g (4 oz) butter or margarine, cut into small pieces

250 ml (9 fl oz) milk

750 g (1 lb 10 oz) granary flour

10 ml (2 level tsp) salt

25 g (1 oz) fresh yeast or 15 ml (1 level tsp) dried yeast and a pinch of sugar

2 eggs, size 2, beaten

75 g (3 oz) currants

50 g (2 oz) chopped mixed peel

30 ml (2 level tbsp) caster sugar

cracked wheat

◆ Put the butter and milk into a small ovenproof bowl and microwave on HIGH for 2-3 minutes or until the butter melts. Stir the mixture well and cool it until tepid.
◆ Put the flour and salt into an ovenproof glass bowl and microwave on HIGH for 30 seconds to warm the flour.
◆ Add the fresh yeast to the tepid milk and butter and stir it until it is dissolved. If using dried yeast and sugar, sprinkle it into the milk and leave it in a warm place for 15 minutes until it becomes frothy. Make a well in the centre of the flour, pour in the yeast mixture and the beaten eggs. Mix the ingredients to form a soft dough.
◆ Knead the dough on a lightly floured work surface for 10 minutes until it becomes smooth and elastic. Place the dough in a mixing bowl and cover it with a clean tea-towel. Leave the dough in a warm place for about 1 hour until it has doubled in size.
◆ Turn the risen dough on to a lightly floured work surface and knead it again for 3 minutes until it becomes smooth.
◆ Divide the dough into 16 equal pieces and shape each one into a flat oval. Arrange these on 2 greased, large flat ovenproof plates in overlapping rings of 8 buns each.
◆ Loosely cover the dough rings with a clean tea-towel and leave them in a warm place until they double in size.
◆ Mix the caster sugar with 30 ml (2 tbsp) water and microwave on HIGH for 1 minute or until it dissolves. Brush this over the dough rings and then sprinkle the cracked wheat over the top.
◆ Microwave, one plate at at time, for 5-6 minutes until the tea-cakes are well risen and cooked and a wooden cocktail stick or skewer inserted in the centre of the dough comes out clean. Or, when the cooked tea cakes sound hollow when tapped on the base.
◆ Allow them to stand for 5 minutes, then move them on to a rack to cool. When cooled slightly, brush with the remaining sugar syrup to glaze.

# BATTENBURG CAKE

### SERVES 10-12

175 g (6 oz) butter or margarine

175 g (6 oz) caster sugar

a few drops of vanilla flavouring

3 eggs, size 2, beaten

175 g (6 oz) self raising flour

30-60 ml (2-4 tbsp) cocoa powder

120 ml ( 8 level tbsp) apricot jam

225 g (8 oz) marzipan

caster sugar for dredging

◆ Grease a shallow ovenproof glass dish about 18 × 23 cm (7 × 9 inches). Line the base with greaseproof paper. Divide the dish in half lengthways with a wall of greaseproof paper.
◆ Cream the butter and sugar together until they become pale and fluffy. Beat in the vanilla flavouring. Add the eggs, a little at a time, beating them well between each addition. Carefully fold in the flour. Add 30 ml (2 tbsp) milk to make a soft dropping consistency.
◆ Spoon half of the mixture into one side of the prepared dish and smooth the top.
◆ Add the cocoa powder, and a little more milk, if necessary, to the remaining mixture. Spoon this into the other side of the prepared dish and smooth the top.
◆ Shield each end of the dish with a small piece of smooth foil, shiny side in. Cover with cling film and microwave on HIGH for 7-8 minutes, giving the dish a quarter turn 3 times during the cooking time.
◆ Remove the foil and cling film, allow the sponges to cool in the dish for 4-5 minutes. Turn out on to a rack to cool.
◆ Neatly trim the 2 sponges to an equal size. Cut each sponge in half lengthways.
◆ Put the apricot jam into a small ovenproof glass bowl and microwave on HIGH for 1½-2 minutes, stirring frequently, until hot.
◆ Spread one side of one piece of the vanilla sponge with apricot jam and then place one piece of the chocolate sponge next to it and press the two firmly together.
◆ Spread more jam on top of the two halves and place the remaining 2 sponges on top, alternating the colours.
◆ Roll out the marzipan to an oblong long enough to go around the sponge cakes.
◆ Brush marzipan with apricot jam and place sponge cakes in centre. Bring marzipan up over sides to enclose sponges. Turn cake over so that join is underneath.
◆ Press the marzipan firmly around the sponges to seal. Trim each end neatly. Use a small knife to decorate the top of the cake with a criss-cross pattern. Pinch the top side edges between thumb and forefinger to give a fluted edge. Dredge with caster sugar and place on a serving dish.

# ENGLISH MADELEINES

### MAKES 8

100 g (4 oz) butter or margarine

100 g (4 oz) caster sugar

2 eggs, size 2, beaten

100 g (4 oz) self raising flour

75 ml (5 tbsp) red jam, sieved

50 g (1½ oz) desiccated coconut

4 glacé cherries, halved, and angelica pieces, to decorate

◆ Grease 8 paper drinking cups. Line the base of each one with a small round of greasproof paper.
◆ Cream the butter and the sugar together until they are very pale and fluffy. Add the eggs a little at a time, beating well after each addition. Carefully fold in the flour.
◆ Divide the mixture evenly among the prepared cups. Place the cups on flat ovenproof plates, 4 to each plate.
◆ Cover with cling film and microwave on HIGH, one plate at a time, for 1½-2 minutes or until the mixture is cooked but just slightly moist on the surface. Quickly remove the cling film. Stand for 1-2 minutes, then carefully turn the cakes out on to a rack to cool.
◆ When the cakes are almost cold, trim the bases, so that they stand firmly and are about the same height.
◆ Microwave the jam on HIGH for 1-2 minutes or until the jam is melted and boiling; stir well.
◆ Spread the coconut out on a large plate. Spear each cake on to a skewer, brush them with the boiling jam and then roll them in the coconut until they are evenly coated.
◆ Top each Madeleine with half a glacé cherry and small pieces of angelica.

# CHOCOLATE FUDGE COOKIES

### MAKES 24

100 g (4 oz) butter or margarine, softened

75 g (3 oz) soft light brown sugar

175 g (6 oz) plain flour

30 ml (2 level tbsp) cocoa powder

◆ Grease and line a flat plate or microwave baking sheet.
◆ Cream the butter and sugar until soft and fluffy. Stir in the flour and cocoa to make a smooth dough.
◆ Roll the dough into balls about the size of a walnut and arrange 6 in a circle on the plate or baking sheet. Flatten slightly and microwave on MEDIUM for 3½ minutes. Leave to stand for 5 minutes, then cool on a wire rack. Repeat with the remaining dough.

## Battenburg Cake and English
### Madeleines
*Two classic tea-time cakes, perfectly cooked in the microwave*
SEE OPPOSITE

# CHERRY AND COCONUT CAKE

## SERVES 8-10

100 g (4 oz) desiccated coconut

250 g (9 oz) self raising flour

1.25 ml (¼ level tsp) salt

125 g (4 oz) butter or margarine, cut into pieces

125 g (4 oz) caster sugar

125 g (4 oz) glacé cherries, finely chopped

2 eggs

300 ml (½ pint) milk

25 g (1 oz) shredded coconut

◆ Grease a 1.3 litre (2¼ pint) ovenproof glass ring mould or microwave ring mould and sprinkle with 25 g (1 oz) of the coconut, spreading any excess evenly in the base.
◆ Put the flour and the salt into a mixing bowl and rub in the butter until the mixture resembles fine breadcrumbs. Stir in the desiccated coconut, sugar and cherries.
◆ Add the eggs and milk and then beat well, adding more milk, if necessary, to make a soft dropping consistency. Spoon the mixture into the prepared dish, smooth the top and scatter the shredded coconut over the top.
◆ Cover loosely with cling film and microwave on HIGH for 10-11 minutes or until the cake is well risen and just dry on the surface, and a wooden cocktail stick or skewer inserted into the centre of the cake comes out clean. Give the cake a quarter turn 4 times during the cooking time.
◆ Allow the cake to stand in its dish for 10 minutes before carefully turning it out on to a rack to cool.

# CHOCOLATE ALMOND CAKE

## SERVES 8

150 g (5 oz) butter or margarine

100 g (4 oz) caster sugar

2 eggs

45 ml (3 tbsp) clear honey

142 ml (5 fl oz) soured cream

100 g (4 oz) self raising flour

40 g (1½ oz) cocoa powder

50 g (2 oz) ground almonds

75 g (3 oz) cooking chocolate drops

15 ml (1 tbsp) brandy

45 ml (3 tbsp) single cream

50 g (2 oz) flaked almonds, toasted

◆ Base line a 1.7 litre (3 pint) round casserole with greased greaseproof paper.
◆ Cream 100 g (4 oz) butter and the sugar together until pale and fluffy. Gradually beat in the eggs, honey and soured cream. Fold in the flour, cocoa and ground almonds.
◆ Spoon the cake mixture into the prepared tin. Microwave on HIGH for 10 minutes until the cake is cooked and a wooden cocktail stick or skewer inserted into the centre of the cake comes out clean. Leave to stand for 5 minutes, then turn out on to a wire rack and remove the paper. Leave to cool.
◆ Place the chocolate drops, brandy, remaining butter and cream in a small bowl and microwave on HIGH for 1 minute or until the butter is melted, stirring once.
◆ Pour the icing over the cold cake, allowing it to run down the sides. Sprinkle with the almonds. Leave until the icing is set and serve the cake cut into thin slices.

# CARROT CAKE

## SERVES 6-8

100 g (4 oz) butter or margarine

100 g (4 oz) dark brown sugar

2 eggs, size 2

grated rind and juice of 1 lemon

5 ml (1 tsp) ground cinnamon

2.5 ml (½ level tsp) grated nutmeg

2.5 ml (½ level tsp) ground cloves

15 g (½ oz) shredded coconut

100 g (4 oz) carrots, peeled and finely grated

40 g (1½ oz) ground almonds

100 g (4 oz) self raising wholemeal flour

caster sugar, for dredging

◆ Grease an 18 cm (7 inch) diameter ovenproof ring mould.
◆ Cream the butter and sugar together until they are very soft, pale and fluffy. Beat in the eggs one at a time, beating well between each addition. Beat in the lemon rind and juice, spices, coconut and carrots. Fold in the ground almonds and the wholemeal flour.
◆ Spoon the mixture into the prepared mould, smooth the top and dredge it with a thin layer of caster sugar.
◆ Cover with cling film and microwave on HIGH for 10 minutes or until the cake is cooked, when it will shrink slightly away from the sides of the mould. Give the cake a quarter turn 4 times during the cooking time.
◆ Remove the cling film and leave the cake to stand for 10-15 minutes before turning it out on to a rack to cool.

# FRUITED BUTTERSCOTCH RING

### SERVES 10

| about 200 ml (7 fl oz) milk |
| 25 g (1 oz) fresh yeast or 15 ml (1 level tbsp) dried yeast and a pinch of sugar |
| 400 g (14 oz) strong plain flour |
| 5 ml (1 level tsp) salt |
| 40 g (1½ oz) butter or margarine |
| 1 egg, size 2, beaten |
| For the topping: |
| 50 g (2 oz) butter |
| 50 g (2 oz) soft light brown sugar |
| 30 ml (2 tbsp) golden syrup |
| 100 g (4 oz) mixed dried fruit |

◆ Grease a 2.3 litre (4 pint) ovenproof glass or microwave ring mould.

◆ Put the milk in an ovenproof measuring jug and microwave on HIGH for about 1 minute or until the milk is tepid. Add the fresh yeast and stir it until it is dissolved. If using dried yeast and sugar, sprinkle it into the milk and leave it in a warm place for 15 minutes until frothy.

◆ Sift the flour and the salt into an ovenproof glass bowl and microwave on HIGH for 30 seconds to warm the flour. Rub the butter into the flour.

◆ Make a well in the centre of the flour and pour in the yeast mixture and the egg. Mix to form a soft dough.

◆ Knead the dough on a lightly floured work surface for 10 minutes until it becomes smooth and elastic. Place the dough in a mixing bowl and cover. Leave the dough in a warm place for about 1 hour until it has doubled in size.

◆ For the topping, put the butter, sugar and syrup into an ovenproof glass bowl and microwave on HIGH for 1-2 minutes, stirring frequently, until melted and boiling. Pour this into the prepared ring mould and then sprinkle it with half the dried fruit.

◆ Turn the risen dough on to a lightly floured work surface and knead it again for about 3 minutes until it becomes smooth. Cut the dough into about 24 small even pieces and shape them into balls.

◆ Arrange the balls of dough in the ring mould in loose layers, sprinkling them with the remaining dried fruit. Cover the dough loosely with a clean tea-towel and leave it in a warm place until it nearly reaches the top of the mould.

◆ Microwave on HIGH for 5-6 minutes until the ring is well risen and cooked and a wooden cocktail stick or skewer inserted in the dough comes out clean. Give the dish a quarter turn 3 times during the cooking time.

◆ Leave the fruited butterscotch ring in the mould for 10 minutes before turning it out on to a rack to cool.

# CHOCOLATE, DATE AND NUT LOAF

### SERVES 10

| 100 ml (4 fl oz) water |
| 75 g (3 oz) stoned dates, chopped |
| 150 g (5 oz) plain flour |
| 25 g (1 oz) caster sugar |
| 2.5 ml (½ level tsp) salt |
| 2.5 ml (½ level tsp) baking powder |
| 2.5 ml (½ level tsp) bicarbonate of soda |
| 25 g (1 oz) butter or margarine |
| 75 g (3 oz) plain chocolate |
| 1 egg, beaten |
| 75 g (3 oz) chopped walnuts |
| 50 ml (2 fl oz) milk |

◆ Grease a 900 g (2 lb) ovenproof glass loaf dish. Place the water and dates in a small ovenproof glass bowl, cover with cling film and microwave on HIGH for 5 minutes. Leave to stand, covered.

◆ Meanwhile, sift the flour, sugar, salt, baking powder and bicarbonate of soda into a mixing bowl.

◆ Place the butter and chocolate in a small ovenproof glass bowl and microwave on LOW for 3-5 minutes or until melted. Add this to the dry ingredients with the dates, egg, walnuts and enough milk to make a very soft dropping consistency. Spoon the mixture into the prepared dish and smooth the top.

◆ Shield each end of the dish with a small piece of smooth foil, shiny side in. Cover with cling film and microwave on HIGH for 8-9 minutes, giving the dish a quarter turn three or four times during cooking. Remove the cling film and foil and microwave on HIGH for 1-1½ minutes or until the cake is cooked and a wooden cocktail stick or skewer inserted in the centre of the cake comes out clean.

◆ Allow the cake to stand in the dish for 5-10 minutes before carefully turning it out on to a rack to cool.

# ALMOND AND CHERRY CAKE

SERVES 10-12

| |
|---|
| 275 g (10 oz) glacé cherries |
| 65 g (2½ oz) self raising flour |
| 225 g (8 oz) unsalted butter, softened |
| 225 g (8 oz) caster sugar |
| 6 eggs, beaten |
| pinch of salt |
| 175 g (6 oz) ground almonds |
| 2.5 ml (½ tsp) almond flavouring |
| icing sugar, to decorate |

◆ Grease a 2.3 litre (4 pint) ovenproof glass or microwave ring mould.
◆ Dust the cherries lightly with 15 g (½ oz) of the flour and arrange them in the bottom of the dish.
◆ Cream the butter and sugar together until they are pale and fluffy. Beat in the eggs, a little at a time, adding a little of the flour if the mixture shows signs of curdling.
◆ Sift in the remaining flour with the salt. Add the almonds and almond flavouring and mix the ingredients together well.
◆ Carefully spoon the mixture on top of the cherries in the prepared dish and smooth the top.
◆ Cover with cling film and microwave on HIGH for 12-13 minutes or until the cake is cooked and a wooden cocktail stick or skewer inserted into the centre of the cake comes out clean. Give the dish a quarter turn 3 times during cooking.
◆ Remove the cling film and leave the cake until it is cold. Loosen around the sides of the cake with a palette knife and carefully turn it out on to a serving plate. Sift icing sugar over the top.

# LEMON GATEAU SLICE

SERVES 2

| |
|---|
| 50 g (2 oz) butter or margarine, cut into pieces |
| 50 g (2 oz) self raising flour |
| 50 g (2 oz) soft light brown sugar |
| pinch of salt |
| 1 egg, beaten |
| finely grated rind and juice of ½ lemon |
| 75 g (3 oz) low fat soft cheese |
| 30 ml (2 tbsp) single cream |
| 15 ml (1 level tbsp) icing sugar |
| 30 ml (2 tbsp) lemon curd |

◆ Line the bases of two 11 × 7.5 cm (4½ × 3 inch), 350 ml (12 fl oz) ovenproof containers with greaseproof paper.
◆ Put the butter into a medium bowl and microwave on HIGH for 15 seconds or until the butter is just soft enough to beat.
◆ Stir in the flour, sugar, salt, egg and lemon rind and beat until smooth.
◆ Spoon into the prepared containers. Cover with absorbent kitchen paper and microwave on HIGH for 1-2 minutes or until the cakes are risen but still look slightly moist on the surface. Turn the cakes once during cooking. Leave to stand for 5 minutes, then turn out and leave to cool on a wire rack.
◆ Meanwhile, make the filling. Beat the cheese, cream and icing sugar together with half of the lemon juice.
◆ When the cakes are cool, spread one with 15 ml (1 tbsp) of the lemon curd. Spread half of the cream cheese mixture on top of the lemon curd, then sandwich the 2 cakes together.
◆ Swirl the remaining cream cheese mixture on top of the cake, then put the remaining lemon curd and the remaining lemon juice in a small bowl and microwave on HIGH for 10 seconds, until just melted but not hot. Beat together then drizzle on top of the cake to make a decorative pattern. Cut the gâteau in half to serve.

# HONEY GINGERBREAD

SERVES 8

| |
|---|
| 100 g (4 oz) butter or margarine |
| 150 g (5 oz) clear honey |
| 100 g (4 oz) soft dark brown sugar |
| 150 ml (¼ pint) milk |
| 2 eggs |
| 225 g (8 oz) plain wholemeal flour |
| 5 ml (1 level tsp) ground mixed spice |
| 10 ml (2 level tsp) ground ginger |
| 2.5 ml (½ level tsp) bicarbonate of soda |
| 30 ml (2 level tbsp) crystallised ginger, finely chopped |

◆ Base line a 11.5 × 23.5 cm (4½ × 9½ inch) ovenproof loaf dish with greaseproof paper.
◆ Place the butter, 125 g (4 oz) honey, half the sugar and the milk in a large bowl and microwave on HIGH for 4 minutes or until the butter has melted and the brown sugar has dissolved. Leave to cool.
◆ Beat in the eggs, flour, spices, bicarbonate of soda and the remaining brown sugar.
◆ Pour into the prepared dish and microwave on HIGH for 7-8 minutes until the cake is cooked, and a wooden cocktail stick or skewer inserted into the centre of the cake comes out clean. Leave to stand until just warm, then turn out on to a wire rack and remove the paper

◆ Place the remaining honey in a small bowl and micro-wave on HIGH for 20 seconds. Brush over the warm cake and sprinkle with the crystallised ginger.

## FRUITY TEA-CAKE

### SERVES 8

| |
|---|
| 75 g (3 oz) currants |
| 75 g (3 oz) glacé cherries, chopped |
| 75 g (3 oz) sultanas |
| 75 g (3 oz) seedless raisins |
| finely grated rind of ½ a lemon |
| 5 ml (1 level tsp) mixed spice |
| 150 ml (¼ pint) cold tea |
| 75 g (3 oz) butter or margarine |
| 75 g (3 oz) soft dark brown sugar |
| 2 eggs, size 2 |
| 175 g (6 oz) plain flour |

◆ Mix the currants, cherries, sultanas, raisins, lemon rind and mixed spice together in a mixing bowl, add the tea and stir well. Cover the mixture and leave it to stand overnight.

◆ Grease a 20.5 cm (8½ inch) soufflé dish and line the base with a round of greaseproof paper.

◆ Cream the butter and sugar together until they are pale and fluffy, then beat in the eggs one at a time, beating them well between each addition. Mix in the soaked fruits and any remaining tea and then fold in the flour.

◆ Spoon the mixture into the prepared dish and smooth the top. Cover the microwave on HIGH for 10 minutes, then reduce the setting to LOW and microwave for 4 minutes, testing after 4 minutes to see if the cake is cooked — a wooden cocktail stick or skewer inserted in the centre of the cake will come out clean. If the cake isn't ready, microwave further. Give the cake a quarter turn 4 times during the cooking time.

◆ Allow the cake to stand in its dish for 20 minutes before turning it out on to a rack to cool.

## PEANUT BUTTER BISCUITS

### MAKES 16

| |
|---|
| 60 ml (4 tbsp) crunchy peanut butter |
| 75 g (3 oz) soft dark brown sugar |
| 50 g (2 oz) butter or margarine |
| 1 egg, size 2 |
| 100 g (4 oz) self raising wholemeal flour |

◆ Cream the peanut butter, sugar and butter together until they are very soft and fluffy. Beat in the egg and then stir in the flour to make a firm dough.

◆ Roll the dough into 16 walnut-sized smooth balls. Place them on large, flat, greased ovenproof plates, about 4 to a plate, spacing them well apart in a circle.

◆ Press criss-cross lines on each ball of dough with a fork to flatten slightly.

◆ Microwave on HIGH for 2 minutes, one plate at a time. Allow the biscuits to cool slightly on the plates, then remove them to a rack to cool completely.

## BOSTON BROWNIES

### MAKES ABOUT 24

| |
|---|
| 100 g (4 oz) plain chocolate |
| 100 g (4 oz) butter or margarine, cut into small pieces |
| 100 g (4 oz) soft dark brown sugar |
| 100 g (4 oz) self raising flour |
| 10 ml (2 level tsp) cocoa powder |
| 1.25 ml (¼ level tsp) salt |
| 2 eggs, size 2, beaten |
| 2.5 ml (½ tsp) vanilla flavouring |
| 100 g (4 oz) walnuts, coarsely chopped |

◆ Grease two shallow 12.5 cm (5 inch) × 18 cm (7 inch) glass ovenproof dishes or plastic dishes. Line the base with greaseproof paper.

◆ Break the chocolate into small pieces and put them into a large ovenproof glass bowl with the pieces of butter. Microwave on LOW for 3-5 minutes or until the chocolate is soft and glossy on top and the butter has melted. Stir well until the mixture is smooth.

◆ Stir the sugar into the chocolate mixture. Sift the flour, cocoa and salt into the bowl and add the eggs and vanilla flavouring and beat well to make a smooth batter. Stir in the walnuts.

◆ Pour half of the brownie mixture into one of the prepared dishes and shield each end with a small piece of smooth foil, shiny side down. Cover with cling film and microwave on HIGH for 5 minutes until well risen, firm to the touch and slightly moist on the surface. Give the dish a quarter turn 3 times during the cooking time. Repeat with the remaining mixture.

◆ Remove the cling film and foil and allow the mixture to cool in the dish. Cut each cake into about 12 squares before serving.

## SMALL CAKES

### MAKES ABOUT 18

150 g (5 oz) butter or margarine

100 g (4 oz) caster sugar

2 eggs

75 g (3 oz) self raising flour

25 g (1 oz) cocoa powder

15-30 ml (1-2 tbsp) milk

100 g (4 oz) plain chocolate, broken into small pieces

◆ Cut 100 g (4 oz) butter into 2.5 cm (1 inch) pieces and put in a large bowl. Microwave on HIGH for 10-15 seconds until slightly softened but not melted.
◆ Stir in the sugar, eggs, flour and cocoa powder and beat well. Add enough milk to make a very soft dropping consistency.
◆ Put 6 paper cases into a microwave muffin pan or into 6 tea cups. Fill the paper cases one third full with cake mixture.
◆ Microwave on HIGH for 1 minute or until the surface of the cakes is almost dry.
◆ Remove the cakes from the muffin pan or cups. Leave to cool on a wire rack.
◆ Place 6 more paper cases in the pan or cups and repeat as above. Then repeat again.
◆ When the cakes are cool, put the chocolate in a small bowl. Microwave on LOW for 3-4 minutes or until the chocolate is melted, stirring occasionally. Stir in the remaining butter and microwave on HIGH for 1 minute. Spread the icing over the cakes to decorate.

## MUESLI BISCUITS

### MAKES 16

100 g (4 oz) butter or margarine

50 g (2 oz) demerara sugar

15 ml (1 tbsp) honey

50 g (2 oz) self raising wholemeal flour

200 g (7 oz) muesli

50 g (2 oz) dried apricots, chopped

1 egg yolk, size 2

icing sugar, for sifting

◆ Cream the butter and sugar together until pale and fluffy. Add the honey, flour, muesli, apricots and egg and mix well together to form a firm dough.
◆ Roll the dough into 16 smooth balls about the size of walnuts. Place them on large, flat, greased ovenproof plates, about 4 to a plate, spacing them well apart in a circle.

◆ Microwave on HIGH, one plate at a time, for 2 minutes. Allow the biscuits to cool slightly, then transfer them to a cooling rack to cool completely.

## PEANUT FUDGE SQUARES

### MAKES ABOUT 25

115 g (4½ oz) unsalted butter

225 g (8 oz) icing sugar

225 g (8 oz) peanut butter

100 g (4 oz) unsalted peanuts

50 g (2 oz) raisins, coarsely chopped

175 g (6 oz) plain chocolate, broken into small pieces

◆ Cut 100 g (4 oz) of the butter into small pieces and put in a large bowl. Microwave on HIGH for 1 minute until melted.
◆ Add the icing sugar, peanut butter, peanuts and raisins to the melted butter and mix well.
◆ Transfer the mixture to a 18 × 28 × 2.5 cm (7 × 11 × 1 inch) deep tin and pat down with the back of a wooden spoon.
◆ Put the chocolate into a bowl with the remaining 15 g (½ oz) of butter. Microwave on HIGH for 2 minutes until melted. Mix together and spread evenly over the top of the peanut butter mixture.
◆ Mark into squares and chill for 10-15 minutes. Remove from the tin and cut into squares.

## CHOCOLATE BISCUIT CAKE

### SERVES 8

125 g (4 oz) plain chocolate, broken into small pieces

125 g (4 oz) butter, diced

15 ml (1 level tbsp) golden syrup

30 ml (2 tbsp) double cream

125 g (4 oz) digestive biscuits, finely broken up

50 g (2 oz) raisins

50 g (2 oz) glacé cherries, quartered

50 g (2 oz) flaked almonds, toasted

◆ Butter a 20.5 cm (8 inch) shallow glass dish. Put the chocolate, butter, syrup and cream into a large bowl. Microwave on LOW for 5 minutes or until the chocolate and butter have melted.
◆ Cool slightly, then mix in the biscuits, raisins, cherries and nuts.
◆ Turn the mixture into the prepared dish, lightly level the top, then chill for at least 1 hour. Serve cut into wedges.

# CHOCOLATE NUT BARS

## MAKES 16

| |
|---|
| 100 g (4 oz) self raising flour |
| 90 ml (6 level tbsp) rolled oats |
| 100 g (4 oz) soft margarine |
| 50 g (2 oz) caster sugar |
| 50 g (2 oz) soft dark brown sugar |
| 1.25 ml (¼ level tsp) salt |
| 2.5 ml (½ tsp) vanilla flavouring |
| 1 egg, size 2 |
| 75 g (3 oz) plain chocolate |
| 50 g (2 oz) chopped mixed nuts |

◆ Grease a 23 × 18 cm (9 × 7 inch) shallow, rectangular ovenproof glass dish.
◆ Put the self raising flour in a large bowl and mix in the rolled oats.
◆ Beat together the margarine, sugars, salt, vanilla flavouring and egg until they are pale and fluffy. Add the flour and oats and thoroughly mix the ingredients together.
◆ Spread the mixture in the prepared dish and smooth the top. Microwave on HIGH for 4-5 minutes until the cake is cooked and a wooden cocktail stick or skewer inserted in the centre of the cake comes out clean. Give the dish a quarter turn 3 times during the cooking time.
◆ Allow the cake to stand in the dish for 3-5 minutes before turning it out on to a rack to cool.
◆ Break the chocolate into pieces and put them in a small ovenproof glass bowl. Microwave on LOW for 3 minutes or until the chocolate becomes soft and glossy on top and stir it well until it is smooth.
◆ Spread the melted chocolate over the cooled cake and sprinkle it with the nuts. Cut the cake into 16 bars just before the chocolate sets.

# JUMBLES

## MAKES 20

| |
|---|
| 150 g (5 oz) butter or margarine |
| 150 g (5 oz) caster sugar |
| 1 egg, size 2, beaten |
| 300 g (10 oz) self raising flour |
| 5 ml (1 level tsp) grated lemon rind |
| 50 g (2 oz) ground almonds |
| 20 whole almonds |

◆ Put the butter into an ovenproof glass bowl and microwave on LOW for about 1 minute to soften it slightly, add the sugar and beat well until the butter becomes soft and fluffy.
◆ Beat half of the egg into the creamed mixture, then mix in the flour, lemon rind, almonds and the rest of the egg.
◆ Form the mixture into 20 walnut-sized balls and place them on large, greased, flat ovenproof plates, about 4 to a plate, spacing them well apart in a circle. Press out with a fork to a thickness of about 0.5 cm (¼ inch). Place an almond on top of each biscuit.
◆ Microwave on HIGH, one plate at a time, for about 2 minutes until the Jumbles are cooked and a wooden cocktail stick or skewer inserted into the centre comes out clean.
◆ Leave to stand for 1 minute, then transfer to a rack to cool.

# CHOCOLATE NUT AND RAISIN COOKIES

## MAKES 24

| |
|---|
| 100 g (4 oz) butter or margarine, softened |
| 100 g (4 oz) soft light brown sugar |
| 1 egg |
| 30 ml (2 tbsp) milk |
| 10 ml (2 level tsp) baking powder |
| 5 ml (1 tsp) vanilla flavouring |
| pinch of salt |
| 350 g (12 oz) plain flour |
| 50 g (2 oz) cooking chocolate drops |
| 25 g (1 oz) nuts, finely chopped |
| 50 g (2 oz) raisins |
| 10 ml (2 level tsp) finely grated orange rind |

◆ Line a flat plate or microwave baking sheet with greased greaseproof paper.
◆ Place the butter, sugar, egg and milk in a large bowl and beat until smooth. Add the baking powder, vanilla flavouring, salt and flour and knead until smooth.
◆ Cut the dough in half. Knead the chocolate drops and nuts into one half, and the raisins and orange rind into the other half.
◆ Shape the dough into 24 walnut-sized balls, flattening slightly. Arrange about one third of the pieces in a circle on the plate or baking sheet and microwave on MEDIUM for 3½ minutes. Cool for a few minutes, then carefully remove from the plate and cool on a wire rack. Repeat with the remaining amount of dough.

# PUDDINGS & DESSERTS

## CHOCOLATE CREAMS

*An elegant dessert to serve, especially in tall glasses, as shown here*

SEE PAGE 183

# Cooking Tips

◆

*Always pierce whole fruits with skins on, such as apples, to prevent them bursting.*

◆

*Steamed suet and sponge puddings cook in a fraction of the time needed for conventional steaming and the results are excellent.*

◆

*Remove sponges from the oven when recommended even if the mixture looks wet. Cooking will be completed during the standing time.*

◆

*Fruit with a high water content, such as rhubarb, will need no additional water but small berries will need a few tablespoonfuls.*

◆

*Fat and sugar attract microwaves and tend to cook before other ingredients. Beware of, for example, a filling in a sweet pie as these can be considerably hotter than the rest of the dish.*

◆

*Soften sugar that has become hard in its original wrapping on HIGH for 30-40 seconds.*

◆

*As well as cooking, a microwave oven can help with the preparation of foods for puddings. Melt chocolate by breaking it into a bowl and microwave on LOW until it looks glossy and is soft on top. Then remove from the oven and stir gently until it is completely melted.*

◆

*Dissolve gelatine by sprinkling it over the water in a small bowl and microwave on HIGH for 30-50 seconds, until the gelatine has dissolved, stirring frequently.*

◆

*To remove the skins and brown hazelnuts, place them in a single layer of absorbent kitchen paper and microwave on HIGH for 30 seconds. Rub off the skins and return to the oven until just golden. To toast flaked almonds place them on a large plate and microwave on HIGH for 8-10 minutes.*

◆

## CHOCOLATE CREAMS

### SERVES 8

15 ml (1 level tbsp) gelatine

30 ml (2 tbsp) rum or strong coffee

100 g (4 oz) plain dessert chocolate

3 eggs, separated

pinch of salt

410 g (14½ oz) can evaporated milk

100 g (4 oz) sugar

300 ml (10 fl oz) double cream

chocolate curls or rice paper flowers, to decorate

◆ Sprinkle the gelatine over the rum or coffee in a small bowl and leave to soften.
◆ Break the chocolate into a large bowl and microwave on HIGH for 2 minutes or until the chocolate melts. Beat in the gelatine with the rum, egg yolks, salt, evaporated milk and 50 g (2 oz) sugar.
◆ Microwave on MEDIUM for 6 minutes or until the mixture is thickened and smooth, stirring several times. Leave to stand at room temperature until cool (do not refrigerate).
◆ Lightly whip the cream and fold half into the chocolate mixture.
◆ Whisk the egg whites until stiff and fold in the remaining sugar. Gently fold into the chocolate cream.
◆ Spoon into individual serving glasses and chill. Pipe the remaining cream on top of the chocolate creams. Decorate with chocolate curls or rice paper flowers and serve.

## BREAD PUDDING

### SERVES 6

225 g (8 oz) stale bread, broken into small pieces

450 ml (¾ pint) milk

175 g (6 oz) mixed dried fruit

50 g (2 oz) shredded suet

10 ml (2 level tsp) ground mixed spice

65 g (2½ oz) soft dark brown sugar

1 egg, beaten

grated nutmeg to taste

caster or brown sugar, for dredging

custard sauce (see p. 216), to serve

◆ Grease a 900 ml (1½ pint) shallow round dish. Put the bread into the dish, pour the milk over and leave to soak for 30 minutes. Beat out the lumps.

◆ Add the dried fruit, suet, spice and the sugar and mix together well. Stir in the egg, and mix to a soft dropping consistency, adding a little more milk if necessary.
◆ Spread the mixture evenly in the dish and grate a little nutmeg over the surface.
◆ Microwave on MEDIUM for 10-15 minutes or until the mixture is almost set in the middle, giving the dish a quarter turn 4 times during cooking if the oven does not have a turntable.
◆ Leave to stand for 10 minutes. Dredge with caster or brown sugar. Serve warm or cold with custard.

## SPONGE PUDDING

### SERVES 3-4

50 g (2 oz) soft margarine

50 g (2 oz) caster sugar

1 egg, beaten

a few drops of vanilla flavouring

100 g (4 oz) self raising flour

45-60 ml (2-4 tbsp) milk

custard sauce (see p. 216), to serve

◆ Beat the margarine, sugar, egg, vanilla flavouring and flour until smooth. Gradually stir in enough milk to give a soft dropping consistency.
◆ Spoon into a greased 600 ml (1 pint) pudding basin and level the surface.
◆ Microwave on HIGH for 5-7 minutes until the top of the sponge is only slightly moist and a wooden cocktail stick or skewer inserted in the centre comes out clean.
◆ Leave to stand for 5 minutes before turning out on to a heated serving dish. Serve with custard.

VARIATIONS
Essex pudding: Spread jam over the sides and base of the greased pudding basin.
Apricot sponge pudding: Drain a 411 g (14½ oz) can of apricot halves and arrange them in the base of the greased pudding basin.
Syrup sponge pudding: Put 30 ml (2 tbsp) golden syrup into the bottom of the basin before adding the mixture. Flavour the mixture with the grated rind of a lemon.
Chocolate sponge pudding: Blend 60 ml (4 level tsp) cocoa powder to a smooth cream with 15 ml (1 tbsp) hot water and add to the beaten ingredients.
Jamaica pudding: Add 50-100 g (2-4 oz) chopped stem ginger with the milk.
Lemon or orange sponge: Add the grated rind of 1 orange or lemon when beating the ingredients.

## SAUCY CHOCOLATE PUDDING

SERVES 4

| |
|---|
| 100 g (4 oz) plain flour |
| 75 ml (5 level tbsp) cocoa powder |
| 10 ml (2 level tsp) baking powder |
| pinch of salt |
| 275 g (10 oz) light brown sugar |
| 175 ml (6 fl oz) milk |
| 30 ml (2 tbsp) vegetable oil |
| 5 ml (1 tsp) vanilla flavouring |
| 50 g (2 oz) walnuts, finely chopped |

◆ Sift the flour, 10 ml (2 level tbsp) cocoa, baking powder and salt into a large bowl. Stir in 100 g (4 oz) sugar.
◆ Make a well in the centre and pour in the milk, oil and vanilla flavouring. Beat to a smooth batter. Stir in the nuts.
◆ Pour the mixture into a 20.5 cm (8 inch) baking dish. Mix the remaining sugar and cocoa together and sprinkle evenly over the batter.
◆ Pour over 350 ml (12 fl oz) boiling water. Microwave on HIGH for 12-14 minutes or until the top looks dry and the sauce is bubbling through.

## FLAN CASE

MAKES A 23 CM (9 INCH) CASE

| |
|---|
| 225 g (8 oz) plain flour |
| pinch of salt |
| 50 g (2 oz) butter or margarine |
| 50 g (2 oz) lard |

◆ Place the flour and salt in a bowl. Cut the fats into small pieces and add to the flour. Rub the fat into the flour until the mixture resembles fine breadcrumbs. Add enough water to bind the mixture together.
◆ Knead lightly for a few seconds to make a firm dough.
◆ Roll out the dough on a lightly floured surface and use to line a 23 cm (9 inch) flan ring set on a baking sheet. Chill in the refrigerator for 20-30 minutes.
◆ Line the pastry with greased greasproof paper and weight down with baking beans. Bake conventionally at 200°C (400°F) mark 6 for 15 minutes or until set. Remove beans and bake for 10-12 minutes until golden brown. Remove from the tin and leave on a wire rack until cool.

*To make enough pastry to line a 20.5 cm (8 inch) case:* use 175 g (6 oz) plain flour and 40 g (1½ oz) butter or margarine and 40 g (1½ oz) lard.

## APPLE CRUMBLE

SERVES 4

| |
|---|
| 100 g (4 oz) butter or margarine, chopped |
| 175 g (6 oz) plain flour |
| 100 g (4 oz) granulated or demerara sugar |
| 700 g (1½ lb) cooking apples, peeled, cored and thinly sliced |
| pinch of ground cloves |

◆ Rub the butter into the flour until the mixture resembles fine breadcrumbs. Stir in 50 g (2 oz) sugar
◆ Spread the apples evenly in a shallow dish. Sprinkle with the remaining sugar and ground cloves.
◆ Cover the microwave on HIGH for 5 minutes until the apples begin to soften.
◆ Sprinkle the crumble mixture over the fruit to completely cover it.
◆ Without covering, microwave on HIGH for 10-12 minutes or until the topping is just set, giving the dish a quarter turn during cooking if the oven does not have a turntable. Brown under a hot grill, if liked.

## STRAWBERRY FOOL

SERVES 6

| |
|---|
| 30-40 ml (2-3 level tbsp) sugar |
| 20 ml (4 level tsp) cornflour |
| 300 ml (½ pint) milk |
| 700 g (1½ lb) strawberries, hulled |
| 300 ml (½ pint) double cream |

◆ Blend 15 ml (1 level tbsp) of the sugar and the cornflour with a little of the milk in a measuring jug or medium bowl. Stir in the remainder of the milk.
◆ Microwave on HIGH for 3-4 minutes or until the sauce has thickened, stirring every minute. Cover the surface of the sauce closely with cling film and leave until cold.
◆ Reserve a few whole strawberries for decoration. Push the remaining strawberries through a nylon sieve to form a purée or put in a blender or food processor and liquidise until smooth, then push through a nylon sieve to remove the pips.
◆ Stir the cold sauce into the strawberry purée. Mix well and sweeten to taste with the remaining sugar.
◆ Lightly whip the cream and fold into the strawberry mixture. Turn into 6 individual dishes and chill for 1-2 hours.
◆ Thinly slice the reserved strawberries and arrange on top of each portion, to decorate.

### STRAWBERRY FOOL
*A perfect summer dessert – making the best use of available fresh fruit*
SEE OPPOSITE

## SPICED PLUM SPONGE

### SERVES 4

75 g (3 oz) butter or margarine

75 g (3 oz) soft light brown sugar

2 eggs

100 g (4 oz) self raising flour

2.5 ml (½ level tsp) ground cinnamon

425 g (15 oz) can plums

custard sauce (see p. 216), to serve

◆ Cream the butter and sugar together until light and fluffy. Gradually beat in the eggs and then fold in the flour and cinnamon.

◆ Drain and stone the plums, reserving the juice. Arrange the fruit in the base of an 18 cm (7 inch) soufflé dish and cover with the sponge mixture.

◆ Microwave on HIGH for 8 minutes or until the sponge is firm to the touch. Serve hot with custard sauce.

## RHUBARB CRUMBLE

### SERVES 4

700 g (1½ lb) rhubarb, trimmed

finely grated rind and juice of 1 small orange

pinch of ground ginger (optional)

75 g (3 oz) demerara sugar

175 g (6 oz) wholemeal flour

100 g (4 oz) butter or margarine

25 g (1 oz) finely chopped walnuts

custard sauce (see p. 216), to serve

◆ Cut the rhubarb into 2.5 cm (1 inch) pieces and place in a deep 20.5 cm (8 inch) baking dish.

◆ Add the grated orange rind and juice, the ginger, if using, and 25 g (1 oz) demerara sugar. Mix thoroughly.

◆ Three-quarters cover with cling film and microwave on HIGH for 4-5 minutes or until the rhubarb softens slightly, stirring occasionally.

◆ Sift the flour into a mixing bowl and rub in the butter until the mixture resembles fine breadcrumbs. Stir in the remaining sugar and the walnuts.

◆ Spoon the crumble mixture on top of the fruit, pressing it down well with the back of a spoon.

◆ Microwave on HIGH for 10-12 minutes or until the topping is just set, giving the dish a quarter turn 3 times during cooking.

◆ Leave the crumble to stand for 5 minutes, then brown it under a preheated grill if desired. Serve it hot with custard.

## CURD CHEESE FLAN

### SERVES 8

50 g (2 oz) butter or margarine

75 g (3 oz) digestive biscuits, crushed

450 g (1 lb) curd cheese

3 eggs

100 g (4 oz) demerara sugar

finely grated rind of 1 lemon

50 g (2 oz) sultanas

142 ml (5 fl oz) soured cream

pinch of grated nutmeg

◆ Place the butter in a bowl and microwave on HIGH for 45 seconds or until the butter melts.

◆ Pour half the butter into a blender or food processor and set aside. Mix the butter remaining in the bowl with the crushed biscuits. Reserve 45 ml (3 tbsp) crumbs and press the rest on to the base of a 23 cm (9 inch) flan dish. Microwave on HIGH for 1 minute.

◆ Add the cheese, eggs, sugar and lemon rind to the blender or food processor and liquidise until smooth. Stir in the sultanas and pour into the flan dish. Microwave on LOW for 20 minutes or until the mixture is set around the edges. Leave to stand at room temperature for 1 hour.

◆ Spread the soured cream evenly over the top of the flan. Mix the nutmeg with the reserved crumb mixture and sprinkle it over the top of the flan. Serve at room temperature.

## CARIBBEAN BANANAS

### SERVES 4

25 g (1 oz) butter or margarine

50 g (2 oz) soft dark brown sugar

4 large bananas, peeled and halved

60 ml (4 tbsp) dark rum

◆ Place the butter in a shallow dish and microwave on HIGH for 45 seconds or until the butter melts. Add the sugar and microwave on HIGH for 1 minute. Stir until the sugar has dissolved.

◆ Add the bananas and coat with the sugar mixture. Microwave on HIGH for 4 minutes, turning the fruit over once.

◆ Place the rum in a cup and microwave on HIGH for 30 seconds, pour over the bananas and flambé immediately. Serve at once, with cream, if liked.

## CREME CARAMEL

SERVES 4

*75 ml (5 level tbsp) caster sugar*

*450 ml (¾ pint) milk*

*3 eggs, lightly beaten*

◆ Place 45 ml (3 level tbsp) caster sugar and 45 ml (3 tbsp) water in an ovenproof jug and microwave on HIGH for 5-6 minutes or until the sugar caramelises. Watch it carefully once it starts to colour as it will then brown very quickly.
◆ Pour the caramel into the base of a 750 ml (1¼ pint) soufflé dish and leave it to set.
◆ Meanwhile, place the milk in an ovenproof measuring jug and microwave on HIGH for 1½ minutes or until warm.
◆ Add the beaten eggs and the remaining sugar and carefully strain this over the set caramel.
◆ Cover with cling film and place the dish in a larger dish with a capacity of about 1.7 litres (3 pints). Pour in enough boiling water to come halfway up the sides of the dish.
◆ Microwave on LOW for 25-27 minutes or until the crème caramel is lightly set, giving the dish a quarter turn 3 times during the cooking time.
◆ Leave the caramel to stand for 5 minutes, then remove the dish from the water, uncover the caramel and leave it to cool for about 30 minutes.
◆ Refrigerate for about 4-5 hours until the caramel is set, then turn it out on to a serving dish to serve.

## SPOTTED DICK

SERVES 4

*75 g (3 oz) self raising flour*

*pinch of salt*

*75 g (3 oz) fresh brown breadcrumbs*

*75 g (3 oz) shredded suet*

*50 g (2 oz) soft light brown sugar*

*175 g (6 oz) currants*

*about 90 ml (6 tbsp) milk*

*custard sauce (see p. 216), to serve*

◆ Mix the flour, salt, breadcrumbs, suet, sugar and currants in a large bowl. Add enough milk to give a soft dropping consistency.
◆ Spoon into a 900 ml (1½ pint) pudding basin and cover loosely with cling film. Microwave on HIGH for 5 minutes. Leave to stand for 5 minutes. Turn out on to a hot serving plate. Serve with custard.

## FRUITY SUET PUDDING

SERVES 4 - 6

*175 g (6 oz) cooking apples, peeled, quartered and sliced*

*175 g (6 oz) plums, halved, and stones removed*

*225 g ( 8 oz) blackberries, hulls removed*

*finely grated rind of 1 lemon*

*15 ml (1 tbsp) lemon juice*

*50-100 g (2-4 oz) caster sugar*

*175 g (6 oz) self raising flour*

*15 ml (1 level tbsp) caster sugar*

*75 g (3 oz) shredded suet*

*milk, to mix*

*custard or ice cream, to serve*

◆ Grease a 1.4 litre (2½ pint) microwave pudding basin. Line the bottom of the basin with a small round of greaseproof paper.
◆ Place the prepared fruits in 3 separate bowls. Add the lemon rind and juice to the apples with 50 g (2 oz) sugar and divide the remaining sugar, if used, equally between the plums and the blackberries. Mix the fruits and the sugar together.
◆ To make the suetcrust pastry, put the flour and sugar into a mixing bowl and mix in the shredded suet. Bind the ingredients together with about 60-70 ml (4-5 tbsp) milk to form a soft but not sticky dough.
◆ Turn out on to a lightly floured surface and shape into a cylinder, wider at one end than the other. Cut into 4 pieces.
◆ Shape the smallest piece of pastry into a round large enough to fit the bottom of the prepared pudding basin. Place the pastry in the bottom of the basin and spoon in the apple mixture.
◆ Shape another piece of pastry into a round large enough to cover the apples. Place on top of the apples and spoon the plums on top. Repeat with another round to cover the plums and spoon in the blackberries.
◆ Shape the remaining pastry into a round large enough to cover the blackberries. Cover the blackberries with this final layer of pastry. There should be space above the last layer of pastry to allow for rising.
◆ Cover the pudding basin with cling film, pleated in the centre to allow for expansion. Microwave on HIGH for 15-16 minutes, giving the basin a quarter turn 3 times during cooking. Allow the pudding to stand in the basin for 5 minutes before turning it out carefully on to a hot serving dish. Serve hot with custard or ice cream.

## Fruit Kebabs with Yogurt and Honey Dip

*A novel way of presenting fruit salad, using firm-textured fruits*

SEE PAGE 190

## APPLE CAKE

*A delicious cake with a pleasing apple topping*

SEE PAGE 190

## FRUIT KEBABS WITH YOGURT AND HONEY DIP

### SERVES 4

1 small pineapple

2 large firm peaches

1 large firm banana

2 crisp eating apples

1 small bunch of large black grapes, seeded

finely grated rind and juice of 1 large orange

60 ml (4 tbsp) brandy or orange-flavoured liqueur

50 g (2 oz) unsalted butter

200 ml (7 fl oz) natural yogurt

45 ml (3 tbsp) clear honey

mint sprigs, to decorate

◆ Cut the top and bottom off the pineapple. Stand the pineapple upright on a board and, using a very sharp knife, slice downwards in sections to remove the skin and 'eyes'. Cut the pineapple into quarters and remove the core. Cut the flesh into small cubes.

◆ Skin and halve the peaches and remove the stones. Cut the flesh into chunks.

◆ Peel the banana and then slice it into thick chunks. Quarter and core the apples but do not skin them. Cut each quarter in half cross-ways.

◆ Put all the fruit together in a bowl. Mix the orange rind and juice with the brandy, pour this over the fruit and cover and leave to marinate for at least 30 minutes.

◆ Thread the fruit on to 8 wooden kebab skewers. Put the butter in a small ovenproof bowl and microwave on LOW for 2 minutes, or until the butter is melted, then brush this over the kebabs.

◆ Arrange the kebabs in a double layer on a roasting rack in a shallow ovenproof dish. Microwave on HIGH for 2 minutes, then reposition the kebabs so that the inside skewers are moved to the outside of the dish. Microwave on HIGH for about 4 minutes, reposition twice more and baste with any juices in the dish. Allow the kebabs to stand for 5 minutes.

◆ Whisk together the yogurt and 30 ml (2 level tbsp) of the honey. Pour the mixture into an ovenproof serving bowl, cover with cling film and microwave on HIGH for 1 minute, stirring occasionally, until just warm. Drizzle over the remaining honey and decorate the dip with a few fresh mint sprigs.

◆ Serve the fruit kebabs with the yogurt dip handed separately.

## APPLE CAKE

### SERVES 6-8

225 g (8 oz) cooking apples, peeled, cored and chopped

100 g (4 oz) sultanas

75 ml (3 fl oz) milk

75 g (3 oz) soft dark brown sugar

175 g (6 oz) self raising flour

10 ml (2 level tsp) mixed spice

2.5 ml (½ level tsp) ground cinnamon

75 g (3 oz) butter or margarine

1 egg, size 2, beaten

2 apples, quartered and sliced

15 ml (1 level tbsp) apricot jam, heated

custard or cream, to serve

◆ Grease a 23 cm (9 inch), 2.3 litre (4 pint) ovenproof glass or microwave ring mould.

◆ Mix the apples, sultanas, milk and sugar together in a bowl.

◆ Sift the flour and spices into a mixing bowl and rub in the butter until the mixture resembles fine breadcrumbs. Add the apple mixture and egg and mix the ingredients together well.

◆ Spoon the cake mixture into the prepared mould and smooth the top.

◆ Cover with cling film and microwave on HIGH for 10 minutes, then remove the cling film and microwave on HIGH for 1-2 minutes until the cake is cooked and a wooden cocktail stick or skewer inserted into the centre of the cake comes out clean.

◆ Leave the cake to stand in its mould for 5 minutes before carefully turning it out. Arrange the sliced apple on top of the cake and brush with the apricot jam. Serve the apple cake warm with custard or cream.

## VANILLA ICE CREAM

### SERVES 8-10

568 ml (1 pint) milk

1 vanilla pod

6 egg yolks, size 2

175 g (6 oz) caster sugar

600 ml (1 pint) double cream

◆ Put the milk and the vanilla pod into a large ovenproof measuring jug and microwave on HIGH for 4-5 minutes or until the milk comes almost to the boil. Remove it from the oven and allow it to stand for 15 minutes.

◆ Put the egg yolks and the caster sugar into a large mixing bowl and beat them together until pale, then stir in the milk. Strain the mixture through a fine sieve into a large ovenproof glass bowl.

◆ Microwave the custard on LOW for 20-22 minutes, stirring frequently, until the custard is thick enough to coat the back of a wooden spoon.

◆ Pour the custard into a well chilled shallow freezer container and cover the surface closely with cling film to prevent a skin forming. Leave the custard to cool.

◆ Freeze the cooled custard for about 2 hours until it becomes mushy, then turn it into a large, chilled basin and mash the custard with a whisk. Lightly whip the cream and fold it into the vanilla custard. Cover and freeze it again for a further 2 hours until it becomes mushy, then mash it again.

◆ Cover and return it to the freezer for about 2 hours to become firm. To serve, thaw the ice cream in the microwave on MEDIUM for 30-45 seconds, then leave it to stand for 1 minute until it is slightly softened.

*Note:* do not whip the fresh cream if you are using a mechanical churn or ice cream maker. Agitate the chilled custard and un-whipped cream.

# ORANGES IN CARAMEL

## SERVES 4

| |
| --- |
| 8 medium juicy oranges |
| 225 g (8 oz) caster sugar |
| 200 ml (7 fl oz) boiling water |
| 30 ml (2 tbsp) orange-flavoured liqueur |

◆ Using a potato peeler, thinly pare the rind from 2 of the oranges, taking care not to peel off any of the white pith. Cut the rind into very fine julienne strips.

◆ Remove the peel and the white pith from all the oranges. Slice the oranges into rounds and remove the pips. In a shallow serving dish, arrange the slices so that they overlap and set aside.

◆ Put 90 ml (6 tbsp) water into an ovenproof dish and microwave on HIGH for 1-2 minutes or until boiling, then add the sugar and stir until dissolved.

◆ Microwave the sugar syrup on HIGH for 5-6 minutes until it turns a golden caramel colour. Immediately pour the boiling water on to the caramel. Add the julienne strips and microwave on HIGH for 4-5 minutes to dissolve the caramel and until the julienne strips are tender.

◆ Remove the caramel syrup from the oven and stir in the orange-flavoured liqueur. Allow the syrup to stand for 10 minutes to ensure that all the caramel has dissolved.

◆ Pour the caramel syrup and the julienne strips over the sliced oranges. Cover and refrigerate them for about 1 hour until they are well chilled.

# COFFEE CHEESECAKE

## SERVES 8

| |
| --- |
| 50 g (2 oz) butter or margarine, cut into small pieces |
| 175 g (6 oz) gingernut biscuits, finely crushed |
| 15 ml (1 level tbsp) gelatine |
| 20 ml (4 level tsp) instant coffee granules |
| 45 ml (3 tbsp) coffee-flavoured liqueur |
| 150 g (5 oz) soft light brown sugar |
| 450 g (1 lb) full fat soft cheese |
| 300 ml (½ pint) whipping cream |
| coffee beans, to decorate |

◆ Lightly butter a 20.5 cm (8 inch) loose-bottomed deep cake tin or spring-release cake tin.

◆ Place the butter in a medium ovenproof bowl and microwave on HIGH for 1 minute or until the butter melts. Stir in the biscuit crumbs and mix together well.

◆ Press the crumb mixture firmly into the base of the prepared tin. Leave it in the refrigerator to chill while making the filling.

◆ In an ovenproof glass bowl, sprinkle the gelatine on to 45 ml (3 tbsp) water. Leave for 2 minutes to soak, then microwave on HIGH for 30-50 seconds or until dissolved, stirring frequently.

◆ Mix the instant coffee, coffee liqueur and sugar with 300 ml (½ pint) water and microwave on HIGH for 1-2 minutes or until the coffee and sugar have dissolved. Stir in the gelatine mixture.

◆ Place the coffee and gelatine mixture in a blender or food processor with the cheese and liquidise until smooth.

◆ Lightly whip the cream and fold half of it into the cheese mixture.

◆ Pour on top of the biscuit base. Chill in the refrigerator for 3-4 hours until set.

◆ Remove from the tin and decorate with the remaining cream and the coffee beans.

## HOT STUFFED DATES

*An exotic date dessert with a spiced nut filling*

SEE OPPOSITE

## HOT STUFFED DATES

### SERVES 2

*30 ml (2 level tbsp) ground almonds*

*30 ml (2 level tbsp) pistachio nuts, chopped*

*pinch of ground ginger*

*large pinch of ground cinnamon*

*30 ml (2 tbsp) clear honey*

*6 large fresh dates, pitted*

*90 ml (6 tbsp) double cream*

*5 ml (1 tsp) rum*

◆ Mix together the almonds, pistachio nuts, ginger and cinnamon. Stir in the honey and mix well together.
◆ Stuff the dates with this mixture and arrange on a small ovenproof plate.
◆ Cover loosely with cling film and microwave on HIGH for 2-3 minutes or until hot. Leave to stand.
◆ Meanwhile, make the sauce. Put the cream and the rum into a heatproof jug. Mix well together and microwave on HIGH for 5-7 minutes or until the sauce is thickened and reduced. Pour the sauce around the dates and serve immediately.

*To serve 4:* double all the ingredients, then follow the recipe as above, but in point 3 microwave on HIGH for 2-3 minutes; in point 4 microwave on HIGH for 5-7 minutes.

## LEMON MERINGUE PIE

### SERVES 6

*20.5 cm (8 inch) flan case (see p.184)*

For the filling:

*45 ml (3 level tbsp) cornflour*

*finely grated rind and juice of 2 lemons*

*200 g (7 oz) caster sugar*

*3 eggs, separated*

◆ Pour 150 ml (¼ pint) water into a medium bowl and mix in the cornflour, lemon rind, lemon juice and 75 g (3 oz) sugar. Microwave on HIGH for 4-5 minutes or until the mixture is smooth and thick, stirring several times.
◆ Beat in the egg yolks and microwave on HIGH for 45 seconds, whisking once. Pour mixture into baked flan case.
◆ Whisk the egg whites until stiff and gradually fold in the remaining sugar. Spoon or pipe the whisked whites on top of the lemon filling.
◆ Place the pie under a hot grill until the topping is golden brown on top.

## GINGER PEARS

### SERVES 6

*300 ml (½ pint) sweet cider*

*100 g (4 oz) caster sugar*

*strip of lemon peel*

*1.25 ml (¼ level tsp) ground ginger*

*6 large eating pears, peeled, left whole with stalks on*

*50 g (2 oz) crystallised or stem ginger, chopped*

◆ Put the cider, sugar, lemon peel and ginger into a casserole dish. Microwave on HIGH for 3-5 minutes until boiling, stirring frequently to dissolve the sugar.
◆ Place the pears in the ginger syrup, spooning it over them to coat. Three-quarters cover the dish with cling film, or with a lid.
◆ Microwave the pears on HIGH for 5-7 minutes until they are just tender when pierced with the tip of a knife, turning the pears and repositioning them in the dish two or three times during the cooking time.
◆ Lift the pears from the syrup with a slotted draining spoon and place them in a serving dish.
◆ Microwave the syrup, uncovered, on HIGH for 15-17 minutes until the syrup is reduced by half.
◆ Pour the syrup over the pears and allow them to cool, then cover and refrigerate the pears until they are well chilled. Sprinkle ginger over the pears before serving.

## BAKED APPLES

### SERVES 4

*50 g (2 oz) sultanas*

*50 g (2 oz) seedless raisins*

*50 g (2 oz) no-soak dried apricots, chopped*

*50 g (2 oz) demerara sugar*

*4 medium cooking apples*

*60 ml (4 tbsp) water*

*15 g (½ oz) butter or margarine*

◆ Mix the sultanas, raisins, apricots and sugar together.
◆ Make a shallow cut through the skin around the middle of each apple. Remove the core from each, making a hole large enough to accommodate the filling.
◆ Stand the apples in an ovenproof dish and fill the centres with the mixed fruit. Pour the water into the dish and dot each apple with the butter.
◆ Loosely cover the apples with cling film and microwave on HIGH for 5-8 minutes, giving the dish a quarter turn 3 times during the cooking time. Allow the apples to stand for 5 minutes before serving.

## APRICOT CHEESECAKES

*Delicious fruit cheesecakes, flavoured with lemon and brandy*

SEE PAGE 196

## WALNUT PIE

*A dark, satisfying dessert with a rich nut filling*

SEE PAGE 196

## WALNUT PIE

### SERVES 8

23 cm (9 inch) flan case (see p. 184)

whipped cream, to serve

For the filling:

50 g (2 oz) butter or margarine

3 eggs

175 g (6 oz) soft dark brown sugar

75 ml (5 tbsp) golden syrup

5 ml (1 tsp) vanilla flavouring

175 g (6 oz) coarsely chopped walnuts

◆ Place the butter in a medium bowl and microwave on HIGH for 45 seconds or until the butter melts.
◆ Beat in the eggs, sugar, syrup and flavouring, then stir in the nuts.
◆ Pour into the flan case and microwave on MEDIUM for 18 minutes or until the filling is set. Leave to cool, and serve at room temperature with whipped cream.

## SUMMER PUDDING

### SERVES 2

5-6 thin slices day-old white bread, crusts removed

150 g (5 oz) strawberries, hulled

150 g (5 oz) raspberries

45 ml (3 level tbsp) sugar

whipped cream, to serve

◆ Cut the bread slices into neat fingers. Reserve about a quarter and use the rest to line the base and sides of two 150 ml (¼ pint) ramekin dishes, making sure that there are no spaces between the bread.
◆ Put the fruit into a medium bowl.
◆ Sprinkle with the sugar and add 45 ml (3 tbsp) water. Cover with cling film, pulling back one corner to allow the steam to escape, and microwave on HIGH for 5-7 minutes or until the sugar dissolves, the juices begin to flow and the fruit softens.
◆ Reserve about 45 ml (3 tbsp) of the juice and pour the remaining fruit and juice into the lined ramekins. Cover with the reserved bread.
◆ Place a small saucer with a weight on it on top of each pudding and refrigerate overnight.
◆ To serve, turn out on to 2 serving plates and spoon over the reserved juice. Serve with whipped cream.

## HOT FRUIT SALAD

### SERVES 4-6

100 g (4 oz) dried apricots

100 g (4 oz) dried figs

2 large firm bananas, peeled and thickly sliced

2 large fresh peaches, skinned, halved, stoned and sliced

2 large oranges, peel and pith removed, and cut into segments

juice of 2 lemons

50 g (2 oz) stoned raisins

5 ml (1 level tsp) ground cinnamon

2.5 ml (½ level tsp) ground ginger

6 cloves

◆ Put the dried apricots and figs into a large ovenproof serving dish and add 450 ml (¾ pint) cold water. Three-quarters cover the fruits with cling film and microwave on HIGH for 10-12 minutes or until the fruits are almost tender. Stir two or three times during cooking.
◆ Add the remaining fruits, lemon juice, raisins and spices and stir well. Microwave on HIGH for 4-5 minutes or until the fruit is very hot but not boiling.

## APRICOT CHEESECAKES

### SERVES 2

100 g (4 oz) Ricotta or curd cheese

1 egg yolk

30 ml (2 level tbsp) ground almonds

30 ml (2 level tbsp) caster sugar

finely grated rind of ½ lemon

20 ml (4 tsp) brandy

400 g (14 oz) can apricot halves in natural juice

15 ml (1 level tbsp) apricot jam

mint sprigs, to decorate

◆ Put the Ricotta cheese and egg yolk into a medium bowl and beat thoroughly together.
◆ Beat in the almonds, sugar and lemon rind. Gradually stir in 10 ml (2 tsp) brandy.
◆ Drain the apricots, reserving the juice. Finely chop one apricot half and stir into the cheese mixture.
◆ Spoon into two 150 ml (¼ pint) ramekin dishes and level the surface. Cut 2 of the apricot halves crossways into thin slices and fan out. Press lightly on top of the cheesecakes.
◆ Microwave on LOW for 15 minutes until the cakes are cooked, or until they shrink away slightly from the edges of the dishes. Leave to stand for 10 minutes then chill.

◆ Meanwhile liquidise the remaining apricots and 30 ml (2 tbsp) juice in a blender or food processor until smooth. Pour into a small bowl and stir in the remaining brandy.
◆ Microwave on HIGH for 2 minutes or until the liquid is boiling. Leave to cool.
◆ To serve, unmould the cheesecakes and put on to 2 serving plates. Put the apricot jam into a small bowl and microwave on HIGH for 30 seconds or until the jam melts. Brush the cheesecakes with the glaze.
◆ Pour the sauce around the cheesecakes and decorate with the mint.

## ORANGE WATER ICE

### SERVES 4

| |
|---|
| 100 g (4 oz) caster sugar |
| juice of 3 oranges |
| finely grated rind and juice of 1 lemon |
| 1 egg white |

◆ Put the sugar and 300 ml (½ pint) water in a large bowl and microwave on HIGH for 3-4 minutes, stirring occasionally, until the sugar has dissolved and the syrup is boiling.
◆ Microwave on HIGH for a further 8 minutes. Strain the orange juice and lemon juice into the syrup then stir in the lemon rind. Leave until cold.
◆ Pour into a shallow metal container, cover and freeze for 1-1½ hours until slushy.
◆ Whisk the egg white until stiff. Turn the mixture into a cold bowl then fold in the egg white. Return mixture to container, and freeze for 3-4 hours until firm.
◆ Transfer to the refrigerator 30-40 minutes before serving to soften slightly.

## SEMOLINA PUDDING

### SERVES 2-3

| |
|---|
| 568 ml (1 pint) milk |
| 60 ml (4 level tbsp) semolina or ground rice |
| 30 ml (2 level tbsp) caster sugar |

◆ Put the milk, semolina and sugar in a large bowl. Microwave on HIGH for 5-6 minutes or until the milk boils. Stir thoroughly.
◆ Three-quarters cover with cling film or a lid and microwave on HIGH for 1-2 minutes or until the milk returns to the boil. Reduce to LOW and microwave for 10-15 minutes or until thickened, stirring frequently.
◆ Leave to stand, covered, for 5 minutes. Stir before serving.

## BANANA AND PASSIONFRUIT UPSIDEDOWN PUDDING

### SERVES 2

| |
|---|
| 25 g (1 oz) butter or margarine |
| 25 g (1 oz) soft light brown sugar |
| 25 g (1 oz) self raising wholemeal flour |
| 1.25 ml (¼ level tsp) ground mixed spice |
| 1 egg, beaten |
| 1 medium ripe banana, peeled |
| 15 ml (1 tbsp) clear honey |
| 1 ripe passionfruit |

◆ Line the base of an 8 × 12 cm (3 × 4½ inch) ovenproof dish with greaseproof paper.
◆ Put the butter into a medium bowl and microwave on HIGH for 10-15 seconds or until it is just soft enough to beat.
◆ Add the sugar, flour, mixed spice and the egg and beat well together using a wooden spoon, until the mixture is well blended and slightly glossy.
◆ Cut half the banana into thin slices and arrange in the base of the prepared dish. Mash the remaining banana and stir into the sponge mixture. Beat together well.
◆ Spoon the mixture on top of the banana slices and cover with a double thickness of absorbent kitchen paper.
◆ Microwave on MEDIUM for 4-4½ minutes until the pudding is cooked or until it has slightly shrunk away from the sides of the dish, but the surface still looks wet.
◆ Leave to stand, covered, for 5 minutes, then turn out on to a serving plate.
◆ Put the honey in a ramekin dish or cup. Halve the passionfruit and spoon the pulp into the dish with the honey. Microwave on HIGH for 15-30 seconds or until warmed through. Spoon over the pudding and serve warm.

## CREAMY RICE PUDDING

### SERVES 4

| |
|---|
| 225 ml (8 fl oz) full cream evaporated milk |
| 50 g (2 oz) short grain rice |
| 25 g (1 oz) caster sugar |

◆ Place ingredients and 350 ml (12 fl oz) water in a buttered ovenproof bowl. Mix well and cover with cling film.
◆ Microwave on HIGH for 5-6 minutes or until liquid boils.
◆ Reduce the setting to LOW and cook for 35-40 minutes or until the rice starts to thicken. Stir it with a fork every 15 minutes and at the end of cooking to break up any lumps.
◆ Leave the rice to stand for 5 minutes before serving.

# PRESERVES & CONFECTIONERY

## LEMON CURD

*A family favourite, perfect with wholemeal bread*

SEE PAGE 201

# Cooking Tips

◆

*Microwave ovens are particularly useful for preparing preserves if you only have a small batch of fruit or vegetables.*

◆

*It is easy to cook small quantities of preserves and confectionary that are difficult to make by conventional methods because of the high risk of burning.*

◆

*During cooking the mixture will bubble up considerably, so always use a large bowl even for making small quantities.*

◆

*Remember to handle bowls with oven gloves as they become hot during the cooking due to the conduction of heat from the food.*

◆

*The jars that are used for preserves can be sterilised in the microwave oven. Quarter fill up to 4 jars with water arranged in a circle in the oven then bring to the boil on High. Remove each jar as it is ready, wearing oven gloves, and pour out the water. Invert the jar on a clean tea towel or absorbent kitchen paper and use as required.*

◆

## ORANGE MARMALADE

MAKES 1.1 KG (2½ LB)

| |
|---|
| 900 g (2 lb) Seville oranges |
| 2 lemons |
| 900 g (2 lb) granulated sugar |
| knob of butter |

◆ Pare the oranges, avoiding the white pith. Shred or chop the rind and set aside.
◆ Put the fruit pith, flesh and pips in a food processor and chop until the pips are broken.
◆ Put the chopped mixture into a large heatproof mixing bowl and add 900 ml (1½ pints) boiling water. Without covering, microwave on HIGH for 15 minutes.
◆ Strain the mixture into another large heatproof bowl and press the cooked pulp until all the juice is squeezed out. Discard the pulp. Stir the shredded rind into the hot juice and microwave on HIGH for 15 minutes until the rind is tender, stirring occasionally. Stir in the sugar until dissolved. Cover the bowl with cling film, pulling back one corner to allow steam to escape. Microwave on HIGH for 10 minutes.
◆ Stir in the butter and microwave on HIGH for 5-6 minutes, stirring once during cooking, until setting point is reached. Remove any scum with a slotted spoon.
◆ Leave to cool for 15 minutes, then pour into hot sterilised jars. Place a disc of waxed paper across surface of marmalade. Cover jars with dampened cellophane, securing with an elastic band. Label.

## LEMON CURD

MAKES 900 G (2 LB)

| |
|---|
| finely grated rind and juice of 4 large lemons |
| 4 eggs, beaten |
| 225 g (8 oz) caster sugar |
| 100 g (4 oz) butter, diced |

◆ Put the lemon rind in a large heatproof bowl. Mix the juice with the eggs and strain into the bowl. Stir in the sugar then add the butter.
◆ Microwave on HIGH for 1 minute, stir, then microwave for 5 minutes until the lemon curd is thick. Whisk well every minute to prevent curdling.
◆ Using oven gloves, remove the bowl from the oven and continue whisking until the mixture is cool. Lemon curd thickens on cooling.
◆ Pour into hot sterilised jars. Place a disc of waxed paper across the surface of the curd and cover the jars with dampened cellophane, securing with an elastic band. Label and store in the refrigerator for up to 2-3 weeks.

## CRUSHED STRAWBERRY JAM

MAKES 700 G (1½ LB)

| |
|---|
| 450 g (1 lb) strawberries, hulled |
| 45 ml (3 tbsp) lemon juice |
| 450 g (1 lb) granulated sugar |
| knob of butter |

◆ Put the strawberries into a 2.8 litre (5 pint) ovenproof glass bowl with the lemon juice. Three-quarters cover the bowl with cling film and microwave on HIGH for 5 minutes or until the strawberries are soft, stirring frequently.
◆ Lightly crush the strawberries with a potato masher. Add the sugar and stir well. Microwave on LOW for 15 minutes or until the sugar is dissolved, stirring frequently.
◆ Raise the setting and microwave on HIGH for 20-25 minutes or until a setting point is reached (when the skin on a small spoonful of jam allowed to set on a cold saucer wrinkles when it is pushed with a tip of a finger). Stir the butter into the jam.
◆ Allow the jam to cool slightly, then pour into hot sterilised jars. Place a disc of waxed paper across the surface of the jam and cover the jars with dampened cellophane, securing with an elastic band. Label.

RASPBERRY JAM

*The perfect jam to make with frozen or fresh fruit*

SEE OPPOSITE

## MANGO CHUTNEY

MAKES ABOUT 450 G (1 LB)

| |
|---|
| *3 mangoes* |
| *2.5 cm (1 inch) piece of fresh root ginger* |
| *1 small green chilli, seeded* |
| *125 g (4 oz) soft light brown sugar* |
| *200 ml (7 fl oz) cider vinegar* |
| *2.5 ml (½ level tsp) ground ginger* |
| *1 garlic clove, skinned and crushed* |

◆ Peel the mangoes and cut the flesh into small pieces. Finely chop the ginger and chilli.

◆ Place all the ingredients in a large bowl and microwave on HIGH for 5 minutes or until the sugar has dissolved. Stir occasionally.

◆ Three-quarters cover with cling film and microwave on HIGH for 20 minutes or until thick and well reduced. Stir two or three times during cooking and after every minute for the last 5 minutes to prevent the surface of the chutney from drying out.

◆ Leave to stand for 5 minutes. Pour into hot sterilised jars, cover and label. Store for 3 months before eating.

## RHUBARB AND GINGER JAM

MAKES ABOUT 450 G (1 LB)

| |
|---|
| *450 g (1 lb) rhubarb, trimmed weight* |
| *450 g (1 lb) granulated sugar* |
| *juice of 1 lemon* |
| *2.5 cm (1 inch) piece of dried root ginger, bruised and tied in muslin* |
| *50 g (2 oz) crystallised ginger, chopped* |

◆ Chop the rhubarb into short even-sized lengths and arrange in a large bowl in alternate layers with the sugar. Pour over the lemon juice. Cover with cling film and leave in a cool place overnight.

◆ Remove the cling film and add the root ginger. Microwave on HIGH for 5 minutes to dissolve the sugar, stirring twice.

◆ Remove the root ginger, add the crystallised ginger and microwave for 14 minutes or until setting point is reached.

◆ Pour the jam into hot sterilised jars. Place a disc of waxed paper across surface of jam and cover jar with dampened cellophane, securing with an elastic band. Label.

## RASPBERRY JAM

MAKES 700 G (1½ LB)

| |
|---|
| *450 g (1 lb) frozen raspberries* |
| *30 ml (2 tbsp) lemon juice* |
| *450 g (1 lb) granulated sugar* |

◆ Place the frozen fruit in a large bowl and microwave on HIGH for 4 minutes to thaw. Stir several times with a wooden spoon to ensure even thawing.

◆ Add the lemon juice and sugar. Mix well and microwave on HIGH for 5 minutes until the sugar has dissolved. Stir several times during cooking.

◆ Microwave on HIGH for 13 minutes, stirring occasionally, until setting point is reached.

◆ Pour the jam into hot sterilised jars. Place a disc of waxed paper across the surface of the jam and cover the jars with dampened cellophane, securing with an elastic band. Label.

# LIME CURD

MAKES ABOUT 700 G (1½ LB)

| |
|---|
| *finely grated rind and juice of 4 limes* |
| *3 eggs, beaten* |
| *250 g (9 oz) caster sugar* |
| *75 g (3 oz) unsalted butter, cut into small pieces* |

◆ Thoroughly wash two 350 g (12 oz) jars and pour 60 ml (4 tbsp) water into each. Set aside.

◆ Put the lime rind and juice in a medium bowl. Gradually whisk in the eggs, sugar and butter, using a balloon whisk. Microwave on HIGH for 4-6 minutes or until the mixture is thickened, whisking frequently.

◆ When the curd is cooked, microwave the jam jars on HIGH for 1-1½ minutes or until the water is boiling. Using oven gloves, pour out the water, invert the jars on to absorbent kitchen paper and leave to drain for a minute.

◆ Meanwhile, whisk the curd frequently for 3-4 minutes or until it starts to cool and thicken further.

◆ Pour the curd into the hot sterilised jars, place a disc of waxed paper across the surface of the curd and cover the jars with dampened cellophane, securing with an elastic band. The curd will keep in a refrigerator for 3-4 weeks.

# LEMON AND GRAPEFRUIT CURD

MAKES 900 g (2 LB)

| |
|---|
| *grated rind and juice of 2 lemons* |
| *grated rind and juice of 1 large grapefruit* |
| *4 eggs* |
| *225 g (8 oz) caster sugar* |
| *125 g (4 oz) unsalted butter, cut into small pieces* |

◆ Place the fruit rind and juice in a large bowl. Using a wooden spoon, beat in the eggs and sugar. Add the butter and stir well.

◆ Microwave on HIGH for 7 minutes, or until the curd has thickened. Whisk occasionally during cooking to ensure even thickening.

◆ Remove from the oven and whisk for about 5 minutes, or until the curd cools and thickens further. Spoon into pre-heated jars and cover in the usual way.

Lemon and grapefruit curd keeps in the refrigerator for 3-4 weeks.

# APRICOT JAM

MAKES ABOUT 350 G (12 OZ)

| |
|---|
| *425 g (15 oz) can apricot halves in syrup* |
| *25 g (1 oz) dried apricots, thinly sliced* |
| *10 ml (2 tsp) lemon juice* |
| *75 g (3 oz) granulated sugar* |

◆ Drain the apricots, reserving the syrup. Put into a blender or food processor with 150 ml (¼ pint) of the syrup, the lemon juice and the sugar.

◆ Liquidise until smooth, then pour into a large bowl. Stir in the dried apricots.

◆ Microwave on HIGH for 10-15 minutes or until the mixture is thick and reduced, stirring occasionally.

◆ Meanwhile thoroughly wash a 350 g (12 oz) jar. When the jam is cooked, pour 60 ml (4 tbsp) water into the washed jar and microwave on HIGH for 1-1½ minutes or until the water is boiling.

◆ Using oven gloves, pour out the water, invert the jar on to absorbent kitchen paper and leave to drain for a minute. Pour the jam into the hot sterilised jar, place a disc of waxed paper across the surface of the jam and cover the jar with dampened cellophane, securing with an elastic band. Label.

## TOMATO CHUTNEY

MAKES 900 G (2 LB)

| |
|---|
| 700 g (1½ lb) firm tomatoes |
| 225 g (8 oz) cooking apples, peeled and cored |
| 1 medium onion, skinned |
| 100 g (4 oz) soft dark brown sugar |
| 100 g (4 oz) sultanas |
| 5 ml (1 level tsp) salt |
| 200 ml (7 fl oz) malt vinegar |
| 15 g (½ oz) ground ginger |
| 1.25 ml (¼ level tsp) cayenne pepper |
| 2.5 ml (½ level tsp) mustard powder |

◆ Put the tomatoes in a large heatproof bowl and just cover with boiling water. Microwave on HIGH for 4 minutes, then lift the tomatoes out one by one using a slotted spoon and remove their skins.

◆ Liquidise the apple and onion to a thick paste in a blender or a food processor. Coarsely chop the tomatoes.

◆ Mix all the ingredients together in a large heatproof bowl. Cover with cling film, pulling back one corner to allow the steam to escape, and microwave on HIGH for 45 minutes or until the mixture is thick and has no excess liquid. Stir every 5 minutes during cooking and take particular care, stirring more frequently, during the last 5 minutes.

◆ Leave to stand for 10 minutes, then stir. Pour into hot sterilised jars, cover and label. Store for at least 2 months before eating.

## MIXED FRUIT CHUTNEY

MAKES 1.4 KG (3 LB)

| |
|---|
| 225 g (8 oz) dried apricots |
| 225 g (8 oz) stoned dates |
| 350 g (12 oz) cooking apples, peeled and cored |
| 1 medium onion, skinned |
| 225 g (8 oz) bananas, peeled and sliced |
| 225 g (8 oz) dark soft brown sugar |
| grated rind and juice of 1 lemon |
| 5 ml (1 level tsp) ground mixed spice |
| 5 ml (1 level tsp) ground ginger |
| 5 ml (1 level tsp) curry powder |
| 5 ml (1 level tsp) salt |
| 450 ml (¾ pint) cider vinegar |

◆ Finely chop or mince the apricots, dates, apple and onion, or chop them in a food processor.

◆ Put all the ingredients into a 2.8 litre (5 pint) ovenproof glass bowl and mix them together well.

◆ Three-quarters cover with cling film and microwave on HIGH for 30-35 minutes or until the mixture is thick and all the liquid has been absorbed. Stir frequently during the cooking time, taking particular care to stir more frequently during the last 10 minutes.

◆ Pour into hot sterilised jars, cover and label. Store the chutney in a cool, dry, airy cupboard for at least 2 months before using.

## APPLE CHUTNEY

MAKES ABOUT 900 G (2 LB)

| |
|---|
| 450 g (1 lb) cooking apples, peeled, cored and finely diced |
| 450 g (1 lb) onions, skinned and finely chopped |
| 100 g (4 oz) sultanas |
| 100 g (4 oz) stoned raisins |
| 150 g (5 oz) demerara sugar |
| 200 ml (7 fl oz) malt vinegar |
| 5 ml (1 level tsp) ground ginger |
| 5 ml (1 level tsp) ground cloves |
| 5 ml (1 level tsp) ground allspice |
| grated rind and juice of half a lemon |

◆ Put all the ingredients into a large bowl and microwave on HIGH for 5 minutes, stirring, until sugar dissolves.

◆ Three-quarters cover the bowl with cling film and microwave on HIGH for 25 minutes, or until the mixture is thick and has no excess liquid. Stir after every 5 minutes during the cooking time to prevent the surface of the chutney from drying out.

◆ Leave to stand for 5 minutes. Pour into hot sterilised jars, cover and label. Store for 3 months before eating.

## CHOCOLATE CHERRY CUPS

MAKES 12

| |
|---|
| 50 g (2 oz) glacé cherries, chopped |
| 30 ml (2 tbsp) kirsch or rum |
| 225 g (8 oz) plain dessert chocolate |
| 1 egg yolk |
| 15 ml (1 level tbsp) icing sugar, sifted |

◆ Marinate the cherries in the kirsch or rum for at least 1 hour before you start.

◆ Make the chocolate shells. Use 24 paper petit four cases to make 12 cases, placing them on a baking sheet.
◆ Break half of the chocolate into a medium bowl and microwave on HIGH for 3 minutes or until it is losing it shape. Stir gently.
◆ Spoon a little chocolate into each case and paint it around the edges to coat. Leave to set. Coat again, making sure the chocolate forms an even layer. Leave to set in a cool place.
◆ Drain the cherries, reserving the kirsch or rum. Peel the paper from the chocolate shells and fill with the cherries.
◆ Put the remaining chocolate into a medium bowl and microwave on HIGH for 3 minutes, then add the egg yolk, icing sugar and reserved kirsch or rum. Beat well.
◆ Pipe the mixture into the chocolate shells. Leave to set.

# COFFEE AND WALNUT FUDGE

### MAKES ABOUT 20

| |
|---|
| 50 g (2 oz) butter or margarine |
| 225 g (8 oz) granulated sugar |
| 90 ml (6 tbsp) milk |
| 45 ml (3 tbsp) coffee essence |
| 50 g (2 oz) walnut pieces |

◆ Oil a 12.5 × 10 cm (5 × 4 inch) rectangular container.
◆ Place the butter in a large bowl and microwave on HIGH for 45 seconds or until melted. Stir in the sugar, milk and coffee essence and mix well.
◆ Microwave on HIGH for 8 minutes or until a drop of the mixture forms a soft ball when dropped in a little cold water.
◆ Remove from the microwave oven and beat in the walnuts using a wooden spoon. Continue beating vigorously for about 4-5 minutes until the mixture is very thick, and has become lighter in colour.
◆ Pour into the prepared container. Using a sharp knife, mark into squares. Cut into squares when cold.

# CREAMY RAISIN AND CHERRY FUDGE

### MAKES ABOUT 20

| |
|---|
| vegetable oil, for greasing |
| 25 g (1 oz) butter |
| 225 g (8 oz) granulated sugar |
| 75 ml (5 tbsp) condensed milk |
| 2.5 ml (½ tsp) vanilla flavouring |
| 25 g (1 oz) seedless raisins |
| 25 g (1 oz) glacé cherries, chopped |

◆ Lightly oil a small rectangular foil dish and set aside. Put the butter into a 2.8 litre (5 pint) ovenproof glass bowl and microwave on HIGH for 30 seconds, or until the butter is only just melted.
◆ Stir in the sugar, milk, 60 ml (4 tbsp) water and the vanilla flavouring and continue stirring for 1 minute or until the sugar is almost dissolved. Microwave on HIGH for 2 minutes, then using oven gloves, give the bowl a gentle shake.
◆ Microwave on HIGH for 6 minutes or until a spoonful of the mixture forms a soft ball when dropped into cold water.
◆ Carefully remove the bowl from the oven, add the raisins and chopped cherries and beat constantly until the mixture is thick and creamy and tiny crystals form. (Do not continue beating after this or the fudge will become candy-like and granular.)
◆ Immediately pour the fudge into the prepared dish. Allow it to cool, then refrigerate it overnight before turning it out and cutting it into squares.

# HAZELNUT TRUFFLES

### MAKES ABOUT 20

| |
|---|
| 50 g (2 oz) chopped hazelnuts |
| 125 g (4 oz) plain chocolate |
| 50 g (2 oz) unsalted butter, cut into small pieces |
| 125 g (4 oz) trifle sponge cakes, crumbled |
| 50 g (2 oz) icing sugar, plus extra for dusting |
| 15 ml (1 tbsp) brandy |
| 75 g (3 oz) chocolate vermicelli |

◆ Spread the hazelnuts on an ovenproof plate and microwave on HIGH for 30-45 seconds or until the nuts are lightly browned, then cool.
◆ Break the chocolate into small pieces and put them into a medium ovenproof glass bowl with the butter pieces. Microwave on LOW for about 1-2 minutes or until the butter melts and the chocolate is soft and glossy on top. Remove the chocolate and butter mixture from the oven and stir it well until it becomes smooth.
◆ Stir the cake crumbs, icing sugar, hazelnuts and brandy into the chocolate and butter, mixing well.
◆ Cover the truffle mixture and refrigerate for about 30 minutes until it is firm enough to handle.
◆ Lightly dust your fingers with a little icing sugar, roll the truffle mixture into about 20 small balls and then roll each one in the chocolate vermicelli to coat completely.
◆ Place the truffles on a foil-lined baking sheet and refrigerate them until they become firm, then cover them with cling film and keep them refrigerated until they are required.
◆ Remove the truffles from the refrigerator 30 minutes before serving and leave them at cool room temperature.

# QUICK CHOCOLATE FUDGE

MAKES 35

100 g (4 oz) plain dessert chocolate

100 g (4 oz) butter or margarine

450 g (1 lb) icing sugar

45 ml (3 tbsp) milk

◆ Place the chocolate, butter, icing sugar and milk in a large ovenproof bowl. Microwave on HIGH for 3 minutes or until the chocolate has melted.
◆ Beat vigorously with a wooden spoon until smooth.
◆ Pour into a 20.5 × 15 cm (8 × 6 inch) rectangular container. Using a sharp knife mark lightly into squares. Leave in the refrigerator for 1-2 hours until set. Serve cut into squares.

# RUM TRUFFLES

MAKES ABOUT 12

50 g (2 oz) plain chocolate

25 g (1 oz) unsalted butter

50 g (2 oz) trifle sponge cakes, crumbled

25 g (1 oz) icing sugar, plus extra for dusting

5-10 ml (1-2 tsp) dark rum

25 g (1 oz) cocoa powder or chocolate vermicelli

◆ Break the chocolate into small pieces and put into a medium bowl with the butter. Microwave on LOW for 3-4 minutes or until the chocolate melts.
◆ Stir well together, then stir in the cake crumbs, icing sugar and rum. Cover and refrigerate for about 30 minutes or until the mixture is firm.
◆ Lightly dust your fingers with icing sugar and roll the truffle mixture into 12 small balls, then roll each one in the cocoa powder or chocolate vermicelli to coat completely.
◆ Put into petit four cases and chill in the refrigerator until required. If storing overnight, cover with cling film. To serve, remove from the refrigerator 30 minutes before serving.

Serve with coffee instead of dessert, or as a special between meal treat.

# COCONUT ICE

MAKES 32 BARS

450 g (1 lb) caster sugar

pinch of cream of tartar

60 ml (4 level tbsp) condensed milk

50 g (2 oz) shredded coconut

100 g (4 oz) desiccated coconut

◆ Put the sugar, cream of tartar, 45 ml (3 tbsp) water and the condensed milk into a large heatproof bowl. Mix thoroughly.
◆ Microwave on HIGH for 3-3½ minutes or until a spoonful of the syrup forms a soft ball when dropped into cold water. Shake the bowl occasionally but do not stir the mixture or it will crystallise.
◆ Stir in the coconut and beat thoroughly until the mixture thickens.
◆ Pour the mixture into a 20.5 × 15 cm (8 × 6 inch) rectangular container. Smooth the top and mark lightly into bars using a sharp knife. Leave in the refrigerator for 1-2 hours until set. Serve cut into bars.

# PEANUT BRITTLE

MAKES 275 G (10 OZ)

vegetable oil, for greasing

175 g (6 oz) caster sugar

75 ml (5 tbsp) liquid glucose

1.25 ml (¼ tsp) vanilla flavouring

25 g (1 oz) butter

150 g (5 oz) salted peanuts

◆ Lightly oil a large baking sheet and set aside. Place the sugar, liquid glucose, 30 ml (2 tbsp) water and the vanilla flavouring in a large ovenproof glass bowl. Microwave on HIGH for 2 minutes, stirring frequently, until the sugar dissolves. Using a wooden spoon, stir in the butter. Microwave on HIGH for 1 minute or until the butter melts.
◆ Stir in the peanuts and microwave on HIGH for 6 minutes or until they are golden brown. Do not stir them during this stage of the cooking.
◆ Pour the peanut mixture on to the oiled baking sheet and allow it to cool and set hard. Break it into pieces for eating.

# SAUCES

## TOMATO AND OLIVE SAUCE

*The olives used here provide a tangy bite to the tomato sauce*

SEE PAGE 211

# Cooking Tips

◆

*Microwave sauces in their serving jugs to cut down on washing up.*

◆

*Providing sauces are whisked or stirred during cooking there is very little risk of lumps forming or of burning occurring.*

◆

*When making sauces thickened with cornflour or arrowroot, make sure the thickening agent is completely dissolved in cold liquid before adding a hot one.*

◆

*Sauces thickened with egg are best cooked on a LOW setting as care is needed to prevent them curdling.*

◆

*Frozen sauces can be reheated straight from the freezer. Transfer to a bowl then reheat, stirring to break up any frozen lumps.*

◆

# TOMATO AND OLIVE SAUCE

MAKES 450 ML (¾ PINT)

| |
|---|
| 25 g (1 oz) butter or margarine |
| 1 large onion, skinned and finely chopped |
| 1 celery stick, trimmed and finely chopped |
| 1 garlic clove, skinned and crushed |
| 450 g (1 lb) ripe tomatoes, skinned, seeded and chopped or 397 g (14 oz) can tomatoes |
| 150 ml (¼ pint) chicken stock |
| 15 ml (1 tbsp) tomato purée |
| 5 ml (1 level tsp) sugar |
| salt and pepper |
| 50 g (2 oz) stuffed olives, sliced |

◆ Place the butter in a large bowl and microwave on HIGH for 45 seconds or until the butter melts. Add the onion, celery and garlic and microwave on HIGH for 5-7 minutes or until the vegetables are soft.
◆ Stir in the chopped fresh tomatoes or canned tomatoes with juice, the stock, tomato purée and sugar. Season to taste with salt and pepper. Microwave on HIGH for 10 minutes or until the sauce has thickened, stirring once or twice during the cooking time.
◆ Leave to cool slightly, then purée in a blender or food processor. Pour the sauce back into the bowl and add the olives. Reheat on HIGH for 2 minutes and check seasoning.

Serve hot with chops, hamburgers, over vegetables or with pasta.

VARIATION
*Fresh tomato sauce:* omit the olives and celery. Sieve the sauce after puréeing in point 3.

# SPINACH SAUCE

MAKES ABOUT 600 ML (1 PINT)

| |
|---|
| 50 g (2 oz) butter or margarine |
| 225 g (8 oz) frozen chopped spinach |
| 30 ml (2 tbsp) milk |
| 225 g (8 oz) Ricotta or full fat soft cheese |
| 25 g (1 oz) freshly grated Parmesan cheese |
| salt and pepper |
| grated nutmeg to taste |

◆ Put the butter into a medium ovenproof glass bowl and microwave on HIGH for 1 minute or until the butter is melted.

◆ Add the frozen spinach to the melted butter and three-quarters cover the bowl with cling film. Microwave on HIGH for 5-6 minutes until the spinach is very hot, breaking up and stirring the spinach two or three times during the cooking time.
◆ Stir the milk and the cheeses into the spinach and season well with salt, pepper and freshly grated nutmeg. Reduce the setting and microwave on LOW for 5 minutes, stirring frequently, until the spinach sauce is hot but not boiling.

Serve with hot pasta.

# ONE-STAGE WHITE SAUCE

MAKES 300 ML (½ PINT)

| Pouring sauce: |
|---|
| 15 g (½ oz) butter or margarine |
| 15 g (½ oz) plain flour |
| 300 ml (½ pint) milk |
| salt and pepper |
| Coating sauce: |
| 25 g (1 oz) butter or margarine |
| 25 g (1 oz) plain flour |
| 300 ml (½ pint) milk |
| salt and pepper |

◆ Put all the ingredients in an ovenproof measuring jug or small bowl and blend well together.
◆ Microwave on HIGH for 3½-4½ minutes or until the sauce has boiled and thickened, stirring after every minute.

VARIATIONS
Add the following to the hot sauce with the seasoning:
*Cheese sauce:* 50 g (2 oz) grated mature Cheddar cheese and a pinch of mustard powder.
*Parsley sauce:* 30 ml (2 tbsp) chopped fresh parsley.
*Hot tartare sauce:* 15 ml (1 tbsp) chopped fresh parsley, 10 ml (2 level tsp) chopped gherkins, 10 ml (2 level tsp) chopped capers and 15 ml (1 tbsp) lemon juice.
*Caper sauce:* 15 ml (1 level tbsp) capers and 5-10 ml (1-2 tsp) vinegar from the jar of capers.
*Blue cheese sauce:* 50 g (2 oz) crumbled Stilton or other blue cheese and 10 ml (2 tsp) lemon juice.
*Mushroom sauce:* 75 g (3 oz) sliced, lightly cooked mushrooms.
*Onion sauce:* 1 medium chopped cooked onion.
*Egg sauce:* 1 finely chopped hard-boiled egg.

## PEANUT SAUCE

MAKES 450 ML (¾ PINT)

| |
|---|
| 90 ml (6 level tbsp) crunchy peanut butter |
| 75 g (3 oz) creamed coconut, crumbled |
| 300 ml (½ pint) water |
| 20 ml (4 tsp) lemon juice |
| 15 ml (1 tbsp) soft light brown sugar |
| 2.5-5 ml (½-1 level tsp) chilli powder |
| 15 ml (1 tbsp) tomato purée |
| 1 garlic clove, skinned and crushed |
| 10 ml (2 tsp) soy sauce |
| salt and pepper |

◆ Put all the ingredients into a medium ovenproof glass bowl and stir them together well.
◆ Three-quarters cover the bowl with cling film and microwave on HIGH for 6-8 minutes until the sauce is boiling and thickened, stirring frequently.
◆ Reduce the setting and microwave the sauce on LOW for 5 minutes or until the sauce thickens, stirring two or three times during the cooking time. Serve hot.

Serve with roast chicken or pork, or with chicken or meat kebabs.

## CELERY BUTTER SAUCE

MAKES 450 ML (¾ PINT)

| |
|---|
| 3 celery sticks, trimmed and very finely chopped |
| 450 ml (¾ pint) milk |
| 125 g (4 oz) butter |
| 45 ml (3 level tbsp) plain flour |
| salt and pepper |

◆ Put the celery into an ovenproof glass bowl with the milk. Three-quarters cover the bowl with cling film and microwave on HIGH for 4-5 minutes or until the milk is boiling. Reduce the setting and microwave on LOW for 4-5 minutes or until the celery is soft.
◆ Strain the milk through a fine sieve into another bowl. Reserve the celery.
◆ Put 40 g (1½ oz) of the butter into a medium ovenproof glass mixing bowl and microwave on HIGH for 45 seconds or until the butter melts. Stir in the flour and microwave on HIGH for 30 seconds. Gradually stir in the strained milk, microwave on HIGH for 45 seconds, then whisk well.

Microwave on HIGH for 3-4 minutes or until the sauce is boiling and thickened, whisking every 30 seconds.
◆ Stir the cooked celery into the sauce and season it well with salt and pepper. Microwave on HIGH for 30 seconds.
◆ Cut the remaining butter into small pieces and gradually beat them into the sauce.

Serve with carrots, onions and other vegetables such as Jerusalem artichokes.

## APPLE SAUCE

MAKES 150 ML (¼ PINT)

| |
|---|
| 450 g (1 lb) cooking apples, peeled, quartered, cored and sliced |
| 45 ml (3 tbsp) lemon juice |
| 30 ml (2 level tbsp) caster sugar |
| 25 g (1 oz) butter or margarine |

◆ Put the apples, lemon juice and caster sugar into a 2.8 litre (5 pint) ovenproof glass bowl. Three-quarters cover with cling film and microwave on HIGH for 5-6 minutes or until the apples are soft, stirring frequently.
◆ Beat the apples to a pulp with a wooden spoon or with a potato masher. If you prefer a smooth sauce, press the apples through a sieve or liquidise them in a blender or food processor until smooth.
◆ Beat the butter into the apple sauce and spoon it into a serving bowl or jug. If the apples are very tart, add a little more sugar to sweeten to taste.

Serve with pork or sausages.

## CRANBERRY SAUCE

| |
|---|
| 225 g (8 oz) fresh cranberries, stalks removed |
| 225 g (8 oz) sugar |
| 150 ml (¼ pint) water |
| 30 ml (2 tbsp) port (optional) |

◆ Rinse the cranberries in a colander under cold running water.
◆ Put the cranberries, sugar and water into a large ovenproof glass bowl and mix well. Three-quarters cover the bowl with cling film and microwave on HIGH for 5 minutes, stirring frequently until the cranberries burst and the sugar is completely dissolved. Add the port, if using. Allow to cool completely before serving.

Serve with turkey or with cold meats.

## BASIC MEAT SAUCE

### SERVES 4

25 g (1 oz) butter or margarine

45 ml (3 tbsp) vegetable oil

2 streaky bacon rashers, rinded and finely chopped

1 small onion, skinned and finely chopped

1 small carrot, peeled and finely chopped

1 small celery stick, trimmed and finely chopped

1 garlic clove, skinned and crushed

1 bay leaf

15 ml (1 tbsp) tomato purée

225 g (8 oz) lean minced beef

10 ml (2 tsp) chopped fresh herbs or 5 ml (1 level tsp) dried

150 ml (¼ pint) dry red wine

150 ml (¼ pint) beef stock

salt and pepper

◆ Put the butter and the oil into a large casserole dish or ovenproof glass bowl and microwave on HIGH for 1 minute. Stir in the bacon, vegetables and garlic and mix well. Cover the dish with a lid or with cling film, pulling back one corner to allow the steam to escape. Microwave on HIGH for 6-8 minutes or until the vegetables begin to soften.
◆ Add the bay leaf to the vegetables and stir in the tomato purée and minced beef. Microwave on HIGH for 3-4 minutes, stirring two or three times to break up the beef.
◆ Add the wine and stock to the dish and stir well to ensure that the meat is free of lumps. Cover with a lid or three-quarters cover with cling film. Microwave on HIGH for 4-5 minutes until boiling, then continue to microwave on HIGH for 12-15 minutes or until the sauce is thick, stirring frequently. Season very well with salt and pepper.

Serve with hot pasta.

## STROGANOFF SAUCE

### MAKES 150 ML (¼ PINT)

25 g (1 oz) butter or margarine

1 medium onion, skinned and finely chopped

125 g (4 oz) button mushrooms, thinly sliced

5 ml (1 tsp) French mustard

50 ml (2 fl oz) chicken stock

150 ml (¼ pint) soured cream

salt and pepper

◆ Place the butter in a medium bowl and microwave on HIGH for 45 seconds or until the butter melts. Stir in the onion and microwave on HIGH for 4 minutes or until the onion begins to soften. Add the sliced mushrooms and microwave on HIGH for a further 2-3 minutes or until the onion and mushrooms are soft.
◆ Stir in the mustard, stock and soured cream and microwave on HIGH for 1 minute until hot. Season to taste and serve hot.

This sauce is traditionally served with fillet steak but is equally good with pork escalopes, chicken breasts, gammon steaks or hamburgers.

## MUSHROOM SAUCE

### MAKES 450 ML (¾ PINT)

450 ml (¾ pint) milk

½ small onion, skinned

1 small carrot, peeled and sliced

1 celery stick, trimmed and sliced

1 bay leaf

4 peppercorns

50 g (2 oz) butter or margarine

125 g (4 oz) button mushrooms, sliced

45 ml (3 level tbsp) plain flour

salt and pepper

15-30 ml (1-2 tbsp) dry sherry (optional)

◆ Put the milk, onion, carrot, celery, bay leaf and peppercorns into a medium ovenproof glass bowl. Microwave on HIGH for 3-4 minutes or until the milk comes to the boil.
◆ Remove the milk from the oven, cover and leave to infuse for 20-30 minutes, then strain and discard the vegetables.
◆ Put the butter into a medium ovenproof glass bowl and microwave on HIGH for 1 minute or until the butter melts.
◆ Stir the mushrooms into the butter and microwave, uncovered, for 1 minute. Stir in the flour and microwave on HIGH for 1 minute. Gradually stir in the flavoured milk.
◆ Three-quarters cover the bowl with cling film and microwave on HIGH for 5 minutes, stirring every 30 seconds or until the sauce is boiling and thickened and the mushrooms are tender.
◆ Season the sauce well with salt and pepper, and stir in the sherry to taste, if using.

Serve with fish or vegetables such as broccoli, new potatoes and cabbage wedges.

## SPICY RAISIN SAUCE

MAKES 300 ML (½ PINT)

75 g (3 oz) stoned raisins

1.25 ml (¼ level tsp) ground cloves

1.25 ml (¼ level tsp) ground cinnamon

good pinch of ground ginger

300 ml (½ pint) water

75 g (3 oz) soft dark brown sugar

10 ml (2 level tsp) cornflour

salt and pepper

25 g (1 oz) butter or margarine

10 ml (2 tsp) lemon juice

◆ Put the raisins, spices, water and sugar into a medium ovenproof glass bowl. Three-quarters cover with cling film and microwave on HIGH for 5 minutes, stirring frequently, until the raisins plump up and the sugar dissolves.

◆ Blend the cornflour to a smooth paste with a little cold water and stir this into the raisins. Season. Microwave on HIGH for 2-3 minutes until the sauce thickens, stirring twice.

◆ Stir the butter and lemon juice into the sauce.

Serve with a cooked bacon joint or gammon rashers.

## CUCUMBER SAUCE

MAKES 300 ML (½ PINT)

50 g (2 oz) butter or margarine

1 large cucumber, peeled, seeded and finely chopped

5 ml (1 level tsp) plain flour

15 ml (1 tbsp) white wine vinegar

150 ml (¼ pint) fish stock or water

10 ml (2 tsp) finely chopped fresh tarragon

salt and pepper

◆ Put the butter into a large ovenproof glass bowl and microwave on HIGH for 1 minute or until the butter melts.

◆ Stir the cucumber into the butter and three-quarters cover the bowl with cling film. Microwave on HIGH for 6 minutes or until the cucumber is very soft, stirring two or three times.

◆ Blend the flour with the vinegar and stir in the fish stock or water, then stir this into the cucumber and add the tarragon. Microwave on HIGH for 3-4 minutes or until the sauce is boiling, stirring frequently. Season well.

Serve with fish.

## TOMATO KETCHUP

MAKES 600 ML (1 PINT)

1.8 kg (4 lb) ripe tomatoes, chopped

225 g (8 oz) sugar

pinch of cayenne pepper

2.5 ml (½ level tsp) paprika

15 g (½ oz) salt

75 ml (5 tbsp) white wine vinegar

◆ Put the tomatoes into a 2.8 litre (5 pint) ovenproof glass bowl and three-quarters cover the top with cling film. Microwave on HIGH for 40-50 minutes until the tomatoes are very well cooked, very thick and reduced. Stir them frequently during the cooking time.

◆ Rub the tomatoes through a nylon sieve into another large, clean ovenproof bowl, then stir in the sugar, spices, salt and vinegar. Three-quarters cover the bowl with cling film and microwave on HIGH for 40-45 minutes or until the mixture becomes very thick and creamy, stirring frequently.

◆ Pour the tomato ketchup into hot, clean jars. Cover the jars with a clean tea-towel until the ketchup is cold. Cover jars and store in the refrigerator for up to 2-3 weeks.

## TUNA FISH SAUCE

SERVES 2

1 small onion, skinned and finely chopped

2 garlic cloves, skinned and crushed

60 ml (4 tbsp) olive oil

4 anchovy fillets, finely chopped

226 g (8 oz) can tomatoes

200 g (7 oz) can tuna, drained and flaked

salt and pepper

30 ml (2 tbsp) chopped fresh parsley

◆ Mix together the onion, garlic and oil in an ovenproof glass bowl. Cover with cling film, pulling back one corner to allow the steam to escape, and microwave on HIGH for 3-4 minutes, stirring occasionally, until the onion softens.

◆ Add the anchovy fillets and the tomatoes, with their juice, to the onion, mashing up the tomatoes with the spoon as they are stirred in. Three-quarters cover with cling film and microwave on HIGH for 5 minutes, stirring frequently.

◆ Stir the tuna into the sauce and season well with salt and pepper. Microwave on HIGH for 5 minutes, stirring occasionally. Stir in the parsley and serve.

Serve with hot pasta.

## BREAD SAUCE

MAKES 450 ML (¾ PINT)

| |
|---|
| 6 cloves |
| 1 medium onion, skinned |
| 4 black peppercorns |
| a few blades of mace |
| 450 ml (¾ pint) milk |
| 25 g (1 oz) butter or margarine |
| 100 g (4 oz) fresh breadcrumbs |
| salt and pepper |
| 30 ml (2 tbsp) single cream (optional) |

◆ Stick the cloves into the onion and place in a medium bowl together with the peppercorns and mace. Pour in the milk. Microwave on HIGH for 5 minutes, stirring occasionally, until the milk is hot.
◆ Remove from the oven, cover and leave to infuse for at least 30 minutes.
◆ Discard the peppercorns and mace and add the butter and breadcrumbs. Mix well, cover and microwave on HIGH for 3 minutes or until the sauce has thickened, whisking after every minute. Remove the onion, season to taste and stir in the cream, if using. Leave to stand for 2 minutes.

Serve hot with roast chicken, turkey and game dishes.

## BARBECUE SAUCE

MAKES 300 ML (½ PINT)

| |
|---|
| 50 g (2 oz) butter or margarine |
| 1 large onion, skinned and finely chopped |
| 1 garlic clove, skinned and crushed |
| 5 ml (1 tsp) tomato purée |
| 30 ml (2 tbsp) vinegar |
| 30 ml (2 level tbsp) demerara sugar |
| 10 ml (2 level tsp) mustard powder |
| 1.25 ml (¼ level tsp) chilli powder |
| 30 ml (2 tbsp) Worcestershire sauce |
| 150 ml (¼ pint) water |

◆ Put the butter into a medium ovenproof glass bowl and microwave on HIGH for 1 minute or until the butter melts.
◆ Stir the onion and garlic into melted butter, cover with cling film, pulling back one corner to allow steam to escape. Microwave on HIGH for 5-6 minutes until onion softens.
◆ Whisk all the remaining ingredients together and stir them into the onion. Microwave uncovered on HIGH for 5 minutes, stirring frequently. Serve hot.

Serve with chicken, sausages, hamburgers or chops.

## HOLLANDAISE SAUCE

MAKES 150 ML (¼ PINT)

| |
|---|
| 5 ml (1 tsp) lemon juice |
| 5 ml (1 tsp) white wine vinegar |
| 3 white peppercorns |
| half a small bay leaf |
| 4 egg yolks |
| 225 g (8 oz) unsalted butter, cut into small pieces |
| salt and pepper |

◆ Put the lemon juice, vinegar, 15 ml (1 tbsp) water, peppercorns and bay leaf into a small bowl and microwave on HIGH for 2 minutes or until boiling. Continue to microwave on HIGH for 2-3 minutes longer or until reduced by half. Leave until cold.
◆ Strain liquid into a large bowl. Add egg yolks and whisk.
◆ Place butter in a small bowl and microwave on HIGH for 45 seconds or until melted. Pour into egg mixture and whisk.
◆ Microwave on HIGH for 3 minutes whisking every 30 seconds until the consistency of mayonnaise. Season.

Serve with salmon or green vegetables.

## SWEET WHISKED SAUCE

MAKES 600 ML (1 PINT)

*4 eggs, separated*

*50 g (2 oz) soft light brown sugar*

*75 ml (3 fl oz) white vermouth or sweet white wine*

◆ In a medium bowl, beat the egg yolks and sugar together until pale and creamy.
◆ Stir in the vermouth or wine and microwave on HIGH for 2 minutes, whisking occasionally, until the mixture starts to thicken around the edges, then quickly remove from the oven and whisk with a hand-held electric mixer until smooth and thick.
◆ Whisk the egg whites until stiff and fold into the sauce. Serve immediately.

Serve with fresh fruit or fruit pies.

## CUSTARD SAUCE

MAKES 568 ML (1 PINT)

*15-30 ml (1-2 level tbsp) sugar*

*30 ml (2 level tbsp) custard powder or 600 ml (1 pint) packet 568 ml (1 pint) milk*

◆ Blend the sugar and custard powder with a little of the milk in a measuring jug or medium bowl. Stir in the remaining milk.
◆ Microwave the sauce on HIGH for 3-4 minutes or until the sauce is thickened, stirring after every 2 minutes. Stir well and serve.

Serve with fruit, puddings and pies.

## EGG CUSTARD SAUCE

MAKES 300 ML (½ PINT)

*300 ml (½ pint) milk*

*2 eggs*

*15 ml (1 level tbsp) granulated sugar*

*a few drops of vanilla flavouring*

◆ Microwave the milk in a large measuring jug on HIGH for 2 minutes or until hot.
◆ Lightly whisk the eggs, sugar and vanilla flavouring together in a bowl. Add the heated milk, mix well and strain back into the jug.

◆ Microwave on HIGH for 1 minute, then microwave on LOW for 4½ minutes or until the custard thinly coats the back of a spoon. Whisk several times during cooking. The sauce thickens slightly on cooling.

Serve hot or cold with sponge puddings and fruit desserts.

## CHOCOLATE SAUCE

MAKES 300 ML (½ PINT)

*15 ml (1 level tbsp) cornflour*

*15 ml (1 level tbsp) cocoa powder*

*30 ml (2 level tbsp) sugar*

*300 ml (½ pint) milk*

*15 g (½ oz) butter*

◆ Put the cornflour, cocoa powder and sugar in a measuring jug or medium bowl and blend together with enough of the milk to give a smooth paste.
◆ Stir in the remaining milk and the butter. Microwave on HIGH for 3-4 minutes or until the sauce has thickened, stirring every minute. Stir well and serve.

Serve with ice creams.

## HOT RASPBERRY SAUCE

MAKES 150 ML (¼ PINT)

*225 g (8 oz) raspberries, sieved*

*45 ml (3 level tbsp) redcurrant jelly*

*15 ml (1 level tbsp) caster sugar*

*10 ml (2 level tsp) cornflour*

*5 ml (1 tsp) lemon juice*

◆ Rub the raspberries through a nylon sieve into a medium bowl. Add the redcurrant jelly and caster sugar. Microwave on HIGH for 2 minutes. Remove from the oven and stir until the jelly has melted and the sugar has dissolved.
◆ Blend the cornflour to a paste with 15 ml (1 tbsp) water and stir into the raspberry mixture. Microwave on HIGH for 2 minutes or until thickened, whisking every 30 seconds. Stir in the lemon juice.

Serve hot with steamed puddings or try serving the sauce warm with ice cream and meringue desserts.

## GOOSEBERRY SAUCE

MAKES 150 ML (¼ PINT)

*450 g (1 lb) gooseberries, topped and tailed*

*25 g (1 oz) butter or margarine*

*45-60 ml (3-4 level tbsp) caster sugar*

*pinch of ground ginger (optional)*

◆ Put the gooseberries and 30 ml (2 tbsp) water in a large bowl and three-quarters cover with cling film. Microwave on HIGH for 6 minutes or until the fruit is soft. Add the butter and caster sugar and stir until the sugar has dissolved.
◆ Rub the fruit with juice through a sieve to remove the seeds.

Serve hot or cold with steamed puddings or ice cream.

## CHOCOLATE FUDGE SAUCE

MAKES 300 ML (½ PINT)

*75 ml (5 tbsp) single cream*

*25 g (1 oz) cocoa powder*

*125 g (4 oz) caster sugar*

*175 g (6 oz) golden syrup*

*25 g (1 oz) butter or margarine*

*pinch of salt*

*2.5 ml (½ tsp) vanilla flavouring*

◆ Put all the ingredients except the vanilla flavouring into a medium ovenproof glass bowl and stir them together well.
◆ Three-quarters cover with cling film and microwave on HIGH for 5 minutes or until the ingredients are boiling hot, stirring frequently.
◆ Stir the vanilla flavouring into the sauce and allow it to cool slightly before serving.

Serve with ice cream, profiteroles and other desserts.

## BUTTERSCOTCH SAUCE

MAKES 150 ML (¼ PINT)

*170 g (6 oz) can evaporated milk*

*75 g (3 oz) soft brown sugar*

*25 g (1 oz) butter or margarine*

*2.5 ml) (½ tsp) vanilla flavouring*

*15 ml (1 level tbsp) cornflour*

*25 g (1 oz) raisins (optional)*

◆ Pour the evaporated milk into a medium bowl and add 30 ml (2 tbsp) water and the brown sugar. Microwave on HIGH for 3 minutes, stirring once. Add the butter and vanilla flavouring.
◆ Blend the cornflour to a paste with a little cold water and add to the bowl, stirring well. Microwave on HIGH for 2 minutes or until thickened, whisking once during the cooking time. Stir in the raisins, if using.

Serve hot with ice cream and puddings.

## JAM OR MARMALADE SAUCE

SERVES 4

*100 g (4 oz) jam or marmalade, sieved if preferred*

*2.5 ml (½ level tsp) cornflour*

*a few drops of lemon juice*

◆ Put the jam or marmalade and 150 ml (¼ pint) water in a medium bowl and microwave on HIGH for 2 minutes.
◆ Blend the cornflour with 30 ml (2 tbsp) water then stir into the heated mixture.
◆ Microwave on HIGH for 1-2 minutes until boiling, stirring after 1 minute. Add lemon juice to taste, before serving.

Serve with steamed puddings.

## THAWING MEAT

Frozen meat exudes a lot of liquid during thawing and because microwaves are attracted to water, the liquid should be poured off or mopped up with absorbent kitchen paper when it collects, otherwise thawing will take longer. Start thawing a joint in its wrapper and remove it as soon as possible – usually after one-quarter of the thawing time. Place the joint on a microwave roasting rack so that it does not stand in liquid during thawing.

Remember to turn over a large piece of meat. If the joint shows signs of cooking give the meat a 'rest' period of 20 minutes. Alternatively, shield the 'thin ends' or parts which will thaw more quickly with small pieces of foil. A joint is thawed when a skewer can easily pass through the thickest part of the meat. Chops and steaks should be re-positioned during thawing; test them by pressing the surface with your fingers – the meat should feel cold to the touch and give in the thickest part.

*Do not allow the foil used for shielding to touch the sides of the oven.*

| Type | Approximate time on LOW | Special instructions |
|---|---|---|
| **BEEF** | | |
| Boned roasting joints (sirloin, topside) | 8–10 minutes per 450 g (1 lb) | *Turn* over regularly during thawing and rest if the meat shows signs of cooking. *Stand* for 1 hour. |
| Joints on bone (ribs of beef) | 10–12 minutes per 450 g (1 lb) | *Turn* over joint during thawing. The meat will still be icy in the centre but will complete thawing if you leave it to stand for 1 hour. |
| Minced beef | 8–10 minutes per 450 g (1 lb) | *Stand* for 10 minutes. |
| Cubed steak | 6–8 minutes per 450 g (1 lb) | *Stand* for 10 minutes. |
| Steak (sirloin, rump) | 8–10 minutes per 450 g (1 lb) | *Stand* for 10 minutes. |
| Beefburgers standard (50 g/2 oz) quarter-pounder | 2 burgers: 2 minutes 4 burgers: 2–3 minutes 2 burgers: 2–3 minutes 4 burgers: 5 minutes | Can be cooked from frozen, without thawing if preferred. |
| **LAMB/VEAL** | | |
| Boned rolled joint (loin, leg, shoulder) | 5–6 minutes per 450 g (1 lb) | As for for boned roasting joints of beef (above). *Stand* for 30–45 minutes. |
| On the bone (leg and shoulder) | 5–6 minutes per 450 g (1 lb) | As for beef joints on the bone above. *Stand* for 30–45 minutes. |
| Minced lamb or veal | 8–10 minutes per 450 g (1 lb) | *Stand* for 10 minutes. |
| Chops | 8–10 minutes per 450 g (1 lb) | *Separate* during thawing. *Stand* for 10 minutes. |

| | | |
|---|---|---|
| **PORK** | | |
| Boned rolled joint (loin, leg) | 7–8 minutes per 450 g (1 lb) | As for boned roasting joints of beef above. *Stand* for 1 hour. |
| On the bone (leg, hand) | 7–8 minutes per 450 g (1 lb) | As for beef joint on bone above. *Stand* for 1 hour. |
| Tenderloin | 8–10 minutes per 450 g (1 lb) | *Stand* for 10 minutes. |
| Chops | 8–10 minutes per 450 g (1 lb) | *Separate* during thawing and arrange 'spoke' fashion. *Stand* for 10 minutes. |
| Sausages | 5–6 minutes per 450 g (1 lb) | *Separate* during thawing. *Stand* for 5 minutes. |
| **OFFAL** | | |
| Liver | 8–10 minutes per 450 g (1 lb) | *Separate* during thawing. *Stand* for 5 minutes. |
| Kidney | 6–9 minutes per 450 g (1 lb) | *Separate* during thawing. *Stand* for 5 minutes. |

## TIME AND SETTINGS FOR COOKING MEAT

| Type | Time/Setting | Microwave Cooking Technique(s) |
|---|---|---|
| **BEEF** | | |
| Boned roasting joint (sirloin, topside) | per 450 g (1 lb) Rare: 5–6 minutes on HIGH Medium: 7–8 minutes on HIGH Well: 8–10 minutes on HIGH | *Turn* over joint halfway through roasting time. *Stand* for 15–20 minutes, tented in foil. |
| On the bone roasting joint (fore rib, back rib) | per 450 g (1 lb) Rare: 5 minutes on HIGH Medium: 6 minutes on HIGH Well: 8 minutes on HIGH | *Turn* over joint halfway through cooking time. *Stand* as for boned joint. |
| **LAMB/VEAL** | | |
| Boned rolled joint (loin, leg, shoulder) | per 450 g (1 lb) Medium: 7–8 minutes on HIGH Well: 8–10 minutes on HIGH | *Turn* over joint halfway through cooking time. *Stand* as for beef. |
| On the bone (leg and shoulder) | per 450 g (1 lb) Medium: 6–7 minutes on HIGH Well: 8–9 minutes on HIGH | *Position* fatty side down and turn over halfway through cooking time. *Stand* as for beef. |
| Chops | 1½ minutes on HIGH then 1½–2 minutes on MEDIUM | *Cook* in preheated browning dish. *Position* with bone ends towards centre. Turn over once during cooking. |
| **BACON** | | |
| Joints | 12–14 minutes on HIGH per 450 g (1 lb) | *Cook* in a pierced roasting bag. *Turn* over joint partway through cooking time. *Stand* for 10 minutes, tented in foil. |

*continued*

| | | |
|---|---|---|
| Rashers | 2 rashers: 2–2½ minutes on HIGH<br>4 rashers: 4–4½ minutes on HIGH<br>6 rashers: 5–6 minutes on HIGH<br><br>12 minutes on HIGH per 450 g (1 lb) | *Arrange* in a single layer.<br>*Cover* with greaseproof paper to prevent splattering.<br>*Cook* in preheated browning dish if liked.<br>*Remove* paper immediately after cooking to prevent sticking.<br>For large quantities:<br>*Overlap* slices and place on microwave rack.<br>*Re-position* three times during cooking. |
| **PORK** | | |
| Boned rolled joint (loin, leg) | 8–10 minutes on HIGH per 450 g (1 lb) | As for boned rolled lamb above. |
| On the bone (leg, hand) | 8–9 minutes on HIGH per 450 g (1 lb) | As for lamb on the bone above. |
| Chops | 1 chop: 4–4½ minutes on HIGH<br>2 chops: 5–5½ minutes on HIGH<br>3 chops: 6–7 minutes on HIGH<br>4 chops: 6½–8 minutes on HIGH | *Cook* in preheated browning dish, or finish off under grill.<br>*Position* with bone ends towards centre.<br>Prick kidney, if attached.<br>Turn over once during cooking. |
| Sausages | 2 sausages: 2½ minutes on HIGH<br>4 sausages: 4 minutes on HIGH | *Pierce* skins.<br>*Cook* in preheated browning dish or finish off under grill.<br>*Turn* occasionally during cooking. |
| **OFFAL** | | |
| Liver (lamb and calves) | 6–8 minutes on HIGH per 450 g (1 lb) | *Cover* with greaseproof paper to prevent splattering. |
| Kidneys | 8 minutes on HIGH per 450 g (1 lb) | *Arrange* in a circle.<br>*Cover* to prevent splattering.<br>*Re-position* during cooking. |

# TIMES AND SETTINGS FOR COOKING POULTRY

| Type | Time/Setting | Microwave Cooking Technique(s) |
|---|---|---|
| **CHICKEN** | | |
| Whole chicken | 8–10 minutes on HIGH per 450 g (1 lb) | *Cook* in a roasting bag, breast side down and turn halfway through cooking.<br>*Stand* for 10–15 minutes. |
| Portions | 6–8 minutes on HIGH per 450 g (1 lb) | *Position* skin side up with thinner parts towards the centre.<br>*Re-position* halfway through cooking time.<br>*Stand* for 5–10 minutes. |
| Boneless breast | 2–3 minutes on HIGH | |
| **DUCK** | | |
| Whole | 7–10 minutes on HIGH per 450 g (1 lb) | *Turn* over as for whole chicken.<br>*Stand* for 10–15 minutes. |
| Portions | 4 × 300 g (11 oz) pieces: 10 minutes on HIGH, then 30–35 minutes on MEDIUM | *Position* and *re-position* as for chicken portions above. |
| **TURKEY** | | |
| Whole | 9–11 minutes on HIGH per 450 g (1 lb) | *Turn* over 3–4 times, depending on size, during cooking; start cooking breast side down.<br>*Stand* for 10–15 minutes. |

# THAWING POULTRY AND GAME

Poultry and game should be thawed in its freezer wrapping which should be pierced first and the metal tag removed. During thawing, pour off liquid that collects in the bag. Finish thawing in a bowl of cold water with the bird still in its bag. Chicken portions can be thawed in their polystyrene trays.

| Type | Approximate time on LOW | Special instructions |
|---|---|---|
| Whole chicken or duckling | 6–8 minutes per 450 g (1 lb) | Remove giblets.<br>*Stand* in cold water for 30 minutes. |
| Whole turkey | 10–12 minutes per 450 g (1 lb) | Remove giblets.<br>*Stand* in cold water for 2–3 hours. |
| Chicken portions | 5–7 minutes per 450 g (1 lb) | *Separate* during thawing.<br>*Stand* for 10 minutes. |
| Poussin, grouse, pheasant, pigeon, quail | 5–7 minutes per 450 g (1 lb) | |

# THAWING FISH

Separate fish cutlets, fillets or steaks as soon as possible during thawing. Like poultry, it is best to finish thawing whole fish in cold water to prevent drying out of the surface. Arrange scallops and prawns in a circle and cover with absorbent kitchen paper to help absorb liquid; remove pieces from the oven as soon as thawed.

| Type | Approximate time on LOW | Special instructions |
|---|---|---|
| White fish fillets or cutlets, e.g. cod, coley, haddock, halibut, or whole plaice or sole | 3–4 minutes per 450 g (1 lb) plus 2–3 minutes. | *Stand* for 5 minutes after each 2 minutes. |
| Oily fish, e.g. whole and gutted mackerel | 2–3 minutes per 225 g (8 oz) plus 3–4 minutes | *Stand* for 5 minutes after each 2 minutes |
| Kipper fillets | 2–3 minutes per 225 g (8 oz) | As for oily fish above. |
| Lobster tails, crab claws, etc. | 3–4 minutes per 225 g (8 oz) plus 2–3 minutes | As for oily fish above. |
| Prawns, shrimps, scampi | 2½ minutes per 100 g (4 oz)<br>3–4 minutes per 225 g (8 oz) | *Pierce* bag if necessary.<br>*Stand* for 2 minutes.<br>*Separate* with a fork after 2 minutes.<br>*Stand* for 2 minutes, then plunge into cold water and drain. |

## TIME AND SETTINGS FOR COOKING FISH IN THE MICROWAVE

| Type | Time/Setting | Microwave Cooking Technique(s) |
|---|---|---|
| Whole round fish (whiting, mullet, trout, carp, bream, small haddock) | 3 minutes on HIGH per 450 g (1 lb) | *Slash* skin to prevent bursting *Turn* over fish partway through cooking time. *Shield* tail with small pieces of smooth foil. *Re-position* fish if cooking more than 2. |
| Whole flat fish (plaice, sole) | 3 minutes on HIGH | *Slash* skin. *Turn* dish partway through cooking time. *Shield* tail. |
| Cutlets, steaks, fillets | 4 minutes on HIGH per 450 g (1 lb) | *Position* thicker parts towards the outside, overlapping thin ends and separating with cling film. *Turn* over fillets and quarter-turn dish 3 times during cooking. |

## THAWING BREADS

To absorb the moisture of thawing breads, place them on absorbent kitchen paper (remove as soon as thawed to prevent sticking). For greater crispness, place breads and the paper on a microwave rack or elevate food on an upturned bowl to allow the air to circulate underneath.

| Type | Quantity | Approximate time on LOW setting | Special instructions |
|---|---|---|---|
| **Bread** | | | |
| Loaf, whole | 1 large | 6–8 minutes | Uncover and place on absorbent kitchen paper. *Turn* over during thawing. *Stand* for 5–15 minutes. |
| Loaf, whole | 1 small | 4–6 minutes | |
| Loaf, sliced | 1 large | 6–8 minutes | *Defrost* in original wrapper but remove any metal tags. *Stand* for 10–15 minutes. |
| Loaf, sliced | 1 small | 4–6 minutes | |
| Slice of bread | 25 g (1 oz) | 10–15 seconds | *Place* on absorbent kitchen paper. *Time* carefully. *Stand* for 1–2 minutes. |
| Bread rolls, tea-cakes, scones, crumpets, etc. | 2 | 15–20 seconds | *Place* on absorbent kitchen paper. *Time* carefully. *Stand* for 2–3 minutes. |
| | 4 | 25–35 seconds | |

## TIME AND SETTINGS FOR RICE AND PASTA

Although there are no real time savings in cooking rice and pasta in the microwave, it may be a more foolproof way of cooking as there is no risk of it sticking to the pan. Add boiling water to cover by at least 2.5 cm (1 inch).

| Type and quantity | Time on HIGH setting | Microwave cooking technique(s) |
|---|---|---|
| White long grain rice 225 g (8 oz) | 10–12 minutes | *Stir* once during cooking. *Stand* for 10 minutes. |
| 350 g (12 oz) | 12–14 minutes | |
| Brown rice, 100 g (4 oz) | 30 minutes | As for white long grain rice. |
| Pasta shapes, 225 g (8 oz) dried | 7 minutes | *Stir* once during cooking. *Stand* for 5 minutes. |
| Spaghetti, tagliatelli, 225 g (8 oz) dried | 7–8 minutes | *Stand* for 10 minutes. |
| 350 g (12 oz) dried | 8–10 minutes | |

## FROZEN VEGETABLES COOKING CHART

Frozen vegetables may be cooked straight from the freezer. Many may be cooked in their original plastic packaging, as long as it is first slit and then placed on a plate. Alternatively, transfer to a bowl.

| Vegetable | Quantity | Approximate time on HIGH | Microwave Cooking Technique(s) |
|---|---|---|---|
| **Asparagus** | 275 g (10 oz) | 7–9 minutes | *Separate* and re-arrange after 3 minutes. |
| **Beans, Broad** | 225 g (8 oz) | 7–8 minutes | *Stir* or *shake* during cooking period. |
| **Beans, Green cut** | 225 g (8 oz) | 6–8 minutes | *Stir* or *shake* during cooking period. |
| **Broccoli** | 275 g (10 oz) | 7–9 minutes | *Re-arrange* spears after 3 minutes. |
| **Brussels sprouts** | 225 g (8 oz) | 6–8 minutes | *Stir* or *shake* during cooking period. |
| **Cauliflower florets** | 275 g (10 oz) | 7–9 minutes | *Stir* or *shake* during cooking period. |
| **Carrots** | 225 g (8 oz) | 6–7 minutes | *Stir* or *shake* during cooking period. |
| **Corn-on-the-cob** | 1 | 3–4 minutes | *Do not* add water. Dot with butter, wrap in greaseproof paper. |
| | 2 | 6–7 minutes | |
| **Mixed vegetables** | 225 g (8 oz) | 5–6 minutes | *Stir* or *shake* during cooking period. |
| **Peas** | 225 g (8 oz) | 5–6 minutes | *Stir* or *shake* during cooking period. |
| **Peas and carrots** | 225 g (8 oz) | 7–8 minutes | *Stir* or *shake* during cooking period. |
| **Spinach, Leaf or Chopped** | 275 g (10 oz) | 7–9 minutes | *Stir* or *shake* during cooking period. |
| **Swede/Turnip, diced** | 225 g (8 oz) | 6–7 minutes | *Stir* or *shake* during cooking period. *Mash* with butter after standing time. |
| **Sweetcorn** | 225 g (8 oz) | 4–6 minutes | *Stir* or *shake* during cooking period. |

## TIME AND SETTINGS FOR FRESH VEGETABLES

Vegetables need very little water added when microwaved. When using these charts add 30 ml (2 tbsp) water unless otherwise stated. In this way they retain their colour, flavour and nutrients more than they would if cooked conventionally. They can be cooked in boil-in-the-bags, plastic containers and polythene bags – pierce the bag before cooking to make sure there is a space for steam to escape.

Prepare vegetables in the normal way. It is most important that food is cut to an even size and stems are of the same length. Vegetables with skins, such as aubergines, need to be pierced before microwaving to prevent bursting. Season vegetables with salt after cooking. Salt distorts the microwave patterns and dries the vegetables.

| Vegetable | Quantity | Approximate time on HIGH | Microwave Cooking Technique(s) |
|---|---|---|---|
| Artichoke, Globe | 1<br>2<br>3<br>4 | 5–6 minutes<br>7–8 minutes<br>11–12 minutes<br>12–13 minutes | *Place* upright in covered dish. |
| Asparagus | 450 g (1 lb) | 7–8 minutes | *Place* stalks towards the outside of the dish. *Re-position* during cooking. |
| Aubergine | 450 g (1 lb) 0.5 cm (¼") slices | 5–6 minutes | *Stir* or *shake* after 4 minutes. |
| Beans, Broad | 450 g (1 lb) | 6–8 minutes | *Stir* or *shake* after 3 minutes and test after 5 minutes. |
| Beans, Green | 450 g (1 lb) sliced into 2.5 cm (1") lengths | 10–13 minutes | *Stir* or *shake* during the cooking period. Time will vary with age. |
| Beetroot, whole | 4 medium | 14–16 minutes | *Pierce* skin with a fork. *Re-position* during cooking. |
| Broccoli | 450 g (1 lb) small florets | 7–8 minutes | *Re-position* during cooking. *Place* stalks towards the outside of the dish. |
| Brussels sprouts | 225 g (8 oz)<br>450 g (1 lb) | 4–6 minutes<br>7–10 minutes | *Stir* or *shake* during cooking. |
| Cabbage | 450 g (1 lb) quartered<br>450 g (1 lb) shredded | 8 minutes<br>8–10 minutes | *Stir* or *shake* during cooking. |
| Carrots | 450 g (1 lb) small whole<br>450 g (1 lb) 0.5 cm (¼") slices | 8–10 minutes<br>9–12 minutes | *Stir* or *shake* during cooking. |
| Cauliflower | whole 450 g (1 lb)<br>225 g (8 oz) florets<br>450 g (1 lb) florets | 9–12 minutes<br>5–6 minutes<br>7–8 minutes | *Stir* or *shake* during cooking. |

| | | | |
|---|---|---|---|
| Celery | 450 g (1 lb) sliced into 2.5 cm (1") lengths | 8–10 minutes | *Stir* or *shake* during cooking. |
| Corn-on-the-cob | 2 (450 g (1 lb)) | 6–7 minutes | *Wrap* individually in greased greaseproof paper. *Do not* add water. *Turn* over after 3 minutes. |
| Courgettes | 450 g (1 lb) 2.5 cm (1") slices | 5–7 minutes | *Do not* add more than 30 ml (2 tbsp) water. *Stir* or *shake* gently twice during cooking. *Stand* for 2 minutes before draining. |
| Fennel | 450 g (1 lb) 0.5 cm (1") slices | 7–9 minutes | *Stir* or *shake* during cooking. |
| Leeks | 450 g (1 lb) 2.5 cm (1") slices | 6–8 minutes | *Stir* or *shake* during cooking. |
| Mange Tout | 450 g (1 lb) | 7–9 minutes | |
| Mushrooms | 225 g (8 oz) whole<br>450 g (1 lb) whole | 2–3 minutes<br>5 minutes | *Do not* add water. Add 25 g (1 oz) butter and a squeeze of lemon juice. *Stir* or *shake* during cooking. |
| Onions | 225 g (8 oz) thinly sliced<br>450 g (1 lb) whole | 7–8 minutes<br>9–11 minutes | *Stir* or *shake* sliced onions. Add only 60 ml (4 tbsp) water to whole onions. *Re-position* whole onions during cooking. |
| Okra | 450 g (1 lb) whole | 6–8 minutes | |
| Parsnips | 450 g (1 lb) (halved) | 10–16 minutes | *Place* thinner parts towards centre. *Add* a knob of butter and 15 ml (1 tbsp) lemon juice with 150 ml (¼ pint) water. *Turn* dish during cooking and *re-position*. |
| Peas | 450 g (1 lb) | 9–11 minutes | *Stir* or *shake* during cooking. |
| Potatoes | | | *Wash* and prick the skin with a fork. |
| Baked jacket | 1 × 175 g (6 oz) potato<br>2 × 175 g (6 oz) potatoes<br>4 × 175 g (6 oz) potatoes | 4–6 minutes<br>6–8 minutes<br>12–14 minutes | *Place* on absorbent kitchen paper or napkin. When cooking more than 2 at a time, arrange in a circle. *Turn* over halfway through cooking. |
| Boiled (old) halved | 450 g (1 lb) | 7–10 minutes | *Add* 60 ml (4 tbsp) water. *Stir* or *shake* during cooking. |
| Boiled (new) whole | 450 g (1 lb) | 6–9 minutes | *Add* 60 ml (4 tbsp) water. *Do not* overcook or new potatoes become spongy. |
| Spinach | 450 g (1 lb) chopped | 5–6 minutes | *Do not* add water. Best cooked in roasting bag, sealed with non-metal fastening. *Stir* or *shake* during cooking. |

*continued*